*To my children and grandchildren,
my husband, family and friends.*

CONTENTS

Introduction	1
On Writing	7
Grandparents	15
Parents	21
Childhood	31
Migration	47
Education - School	57
Education - University	67
Religion	79
Work	89
Boyfriends	101
When Harry Met And Married Agnes	115
My Three Sons	127
From My Children	143
Family	155
Friends - Part 1	171
Friends - Part 2	183
Homes	203
Music	217
Old Age	227
Conclusion	235

INTRODUCTION

My original intention was to inform my sons and perhaps my grandchildren about my past and the person not necessarily familiar to them before we met. However, in the process of writing I lost sight of my readership and allowed my narratives to wander. Although lacking in any great philosophy or wisdom, I am happy to share with all who may be interested. If not, just turn the page.

Good writing is timeless, whereas my vignettes are dated to when I wrote them. Since some were written over a long time in part or whole, much has happened that influenced their content, tone and all else. Hence the collation of my mixture may not blend. The many styles are a kind of assortment of recordings which may be repetitious even tiresome. But life does not run smoothly, so why should the record of mine, even if my life ran a rather even course.

As I sit at my desk in our Bowral home, I feel extremely privileged to be able to enjoy the lifestyle that my husband Harry has created for us. He always wanted a sylvan setting which now surrounds our home in the country. Once it was a barren blue stone quarry and now it is a vision of mixed greeneries. The cherry trees blossoms are followed by the flowering of lavenders, blue irises, and the blooming of a variety of rose bushes. Our home will soon be enveloped in bright color. Very different from the world in which I grew up.

I was born in Budapest, once known as "Little Paris," a cultural and social center of Europe. The city boasts of the oldest and busiest Metro system, early electrical lighting, and the largest Synagogue in Continental Europe, as well as the many therapeutic thermal spring waters and a high culture. It has a rich history of having been conquered, last ruled by the Hapsburgs when it was part of the Austro-Hungarian Empire. That was well before I was born.

Budapest 2018

My memories of living in Budapest are many, clear, and very positive of a happy childhood. The capital of Hungary was very much like most European cities. Our lives were quite ordinary, and communism had very little effect on me, other than having received a high standard of education till I was ten years old, when we left illegally. The story of our immigration may be of interest to some and shared by those who left at the same time in a similar manner.

We have often returned to Budapest, and even saw more of the countryside than when we lived there, but our main intent was to visit our relatives. We may have felt a certain attachment to our city of origin because we referred to it as "back home" for a time after we left it. I recall most buildings as dark, riddled with bullet holes left over from the World War II and the Hungarian Revolution of 1956 until the government cleaned up those on the tourist routes as Budapest was the gateway to the Communist bloc. But unlike on previous occasions, on our last trip, all those old ornate historical buildings stood unusually clean and shining bright in their summer splendor. A rather nice image to hold onto for the future.

Like my parents and I, after the 1956 Revolution most of the refugees fled through Austria. We stayed in camps outside Vienna and in Salzburg enroute to being shipped to Australia. For a short time on arrival, we lived in Sydney's then famous Kings Cross until we moved to Bondi Junction, where my parents established and built their manufacturing business. But all that is recorded in *The Forbat Story*.

Bondi 2000

Bondi was and is renowned for the golden sands of Bondi Beach, and for the easy cosmopolitan lifestyle with cafes and restaurants. It welcomed each wave of migrants that flocked to an area where they shared their common language and culture. Although not quite the ghetto, Café de la Paix and Mon Bijou were popular meeting places for the northern Europeans who reproduced their Café Society of Budapest. Those who came earlier offered support of camaraderie, advice, and even practical assistance to newcomers.

It was in Bondi that my parents and I had our first home, without it being part of our workplace also and where I had my own room for the first time. Since it was located in the Eastern Suburbs, the move to Rose Bay and then to Vaucluse was but a small step. Then, as prodigals do, my family returned to North Bondi where we stayed in the same house for over thirty years.

Bowral was a small provincial town in the Southern Highlands of New South Wales, where my husband Harry and I spent several weekends each year from the early 1980s. The attraction was the charm of the Australian country with its slow pace, serene surroundings, and historical sites. It was also a chance to have a break from the stresses of work and even our lovely three sons, Richard, Robert, and Ronald. It was so appealing that later we purchased a property and made our

Our Bowral 2004

home there. That was over twenty years ago when Harry created our little paradise where we are fortunate to spend as much time as possible, and I am forever grateful for our contented lifestyle. As I look out at our peaceful landscape, it seems that all is well with the world.

In November 2013 we had our 50th school reunion. We were asked to write about a page summary of our personal and educational background for a small handbook for the students. I wrote it on what was my business letterhead at the time.

Agnes V Czeiger

B.Soc.Wk., B.A. (Hons), Dip. Ed., M.Ed.

There is a full moon tonight and as I sit in our study in the Southern Highlands, I think it is the ideal setting for reflection. I always find it pleasant and nostalgic to look back, but to condense 50 years into one page seems a daunting task.

There were two students who left Darlinghurst Public School at the end of 1958. One went to Sydney High School, and I was accepted at Dover Heights Girls' High School. A most proud achievement with my bare passes, and which foreshadowed my future scholastic results. The acquisition of hats and gloves added further to my pride. Although in the "B" stream for all classes for five years, I remember fondly each and every one of my teachers, despite some altercations with each and every one of them. My principal roles in Gilbert and Sullivan productions, were the most memorable and the most rewarding experience of my high school days. I can still hear Miss Graham 'succinctly' articulating 'really' to rid my American 'r' from the English musical, and Mrs Desmond's insistence on the pronunciation of every syllable in tune and on time. Those rehearsals and the performances often linger in my mind.

With six "B"s, I entered the University of New South Wales in 1964 and there I stayed on and off, for over forty years as student and casual staff member. I was in the first class to graduate as Bachelor of Social Work, and worked in medical, family, community, and other fields for over six years, the last being Team Leader of a Psychiatric Day Care centre. Halfway through a Master program in 1973, I left for overseas, specifically for husband hunting.

I do believe that the two principals tried to instil self-discipline and self-pride into all the girls. Miss Payne who was tall, just, and warm, and later Miss Martin, who was short and strict as a sergeant major with her Cossack fur hat and considered boys as 'undesirable elements,' were responsible for my respect for schooling. During numerous assemblies, the latter taught me how to stand for lengthy periods, by putting "equal weight on two feet, two inches apart". That stood me in good stead at my wedding ceremony to Harry Czeiger in 1974. He and I managed Forbat Styles, manufacturing ladies fashion business for 27 years. Our three sons were born in 1975, 1977 and 1979. They are married and so far, have produced two grand grandchildren.

As the boys were growing up, I tried to impart to them some of what I gained from my teachers, such as that there is beauty in numbers, as Miss Butler proved; that there is beauty in words of Wordsworth, as Mrs Lloyd-Jones demonstrated; that there is value in high culture and waltzing (learnt Ballroom dancing instead of sports); and that just because we had to eat the junket we cooked, it was not compulsory in the real world where licking chocolate from bowls was acceptable. Once the boys were all in school, I returned to UNSW part time. While they slept, I wrote assignments, until I graduated a few times. For about ten years till 2007, I was tutoring Bachelor of Education students.

I have left at least three footprints. If I have left any others with my clients and students, I rejoice. But why I was voted as Senior Prefect at Dover Heights Girls' High School, is still a mystery.

PO Box 1750, Bondi Junction, NSW, 1355   Phone: 02 9365 4011   Fax: 02 9365 3199   Mobile: 0411 715 060   Email: aczeiger@forbat.com.au

Family has always been important to me. I spent considerable time and effort to find a suitable husband. After I married Harry, he built all our homes. As with most of his artworks, the creator in him designed and produced, while I merely criticised. And yes, it might be said that my life is very much in terms of my significant others, Harry being one of the most significant others after my three sons and amidst my parents.

I wrote about my background so that there is some notion of my origin. I wrote the little I know of my grandparents. I wrote of some of what I know of my parents, mostly from the anecdotes they told and my memories of living with them. They died relatively young, so my children didn't know them. Sadly, many of those who did, are no longer. And most of my memories of my parents will remain mine alone.

There are extended family members some of whom played a more important part than others. Naturally they are too many to introduce in detail and a family tree may need to be consulted. But they all played significant roles in my life, many from my childhood and youth.

My children, or should I say our children, should know their origins. Well, herewith some of the stories from their very beginning to which they may call out that it is just too much information. Still, they may recognise themselves within or their memories may be awakened. Perhaps they may even correct my memories of them. I must add that I not only love my children, but I also like them. Most of the time.

Friends are most important to me, and we have been blessed with a large number who are still dominant in our lives after many decades. There is no list, and some are merely mentioned while others are not included here. Hence there may be those who will be offended even though they played just as prominent a part in our lives as all the others.

I thoroughly enjoyed returning to my youth, and my experiences with my boyfriends and friend boys. I even like the way I looked. While my young single life may have been long in relation to that of others, I took full advantage of it. But through it all, I also did work which I began at the young age of nearly eleven and continued till shortly before Covid arrived.

Then there are my musings. Although totally apolitical on that subject which causes more arguments over dinner tables than others, I do have some opinions. And I discovered that I could become quite vocal about religion on occasion.

If only I were an artist, then I could express adequately how I feel whether with words or with music. Sadly, I lacked the passion that many possess, although I may have had some talent in music. Up to this aged age of mine, I have lived with G-d's language of music, which I may not be able to speak, but I appreciate it, and it moved me all my life.

It is probably timely that my compilation of recollections and reflections on a life past are recorded. For if not now, then when. I loved the nostalgia of the process and took great delight in revelling in my memories.

November 2024

Chapter One
ON WRITING

"We write to taste life twice, in the moment and in retrospect."

Anais Nin

Everyone is writing a book. They say, whoever 'they' are, that everyone has a book in them. I had in mind a kind of memoire, a narrative on life matters, a long reflection and one possibly on my life with Harry. The last because I spent so much of my life with him. Also, perhaps because people think we are a good act, and our usual repartee would make for a good play. Comedy if you like.

But where to begin? With some interesting beginning. Perhaps with a quotation or with a well-known, "It was the night before Christmas, ...", or "I was born ...". Or something original? But from me? So, how to start? Perhaps at the beginning and follow in chronological order; or perhaps start in the present with flashbacks; or ignore time, be adventurous and rummage through the past or, however.

On the one hand, there is nothing worse than a blank page. One can sit in front of emptiness for hours and either key a single letter, or a few words or sentences, only to delete them, then repeat the process a few times, and even give up.

On the other hand, there is nothing more inviting than a blank page. It offers unlimited scope for the writer. One can start with anything that can always be changed and edited, redrafted, and rewritten and so on. It reminds me of Harry's "The Island." While I may have ruminated about my writing for what seems ages, he wrote his novel effortlessly just over some weekends, well within a year, but which I thought needed to be corrected and edited. I spent years working on it, and when published, it added another plume to his creations.

I must mention I actually started numerous diaries. On rereading them, they all sounded so trite, childish ramblings about mundane events and full of descriptions of juvenile emotions. Even in my early twenties, no gems of wisdom. In fact, nothing of import and I destroyed them. I was in awe of those who wrote. Ah, fascinating Pepy's Diary, and how treasured you were by Anne Bancroft's character in "84 Charring Cross Road."

I must write down some things because according to my three sons, I have not had a life. I have never been young. I never had any boyfriends because I didn't show any photos of them. And although they acknowledge my having married their father, that is because they heard the story of our meeting, engagement, and wedding many a times, and they have seen the photos. They may deny that I was ever even a mother of three boys, they know naught about any career I may have had or that I have ever done anything. Well perhaps they are right.

Everyone posted on Facebook or some social media, so why shouldn't I? I believed that I had something to say, considering that I always said something about most things. I believed that because I had a past and some experiences, I could offer some advice, none of which was ever taken kindly either by my sons or their spouses, or anyone else for that matter. Who likes to hear some truths? But who am I to be an expert on anything?

Early in the history of the 'Blog', my oldest son Richard set up a site for me and called it *Lady Maleficent*. I posted three items though sometime later they disappeared never to be reclaimed.

Herewith one of **Lady Maleficent's Blogs**:

Christopher Hitchens wrote,

"Never be a spectator of unfairness or stupidity.
The grave will supply plenty of time for silence."

Never truer words have been spoken. And I live up to them almost all the time. Although my mother warned not to seek fairness and justice, I still do. I have always said that "I can't stand stupidity." And when I perceive it, then I address it with words. Ah, the power of the 'word'. The written word appears to have more sting than the spoken word though neither can be retracted. And once it is written, it cannot be denied. Perhaps it can be explained away, but as when Ramses declared, "let it be written, let it be done", once written, it is done and remains down.

Someone once said that "words are cheap." I think not. I think that that is unfair if not stupid. Words are of our language. And language is our primary means of communicating with each other. Words have meaning, whether they denote or connote, or both. And whether they are spoken or written, they can be and often are misunderstood. And when they are misunderstood, oh, what damage!

Jodi Picoult stated that,

"Words are like eggs dropped from great heights;
you can no more call them back than ignore the mess they leave when they fall."

And frequently, I have left a whole mess behind. Yet, I feel no egg on my face. Like Horton the elephant, I say what I mean and mean what I say.

I will not be silenced. I will "not go gently into that good night" without saying the truth, even if it hurts. And as someone keeps repeating that I am "brutally honest", honest I will remain. Although at times I may be forced to refrain till the cup runneth over. In an interview, Susan Sontag advised would be writers to "love words." And as readers, we should view words in that vein. Oh, were that but true.

Some experts advise that one should write about what one knows best. Well, I think I know best about myself and my life. I also think it has been a remarkably unremarkable life, perhaps quite an ordinary life. It could even be summed up as born, educated, worked, married, bred, worked, and retired. But everyone wishes to leave their footprints. In a way so do I, even if they are flat footed ones. Hence the collection over many years of my 34 shopping bags which abounded in material, about me, of course.

In the early 1980s I looked at writing courses and through the Workers Adult Education program I found one located in Vaucluse Boys High School. It seems ironic that I should have started to learn about writing on the spot where I am writing now, as we live in Mark Moran which is a complex built on the grounds of that school. My first lessons were with Susan Yorke, author of the novel *The Widow*, which may have been adapted to film. She tried to instil writing methods, and it was reflected in the exercises she gave her students.

Susan Yorke began with simple tips for writing such *as keep the reader turning the page, be specific, include emotion or sentiment, eliminate padding, stay out of the mind, the reader needs to identify with someone, the opening needs to get attention, avoid clichés, and so on.* She offered a lot of instructions that were a lot to grasp at once and not easy to remember to use all at once. *Short Stories are usually 1000 -5000 words and need one plot, to be complete and condensed with few characters, with point or action and conflict, ... and the ending needs to be implicit in the beginning.*

Her list was practical and by no means exhaustive. It all sounded simple, but to apply it all in practice was not simple. And one needed to learn the 'how' to write. Most important and valuable were the comments on the written pieces. One of the first exercises required writing a paragraph on '**old**.' One would think that such a short piece was not difficult. But it was not easy either. All the exercises were experiences in themselves.

Her face was wrinkled, her eyes were watery. She has been colouring her hair for many years but invariably the roots showed the dense grey. Her movements were slower and at times she was clumsy. Certain fears of death were implied, but never spoken outright. Though her activities grew fewer, her warmth remained.

Susan Yorke's comment was about any 'implication' and the combination of action and emotion in the one sentence. Later I learnt from my youngest son that writing should 'show' not tell. But her criticism was *'not bad for a first attempt.'* Not a bad criticism!

Another exercise required writing a short piece on '**a favourite article of clothing.**'

Eyes stared at the ankle-length shimmering golden creation as he escorted me into the Ball Room and the sheer tulle flowed as we danced. My mother spent many a night carefully stitching back the edge of the low-cut décolletage. When the soft knit lamé clung to my body, he said it resembled the attire of a star. Every year at least once, the shapely glittering gown receives a viewing. For me the nostalgia continues to be overwhelming, but for him, that shining jewel of a dress simply hid my knock-knees.

Her comment was, *"Perfect"*. That was most encouraging! With practice and constructive criticism, the writing improved.

Over the years what I found very common in writing courses was an exercise in which one person wrote a paragraph, and each member of the group added another to continue the story. The complete work was quite a product and a good tool to use to teach how the meandering stories can grow and develop into the unexpected.

Interesting was the work in which each and every adverb and adjective was to be replaced with a synonym. But the most memorable one was to write a story without the most common letter of the alphabet, namely "e".

It was necessary to rewrite it several times as the little vowel kept creeping in, until finally it was totally absent. I thought the writing was perfect. And the story flowed without an 'e'. I was so delighted that without thinking twice I signed my name. But that contained the wretched 'e.'

Much later in some spare time I wrote about chocolates. The short piece I wrote about my pleasurable habits or life's consumption I sent for publication under a pseudonym.

HABITS PLEASURABLE

In our lives, food is not merely fuel for energy for sustenance. It is a cult. It serves and is served for social reasons or just for sheer pleasure. While millions starve in some cultures, millions have 'eloquent sufficiency' or in short, are 'stuffed'. Ever since I can remember I was a disciplined eater because 'moderation' was the guiding principle in my upbringing. And so it was that from an early age I began eating chocolate, moderately.

The large block of Boci milk chocolate, wrapped inside pictures of big full patchy Hungarian 'Jerseys' freely grazing in lush green meadows under white fluffy clouds floating in deep blue skies, was always within my reach, resting between layers of white damask sheets in the cupboard. But I never touched it. One square of chocolate was dealt out to me. It was my daily potion. On special occasions I received an added small thin block of 'Tibi.' It came in light milk or dark bitter chocolate, enveloped in multi-coloured wrappings, which were accumulated in numerous borrowed shoe boxes, to be converted into bracelets, necklaces, and chain decorations for Christmas trees.

Each Sunday's midday meal was preceded by 'espresso meetings.' After the morning ritual visit to my grandmother, who never ever gave me a bite of chocolate, I accompanied my father to meet with one or both of his brothers. In summer, we sat outside somewhere on the shore of the Danube. While they talked and sipped their 'short black' espresso, I hurriedly ate my chocolate ice-cream before it became a melted mess. When they ordered 'long black', I may have ordered a crisp pretzel followed by more chocolate ice-cream.

There was a wide selection of chocolate concoctions awaiting in the winter warmth of various espressos. One favourite was the 'pyramid', an inverted cone shape of soft chocolate cream with a biscuit base. Another was Rigo Jancsi, and layers of chestnut puree and the chocolate never ceased to transport me into other worlds. All through the years I have been wondering what the men talked about, for all those hundreds of hours.

Every year till I was ten, my adopted Nagymama or grandmother created a birthday cake. The ingredients were pure chocolate, layered with thick chocolate cream, some chestnut cream, and decorated with chocolate pieces. It was the highlight of all my parties, anticipated and enjoyed by parents and children alike. All the preparations, mixing, baking, decorating and the washing up were shared with Nagymama, but the licking of the chocolate bowl was mine alone.

Even during the Revolution of 1956, when food was scarce, she managed to bake a small chocolate cake; but we were unable to share it with all our family and friends. There is something to be said for the Revolting Hungarians. I ate most of my birthday cake by myself; rationed, of course.

Six weeks later, after twenty-four hours of street walking, train rides, walking in knee high mud in snow covered farm fields, some tripping and falling, hiding in haystacks, some more walking without eating or drinking, we crossed the border into Austria. A Volkswagen bus landed us in a barn of a shelter, set up for the sole purpose of providing refuge for Hungarian 'fluchtlings' or refugees. Before continuing our transportation to Wien, we were fed hot chocolate drinks, and bars and bars of small chocolates.

During our five months stay in Austria, I was introduced to Lindt, and I enjoyed my portion of one square of chocolate per day, till at least once I consumed the whole block. Looking back on our four weeks voyage to Australia, it seems to have been one large grey mass of steel, named The General Harry Taylor which was scattered with Pepsi machines and Hershey Bars which were a novelty to me. While we sailed through starving Aden, touched the land of plenty in Fremantle and landed in Sydney, we munched on America's national confectionery.

For some time, our life in Australia was extremely modest and so was my intake of chocolates. However, by the time I was in senior High School I had a regular supply. Today, friends remember me with the singular distinction that next to my Senior Prefect badge, constantly protruding from my blazer's pocket, was a small dark 'Men's Club' chocolate.

At University, to prove that I was not an addict, I won a bet for stopping smoking for three months. The minute the clock struck the hour, I lit a cigarette and broke the seal on my winner's prize which was a small box of Baci. Later I graduated to the finest of nougat chocolates, Bouchee's 'Cote d'Or,' which I nicknamed. So, when someone offers you an 'elephant', take it. It is bound to be an orgasmic experience.

Once I was told that chocolate has a vital, even nourishing quality. My working life was usually quite hectic and my eating habits erratic. When I missed meals, a couple of bites of pure chocolate raised my blood sugar level. This treatment was recommended to me by a paramedic with total disregard for my increasing cholesterol level.

Much later in life regarding my increasing weight, a friend suggested a reducing diet of whiskey and chocolates only. Although the residual headache is not worth the fleeting ecstatic stupor, it may well have been handed down by some member of the worldwide organization known as 'Chocoholics Anonymous'.

While travelling overseas, I sampled a multitude of chocolates, ranging from 'M&Ms' to unpronounceable. One would have thought it my vocation, but an expert I did not become. Instead, on my return, I settled with my unique taste buds for a regular supply of Nestles' 'Choc Bits,' mostly 200 mg packs of dark chocolates, usually used to decorate children's birthday cakes and always found in choc-chip biscuits. It was cheap, readily available and loaded with addictive ingredients as were Darrell Lea's dark chocolate covered sultanas, which became my post graduate choice until they were discontinued.

However, it is inadvisable to eat such small bits of chocolates while in bed, at the movies or driving. Invariably, the little objects are accompanied by danger as they unobtrusively drop into one's lap, melt there and leave small dark brown stains in embarrassing places. Further, one ought not to offer cooking chocolate to guests. It is definitely more socially acceptable to offer an elephant.

My home is still a store house for bits of chocolates strategically placed for instant retrieval. The rare event has occurred in the past that my cravings outweighed my stock, and the hunt began for all the odd bits of chocolate deposited in various areas. The scavenger in me rummaged in likely and unlikely hiding places, as is characteristic of the absent minded and desperate addict. When unsuccessful, I speedily drove many miles to the first open food market where the shelves openly offered a multitude of chocolate choices. With my modest selection of strictly plain dark chocolate, I proceeded home. There, in the confines of that secure and secluded environment, I consumed my bits of pleasure until I had 'eloquent sufficiency.'

Veronica Kennedy

The letter of rejection was brief indeed and totally uninformative. However, it had no effect on my chocolate consumption whatsoever. And it had no effect on my writing efforts when prompted by need or circumstance. Over the years I sent a multitude of photographs to family and friends, and all of them were accompanied by explanatory letters which were many pages long of which copies were collected in many thick folders. When photographs became digital and I stopped printing them, I stopped writing the letters, which to this day are lamented and missed by those still very appreciative family members and friends.

At university I wrote numerous essays of varying lengths, and they were specific to the required academic format. The grades I achieved varied, but they were of a most satisfactory level depending on the time I spent on them. Some subjects were more attractive than others and I was credited accordingly.

A major project of mine was the story of *Forbat Styles*. It was prompted by what I considered some injustice. I was not contacted to be interviewed by the organisers and the truth about the hard work of my parents to establish and develop the *Forbat* business was not acknowledged. I felt I owed it to my parents' memory to correct the misinformation.

"In the year 2013, the Sydney Jewish Museum held an exhibition titled 'Dressing Sydney: The Jewish Fashion Story'. It was a two-year joint project by the Museum in cooperation with the University of Technology Sydney, under Professor Peter McNeil who led a team in co-creating and curating the history of Jewish immigrants in the Sydney clothing trade between 1945 and 1990.

Interestingly, the exhibit for Forbat Styles took centre stage in the advertisement of the

Sydney Jewish Museum Temporary Exhibition Site. Sadly, besides a short text about Mr Ernie Friedlander much of which was a personal reminiscence, the exhibit was merely an empty clothes hanger, with the Forbat company name printed on it.

I believe that the history of Forbat Styles should be told in its entirety, from when Mr and Mrs Forbat started the business with the sale of their first skirt, to when the last thousands of locally manufactured garments were delivered. Most of the historical material source is retrospective memorial but with witness testimony, and a few visual images. It is unfortunate that the very relevant and detail documentations of a large part of the company's past, were destroyed in the hailstorm in 1999. Nonetheless, I believe that the 44 years history of the identity of Forbat Styles deserves to be recorded."

So I did. The above was my Introduction to *The Forbat Story*. My husband Harry organised to print and publish it professionally and so, *The Forbat Story* was registered in 2017. I am happy in the knowledge that it is sitting in the National Library, and that there is a copy in the NSW State Library and one in the Jewish Museum Library with several copies in the bookshop of the SJM. Today I am proud of my publication and that it created some interest even today in my book clubs.

The first book club I joined originated from a lunch time play group of mothers who discussed books while their young children played. Then in 1981 two Melbourne ladies Susan and Vera, settled in Sydney and started an evening book club. We now meet in different homes each month to discuss a different book we read each month. We also spend time discussing other topics such as our grandchildren as well as problems of the world.

Early in the history we borrowed copies of the same book for each member and at some point, an English lecturer from Sydney University was our guide and tutor who read and commented on the report of our discussion on the literature as recorded by our elected scribe. For over the forty years a core group remained constant. We became very supportive of each other through some traumatic events. Today we still tend to discuss the selected book but not as intensely as in the past.

That is quite understandable. We have come to know each other so well, that we know how everyone thinks and what everyone likes. Similar to the gaol inmates who after many years of telling the same jokes, knew them so well that they just numbered them. Then all they needed to do was call out a number and they all knew the joke. In our case, at times we merely take a census of those who liked the book or those who did not.

The second book club I joined some years ago is very different. I called it my analytical book club as each book is thoroughly analysed and discussed. The members include teachers, librarians and one lovely journalist lady who is now a double PhD. All were well versed in literature, and I was forced to be more articulate during the discussions.

To that end, I wrote down my comments which were ordered and relatively all-inclusive of my thoughts. My initial purpose was to make notes for myself so that I would remember some of the more relevant points. When it came to my turn to speak on the book, I just read out my opinions. It surprised me that all the ladies were appreciative of my written presentations. And I became most appreciative of my book clubs that forced me to read at least two good books a month for many years.

Writers vary in their opinion about reading and writing. I should think that reading while writing would influence one's writing and may even interfere with it. And writing being a solitary task, may be a lonely one. It may even be self-indulgent.

Writing is not easy. It is not easy for me. I find it hard work. But whatever it is, it must always, always, be gratifying.

"Love words, agonize over sentences. And pay attention to the world."

Susan Sontag

Chapter Two
GRANDPARENTS

*"Grandparents are like stars.
You don't always see them, but you know they're there."*

My recollection of what my parents told me about my grandparents is sketchy by far, as is what they told me about their own youth and wartime experiences. It is strange how children are so focused on their own lives, that even when they listen to anecdotes about the life of their parents, they hear little. I certainly did not hear enough, and it is a shame that I did not ask any more questions than I did while they were alive.

I never met my maternal grandparents at all. They were transported to and murdered in *Auschwitz*. My maternal grandmother was Klein Hermina (nee Kellerman) and my maternal grandfather was Klein Geza. Together they had three children, Erno was the oldest, my mother Ibolya or Ibi was the girl in the middle between two boys, and Gyula was the youngest. They had what must have been a comfortable family home with a spacious garden in Ujpest and they must have had a nice life till the war.

Hermina (Kellerman) and Geza Klein   c 1942   Erno, Ibolya and Gyula Klein

I always had the impression that the Kleins were an attractive and close-knit family. In most of the photographs Hermina appears as a solid shortish figure with a pleasant face, while Geza looked quite the opposite, a tall slim man with an almost 'Huszar' moustache. The boys grew tall like Geza, while my mother was taller than Hermina. About the personalities of the grandparents, I can only hypothesize from their photographic appearances and from the little my mother told me, but they seemed different also. While she was reported to be somewhat distant, he was warm and friendly, and had a close relationship with their children.

Hermina did not speak Hungarian and communication was mostly in German having been born somewhere in the Austro-Hungarian empire. She was fully occupied with house and home, cooking and cleaning for three men. There was always a lot of washing; the boiling of linen and scrubbing men's clothes was all hard work. She kept a *Kosher* (according to Jewish law) kitchen and was believed to be quite religious. Her husband on the other hand was complicit with the children in hiding the fact that they ate *Trejf* (non-Kosher) foods. The children and their father tried to avoid the Jewish rituals.

My grandparents must have treated their children equally, although my mother did mention that the youngest Gyula was spoilt by the whole family. He was good looking and charming. When my mother was married, she received a heavy gold chain bracelet from her parents and identical bracelets were made for and given to the two daughters-in-law as wedding presents.

Geza Klein's Rubber Repair Workshop in Ujpest

Geza had a small rubber repair factory. Retreading tires was very good business and the two boys worked with their father. But the children were also educated. My mother attended secondary school at the Scottish Ladies college. Her older brother Erno was a reader and a studious young man who even studied the classics. Gyula may not have been the best of students, but in his adult life he gained tertiary qualifications as an engineer. The three children were very close to each other from their early childhood to the very end of their lives, and they spent much time together in their youth.

From all accounts the Kleins were very hospitable people. Many weekends were spent with their house full of extended family members. Members of my father's family were invited for many Sunday lunches. There is evidence of my father's mother and brothers the Freunds and their families the Fischers being in Ujpest house.

Misi (my father), Hermina, Geza, Karolina and Ibolya c 1939

That was the balcony of the house that my grandmother Hermina refused to desert when my father wanted the whole family to leave the country with the rise of Nazism. When the threat was imminent, someone buried the small, treasured family possessions which were nothing of any significant monetary value, but of considerable sentimental value. Of the few pieces that were dug up after the war one third was given to my mother. It comprised of a blue Czechoslovakian crystal ashtray, a small silver jewelry box, a silver picture frame, and a pair of hollow silver candle holders, with fine floral engravings, that once adorned my grandmother's *Shabbat* or Sabath table.

Erno, Ibolya, Hermina, Gyula and Geza (c1933)

My paternal grandparents were Freund Mor and his wife Freund Karolina (nee Stern). They had four sons, Laszlo or Laci, Erno, Bela and Miksa or Misi who was my father.

I never met my paternal grandfather who died long before the war. None of the Freund grandchildren know about him, except that he was an alcoholic. He beat up his wife and that was when one of his sons, Bela threw him out of their home. For some time his wife, our grandmother looked after him even though he was not living with her, and she even supported him financially. As no one spoke of him and since there is no photograph of him, we have no visual image of him.

Misi, Grandmother Karolina, Olga and husband Laci (c 1933)

There are no photos of all the Freund family members together. Although I met my only living Grandmother Karolina regularly, I never really knew her and knew precious little about her.

We knew that she was in close contact with one sister who she mentioned frequently. Some of her grandchildren still don't know much about her.

But we knew that she supported the Communist Party. We knew that she was a hawker selling linen mostly to hospitals. We knew that she took in ironing at times. More significantly we knew that she brought up four boys on her own quite remarkably and that they were all decent human beings and family men.

On one or two New Year's Eves Grandmother Karolina looked after me, when my cousin Zsuzsi (Erno's daughter) came over to stay the night while our parents celebrated together. On the many Sundays that I visited her and placed some money between the sheets in her cupboard, it was very much a meeting for mother and son. Yet my father was not her favourite, because he caused her to have a prolapsed uterus after his birth. But in any event, she didn't particularly like my mother.

However, like a good mother, she did provide my father with clean sheets and towels whenever he took his lady bed friends on weekends to Romai on the Danube shores. Thus, she contributed some excellence to his youth despite the family's lack of financial wealth.

What I remember about her was that she was always dressed in black with black high ankle shoes. She always wore a dark scarf to cover her sparse hair which sadly I inherited. She always sat on her bed, and she always complained about her legs, and that she had to wrap the *fasli* or bandages around her legs daily. Later she needed help with it.

Once communism planted its feet solidly, the authorities promptly planted a family of three into one of the two rooms of my grandmother's flat. Before the war that room was occupied by Laci and his family, and later by his two orphaned daughters after their parents were taken away by the Nazis. Later still, that room was the home of granddaughter Eva and her family until they had their own flat not far from her.

It was fortunate that the young woman planted in her flat happened to like my grandmother and looked after her very well. But then she did get extra *aponans* or payments on the side. Besides, the flat was left to her and her family.

When we received the news of her passing, we left my father alone to grieve. My mother said that it is when his mother dies, that a man becomes a grown-up man. And of course, that is different with women; we are born grown up.

Bela, Erno, Misi 1973

Chapter Three
PARENTS

"A parent's love is whole no matter how many times divided."

Robert Brault

My parents were born in Hungary. My mother Klein Ibolya was born on 14th October 1910 in Budapest and my father Freund Miksa was born on 6th October 1910 in Budapest. I never knew how they met but my mother often attended what was called a 'dancing school' which was more like a club. It was a safe way of meeting eligible young men, and my mother danced with a few. She must have been very much a social being from a young age.

I don't know the exact level of school my mother finished but it was in the Scottish Mission School for Jewish and Christian girls in Vorosmarti Utca. It was also a boarding school and during the war a refuge for Jewish children. I understand that she may have received her school certificate before she started work as a dressmaker. And she must have been an attentive student. Where else would she have learnt about Damocles, whose swords often dangled above her head and subsequently mine too.

My mother looked most elegant as all the photos of her illustrate. She said she liked to sew from a very early age, and she made all her own clothes. She also said she wanted to have a daughter so she could sew clothes for her. Her wish was granted, and she made all my dresses while she was alive.

Her taste in fashion was that of simple elegance. While I always stood out from my peers because I looked different, I was secretly proud of my lovely clothes made by my mother. We designed my ball gowns together too and each one was especially unique. I felt simply beautiful in everyone of them. My mother was not yet twenty years old when she had her own dressmaking salon.

I always thought of my father as a handsome young man who was a gentleman and had a great sense of humour. I don't think he graduated from high school, but he was self-taught. He was very well read and very well informed. He had a wealth of general knowledge, particularly of history. He taught himself the violin and when he was very young, he played on street corners to earn extra money. He also sold shoelaces and other goods in his early teens when he started his *gescheft* or business transactions. I assume that it was on street corners and at the market where he began his career as a man of trade.

When he was old enough, my father became an apprentice at *Herceg es Fodor*, which was a relatively large men's store. He did all the work that was asked of him from sweeping the street in front of the shop and window dressing, to being in charge. He spoke fondly of his valuable experience at that store, where he also met the man who became his lifelong best friend, Gal Andi. I was told that as a young man, my father started a number of businesses on his own, but none were successful.

However, he was successful with women. He must have been a charming young man, when he wrote notes to his lady friends, and treated them well. Because he really could not afford expensive evenings, he bought the one ticket for the lady and dropped her off at the theatre or movies. Later he returned to pick her up at the end of the performance, claiming that he 'finished the stock take' or whatever excuse he provided. It seemed to have worked well for him for many years.

My mother received many notes from him during their long courtship. The reason for that was probably that he needed time to establish himself in his trade. So, for five years my parents dated but in their social circle of many friends, they were known as cousins, while my father had his lady bed friends in Romai. My mother knew about the ladies and was even acquainted with some personally.

c 1935

During that time as well as afterwards, my parents skied, rowed, played tennis and other sports. My father was particularly athletic, and it was a great revelation for me who was and is totally nonsporting, to see him on the parallel bars. And surprisingly, even at 63 years of age, he could jump up onto a cutting table in his factory, in one leap!

c1934

In his youth he somehow acquired a motorcycle with a side carriage. There were stories about how the motorcycle stalled every time it saw my mother. I doubt that he could fix it as he was neither handy nor mechanical. I was always the one to change the light bulbs and use a screwdriver in our home. I am sure that it was my uncle Gyula in Ujpest who repaired it each time.

My parents married on 25th August 1935 in the famous and beautiful Dohany Utca Temple. It is the biggest Synagogue in Europe, bombed in 1939 by the Hungarian Arrow Cross and restored by the end of the twentieth century. When I was in Budapest, I visited the synagogue and took a couple of photographs of where my parents held their wedding. I also visited the silver tree which is a Memorial to those who perished in the Holocaust. My cousin Marti founded a silver leaf for her parents, my uncle Laci and his wife Olga. The Memorial was established with the total support of the Hollywood movie actor Tony Curtis who changed his name from Bernard Schwartz which was originally his Hungarian name.

Freund Ibolya and Miksa 1935   Dohany Utca Temple c 1998

As a couple, my parents complemented each other, and I do believe that they were happy together throughout their lives. They enjoyed their youth together. Their honeymoon seemed idyllic, and they had many happy holidays including their tour to France shortly before the Germans invaded Paris. I must admit that I really liked the look of my parents as a married couple when on their honeymoon.

There is one photo of my parents with backpacks on one of their hiking tours. As a small girl I watched the peddlers every time they wheeled their pushcarts into our courtyard, filled with pots and pans and other wares. They wore similar backpacks full of more utensils and goods. Many was the time when looking at this photo, I asked my parents if they too were *Oszeresek*, peddlers or hawkers.

(1935)   (1935)

Before my parents were separated by the war, my mother had a miscarriage. She said that had he lived, I would have had a brother, unless of course he would have perished in the war. I was always quite happy being an only child though it would have been nice to have a brother who I imagined as a child, would have introduced me to boyfriends. And much later in life, it would have been a tremendous help to have another sibling when both my parents became seriously ill at the same time.

Both my parents were Holocaust Survivors. My father was always an optimist. He always spoke freely of his war time experiences at dinners. He wanted to emigrate as early as 1938. He wanted all family members, his and my mother's family to leave Hungary. He saw the developments in Germany, and even predicted the consequences. He saw that Europe was headed for the disaster which eventually occurred, and he wanted to escape it.

He had done his research on the people and the culture of the "big pink land at the bottom" of the world map, and he wanted to emigrate to Australia. However, my mother did not want to leave her family particularly her parents, who did not want to leave their home. So, they all stayed and faced their fate. The Hungarians gave the Jews freely to the Germans and my grandparents were taken to *Auschwitz* in June 1944 where they perished in August 1944.

All the men, my father, his three older brothers and my mother's older brother were sent to various forced labour camps. Her younger brother Gyula was an exceptional man. My mother avoided deportation by hiding as a Gentile with false identification papers which my uncle Gyula was instrumental in obtaining. She told me of some of her experiences while hiding in Budapest with false papers, but without any great detail.

She was a public toilet cleaning lady for a while. As she was a dressmaker, she made clothes for the ladies in a brothel. The Madam liked her and protected her from her clientele especially from German military. Thus, she was safe from the Nazi transportation. On one occasion she was on her way to visit my father in one of the forced labour camps, when she found herself in the same town as the real Kalman Anna whose name was on her false documents. On another occasion she was saved by accepting to ride on a truck with some German soldiers. A brave woman and as many would have it, a lucky one.

My father moved from one camp to another across Europe including Mauthausen. He worked on railway tracks much of the time. He told of some harrowing events of narrow escapes. Whether he acquired injections for his knee to incapacitate him not to be transported out of the camp where he was held, or as on another occasion he purposely contracted typhus to be moved out of camp where he was held, most of the time he seemed to have been ahead of the transport to *Auschwitz*. And he made them all sound as if they were just ordinary stories.

He was a practical man and the many lessons he learnt, he passed on to his fellow inmates. Important was to always eat slowly even the small rations and to keep clean even if the snow with which they washed was icy in the cold winter. One of his lifesaving lessons was that no matter what ill treatment or beating one received, men must not fall down. Once on the ground, few survived the Nazi boots. Despite that my father was kicked in the head and was left with very limited hearing in one ear.

He helped wherever he could as we were told by those who knew him before and during the war. He was a barrack's leader or a *Kapo*. Since he spoke German, he befriended the German *Kapos* and obtained extra rations for the men in his barracks. A tradesman by nature he traded a cigarette for a potato, some potatoes for a block of cheese and so on. He divided and rationed everything equally to all including himself, and because of that he was highly respected.

When liberated from Turkheim Concentration Camp by the American armed forces, my father assisted them as best he could. Since most prisoners were starved, he prevented many from eating all at once what was given to them by the generous Americans. At the beginning he rationed very small portions and then increased the quantities slowly to build up the prisoners' strength gradually after long periods of starvation and malnutrition.

My father met Ilonka, his brother Bela's wife in the hospital where she was treated for her eye injury. He obtained some khaki American army uniform fabric and had tailor made three-piece outfits for both of them by some of the prison inmates. Later he teased his listening audience that they were the best and most elegantly dressed surviving prisoners to return from the Camps. Those suits lasted for many years and Ilonka's skirt was worn by her daughter Marika when she emigrated after the 1956 Revolution.

He always said that he "toured much of Europe", meaning that he was moved through many concentration and extermination camps. After the War, both my parents changed their surname, to make it sound less Jewish and more Westernised or whatever. I supposed there was much fear lingering amidst Hungarian and European Jews. My mother's maiden name of Klein became Kenedi and my father's name was changed from Freund to Forbat, which was distinctly neither Hungarian nor English. I was born Forbat.

Much of Budapest was bombed during the war. At the end of the war, my parents searched for somewhere to live. Until I was born, they shared a small flat in Visegradi Utca. They believed that it was not possible for them to take in either of my cousins, who were left without their parents. The cousins were looked after by an aunt and by our grandmother. There is still some debate and perhaps some negative feeling about why the cousins were not adopted by my parents. Much later my parents moved to Csaki Utca.

Both my parents worked in the clothing industry. My father was head of the department for men's shirts, men's and women's nightwear at DNV (Divataru Nagykereskedelmi Valalat). My mother was head of one of R.T.V.'s (Ruhaipari Tervezo Valalat) departments, which created samples and produced women's and children's clothing for export.

My mother was an expert dressmaker and became well versed in the process of manufacturing from design through to the assembly line production. She also purchased a couple of sample dresses for me that were much larger than my size at the time. She would alter them to fit me by taking in the sides and taking up the hems. As I grew, she would alter them by letting them out and letting them down. So, I wore those dresses for many years as was the case with one lovely white dress which I wore from when I was seven or eight years old until I was about fourteen years old.

My parents' lives were dominated by work always and I believe that I inherited their work ethic. One must work to earn a living, and one must do a good job. It seemed as though my father always had to fight to stay in his position from which someone wanted to remove him. One such occasion was the rusty pin incident which was a long story told many times. In short, one of the storerooms had a water leak about which my father warned his superiors many times and sent multiple reports about the consequences to the appropriate departments. With one heavy down pour, there was major damage; the pins that held together the folded shirts had rusted. He was able to prove that he predicted the event, that he warned his superiors well ahead of time and was freed from any blame. Thus, he retained his position.

In the first ten years of my life, my parents' biggest grievance was the amount of time and effort they put into their jobs for which they were never recompensed. They had little time together. Due to their shift work they missed each other often and communicated by notes left in a vase on our dining table. Despite the fact that they adhered to a tight budget for essentials, the money they earned was never enough.

As soon as they received their monthly wage, they paid the rent for our apartment and there really was not much left for the rest of the month. So, my parents would borrow money from the family and close friends, from my mother's brother Gyula, from my father's brother Bela, from their best friends the Gals and from our dear friends and neighbours the Sakardis. When they received their pay the following month, they would pay the rent and all that they owed to the families and friends from who they borrowed. Then the vicious cycle would start again. That continued for years.

The second ten years of my life were in Australia and whenever my parents argued it was over the accumulation of raw materials and ready garments in their women's clothing manufacturing business. That was my mother's grievance most of their working life. Otherwise, they were a most harmonious couple, and we were a happy family.

As time passed, the business grew as did the staff numbers. Neither of my parents needed to be in the factory on the weekends and they were not as busy constantly as in the first decade. Although range time was always very pressured, my parents' work decreased. And my parents did take holidays. They always tried to combine their overseas business trips with visits to relatives especially in Budapest. They established a pleasant social life with friends and had series tickets to the operas and concerts. One might say that they had carved out a comfortable existence and contented life in our new country.

Surfers' Paradise 1965

My parents were always very close to each other. They always discussed everything openly, so I was witness to everything that happened in my family. My mother said that I can ask her about anything and everything, and she discussed sex very freely. My father was always a wealth of information on any subject. They had a good marriage despite the opinion of one of our relatives. Yes, my parents did argue. However, their arguments were always always work related. But they loved each other and respected each other.

I witnessed them exchanging little very private understanding glances and gently touching each other on the arm or shoulder that seemed as if they spoke to each other without words. And they held each other's hand when they crossed the road. Much like young lovers. What seemed unique about my parents amongst the people of their generation was that they not only loved each other but that they liked each other also.

As parents they were loving, caring, understanding and they gave me an emotional security that I value highly to this day. That was rare in the lives of my friends. I remember telling my friends that if they believed that their parents didn't understand them (as most teenagers did believe), then they should organise a date with their parents for coffee, sit and just talk.

Those who made the effort developed a closer relationship with their parents. There was nothing that I could not discuss with my parents. My mother always said that while I could see them, I had nothing to fear. And I feared nothing while they were alive until my children were born. Then I feared for them. She also told me not to be as modest and humble as I was, though her favourite word was 'moderation,' and she tried to steer me in that direction.

She taught me to smoke a cigarette at age 16 years, because she did not want me to smoke behind her back. That was a mistake. By the time I was twenty-five I smoked two packets a day of a menthol cigarette called *Consulate*. But I gave up smoking completely from one cigarette to the next just after the birth of my third son.

My parents had a solid seventeen years of mostly work in Australia after which they continued life at a much more relaxed pace, but illness struck them both. My mother was fifty-three when first she was diagnosed with lymphosarcoma. Post surgery radiation treatment was successful and gave her an extra ten years of life. Then the disease resurfaced. Unfortunately, at that time I was overseas, and she waited till I came home. She also insisted that my father have his surgery before she had hers. By then she lost too much time.

My father had a prostatectomy that went wrong because the surgeon was intoxicated. The surgeon subsequently fell down the stairs at St Vincent's Private Hospital sustaining leg injuries that ironically landed him in the room next to that of my father. For days no one believed that my father had internal bleeding until he was unconscious. Then the repair post-surgery period was long, as was the convalescence. But he did make a full recovery.

When at the end of 1973 my aunt and uncle arrived from Budapest, Klari and Gyula found my father rather weak and my mother bedridden. I drove my relatives around the country but could not replace my parents. Although their stay in Australia was not the same as planned or expected the time the family spent together was most memorable and especially precious for my mother.

Harry and I met a few days after Klari and Gyula left Sydney and within eight weeks we were engaged to be married. For the following year my mother was ill and hospitalised frequently. Since only I knew her very poor prognosis, I hoped that she would be well enough to be present at our wedding. She was, though she sat through the marriage ceremony.

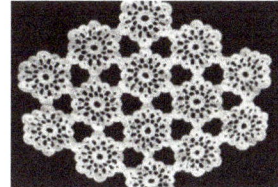
For well over a year of being in and out of hospital, my mother directed the business of pattern making, cutting and production in the factory from a distance. She also embroidered my married monograms on my new bed linen and crocheted a few doyleys for family and friends as her last gift to them.

My mother died in 1975 at the age of sixty-four. She always said that her mother never saw her grandchildren and she didn't think she would see hers. However, she was content in the knowledge that I would have children because I was five months pregnant.

A few weeks before she died, my father had a heart attack and a stroke as a result. There is a saying that 'it is not what you know but who you know.' Because the cardiologist gave up on my father, I called on my colleague Dr Ben Maroszeky, who at that time was in charge of Rehabilitation at Prince Henry Hospital. Coincidentally, his mother was our dentist in Budapest. She was a large lady, a painful tooth filler and an even more painful tooth extractor, despite her free use of 'freezing' which was the anaesthetic that never worked for my cousin or me.

Dr Ben was more positive about my father's prognosis with some reservation. After much therapeutic treatment, my father was able to walk a few steps slowly with a quad stick and eventually did manage to negotiate a whole flight of stairs. At one stage, my adoring father who was afraid to pick me up as a baby for fear of dropping me, pushed me to the floor while I was heavily pregnant. For over three years, my father was trapped in a disabled body with no speech. During all that time my husband was an incredible help and support. Although it is a hazy one, my first-born son has a memory of his banana sharing with my father, who died in 1978 at the age of sixty-seven.

(1975)

It was a very sad and relatively early ending to the lives of the two most important people in the first and a very significantly large part of my life. It is a shame that the last few ill years have left such an indelible mark in my memory. Though I never placed them on a pedestal or ever praised them more dead than alive, I do believe that they were genuinely decent caring beings. I loved my parents, and I liked them. And I am grateful for their unconditional love.

Violet and Michael Forbat 25th August 1974

Chapter Four
CHILDHOOD

> *"The two most important days in your life are the day you were born and the day you find out why."*
>
> Mark Twain

One might say that my childhood was an idyllic one. I wanted for nothing, and I was very much loved. I was always protected, and, in many ways, I had a sheltered life. My mother always said that I had nothing to fear while I could see my parents. Hence, I had what I would call a contended and an emotionally secure life.

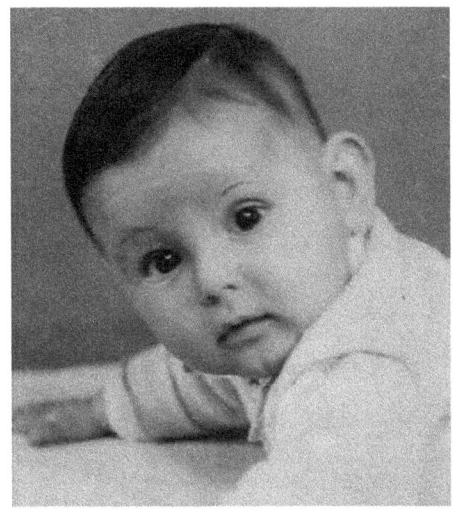

A long-awaited child, I was a very much wanted. Intrauterine, my condition was troublesome, and the doctors advised my mother that there was threat to her full-term pregnancy, due to a number of factors. She had surgery to remove a myoma in the sixth month of her pregnancy and had war time residual malnutrition. Also, she was a 36-year-old woman, relatively old in those days.

However, the foetus that was 'I' survived and after what was for my mother an eternally long thirty-six hours of labour, I was delivered with forceps. Such instrumental interference to my earthly arrival, always causes at least one of my sons to comment, "So that is what went wrong." I have not yet told them that forceps also assisted their births.

My parents knew that it was 'I' who was going to be born to them, or so my father always said. As I was growing up, he not only never threatened me, but he always made me feel as if I were the most important thing in my parents' lives. Yet, on numerous occasions he said that he could not sell the long awaited me at any market for the paltry sum of five *fillér*, the smallest currency in Hungary. When I threatened my sons with Bill Cosby's "I brought you into this world, and I can take you out," they just laughed.

My father adored me and sometimes his mere smile so informed me. My mother told me that after I was born, he rarely picked me up for fear of dropping me. But from the day I stood on my own two feet, whenever we walked together, my hand was held by his hand, the warmth of which I think I can feel still.

My cousin Marika had always said that she was present at my birth. She was ten years old when she visited the hospital after I was born, and to this day she remembers me as a very nice-looking baby. Personally, I believe that all babies are rather unattractive little creatures at birth. They may grow into lovely if not beautiful children as my grandchildren and even attractive adults, much like my sons.

I know that from the time I was born, I was surrounded with affection from everyone around me. I was also very carefully watched by my parents. I must have been about one year old when I started sliding on my potty. I was very quickly taken to a specialist who must have very quickly diagnosed my displaced hip joints and promptly plaster casted me from waist down to my knees. Later the doctors decided that I was misdiagnosed, but by then I was walking normally.

I had live-in Nannies from an early age while my mother worked full time. The first lady was the tiny Mariska who had a limp from Polio, which had a stigma my mother seemed to have ignored. She treated me as if I were her own child as did the others who looked after me. She hid from my parents the more expensive foods like ham and veal, so that I could have more.

Going to kindergarten was a rude shock to the system. But there were some very interesting new activities. We wrapped buds of chives, shallots, and potatoes in cotton wool in small containers and placed them between the double windows which were sunny but sheltered. I knelt on a window seat daily as I watched little shoots sprout from the white fluff and eventually grow into plants overshadowed by patterns of ice crystals on the glass, while I longed to be back home.

Every winter my ears, nose, and hands were freezing despite having my warm woollen hats with earpieces attached and matching mittens. I longed for fingered gloves which were much more attractive, like those of other children, and because not much can be done with only a thumb. The mittens may have been clumsy but later I found out that they were much warmer than the fingered gloves.

As winter approached, so did our fuel supplies. I stood freezing in the cold, as I waited and watched the unloading of the wood and coal. They were carried through the courtyard, down into the basement and stacked in our storage space. When during the 1956 Revolution the radio announced imminent air raids, we were forced to huddle on our wood pile in the basement. We were fortunate that no bombs struck our house. Standing and waiting in line for bread, I was freezing cold. Standing and waiting for the bus or trolley, I was freezing cold.

But I was not freezing when my friend Kertai Juli and I skated together at the Ice Rink in *Varosliget's* lake which was artificially frozen even in winter. Unlike everyone I knew who had proper white shoe skates, I had metal skates that I attached to my shoes with leather straps. I was hot and properly perspiring from exertion when I struggled to slide my feet with the old blades, keeping up with my friend and avoiding the speed skaters. But I persevered and eventually I managed to skate backwards and even do a figure eight after a fashion, though each experience resembled a mild torture for me.

Varosligeti Lake frozen lake

Juli had a most mischievous younger sister. On a few occasions when we reached the *Liget*, her little sister would shout, "End of the line! Everybody out!" All the passengers would get off and the tram or the trolley would continue empty to the end of the line, leaving the passengers stranded. She was small and disappeared between the legs of the adults and was never caught.

It was dark and it was chilly at the start of winter days in Budapest. Every second week I dreaded getting ready for the morning session of school. We had warm water once a week usually on Sundays. The daily washing of hands, face, underarm and undercarriage was fine in summer but in winter it was bitterly cold. I even tried to avoid brushing my teeth in the cold water. That was to my detriment later in life. Then I had to walk to my school.

On those freezing days the roads were icy. I walked leaning against building walls. Crossing was difficult with no props. It was not a matter of bracing myself, taking a deep breath, counting, and then hurrying across the road. Running on ice was never an option. But I had to hurry. The sight of me slipping and sliding must have been like watching some comedian doing a shoe skating dance on ice. It was fortunate that my school was literally around the corner in Csanadi Utca. The distance was short but always a challenge and spectacular.

My parents and I lived in a typical six-storey u-shaped building with a cobble stone central courtyard which extended into the garden in Csaki Utca 37, in Budapest. Ours was one of the smaller of five apartments on the first floor and consisted of two rooms, bathroom, toilet, kitchen, and a maid's room which was rented out for many years. Oh, and there was a *Licht Hof* or 'light court' which was an open building shaft space we shared with our immediate neighbour and where we kept food for cold storage.

The kitchen had a coal burning stove, an 'icebox' which needed to be stacked daily with blocks of ice in summer, and I shall never forget the *fregoli* or clothesline that normally slept on the ceiling. We spent many summer Sundays, bottling fruits and vegetables for winter. Dozens of tomatoes, pickled cucumbers, apples, pears, apricots, and peaches among others were cooked, placed in jars and sealed. They were shelved in the *speise* or pantry next to the kitchen. We also 'cooked' or boiled our bed linen and hung them on the *fregoli* that travelled down and up. Once dry, they were ironed with one coal filled iron while another coal filled iron was warming on the stove. It was easy for all those delightful aromas from all the kitchen activities to have permeated our small home.

My window above the entrance to the basement looked down to the garden and onto the *porolo*, or carpet rack/hanger which was for beating the dust out of carpets and rugs. It was made of two horizontal wooden planks attached to two upright ones on either side. I always had difficulty climbing up onto it and greater difficulty staying on the narrow planks. It served as our magic vehicle which transported us to different worlds, and we may have stayed there for hours, with or without a carpet.

The Manager lived on the ground floor with her twins, Karcsi and Juli (like Jack and Jill) who were my age. Karcsi kept breaking one of my toys. The caretaker of the building lived on the top floor, above which there was a very dark dirty smelly attic. The place was ideal for hiding and playing. I disliked it intensely but was never brave enough to say anything and joined in as children do. I could always look forward to my refuge two floors below to the two little old ladies, who welcomed me every time.

The home of the Klein sisters was filled with old paintings and antique furniture which had crocheted doylies on the backs and arms of the chairs. They were always busy with their hands and one of them was constantly knitting. I used to sit on a stool at her foot, roll wool into balls and watch her hands move for hours while I listened to her stories, none of which I remember. She was particularly clever using four or five or more needles at the same time when knitting the fingered gloves.

We had other good neighbours, and I spent many happy hours with most of them. One was an officer in the AVO which was the much-feared secret police. I never thought I had to be frightened of him, and he taught me canasta. We spent a lot of time playing cards especially during the Revolution, sometimes in the basement.

But the most wonderful of neighbours were the Sarkadis who lived next door. I attended school for six days and stayed with the Sarkadis while my parents were at work. I never knew my grandparents, so I adopted the couple next door. My adopted *Nagymama* or grandmother was a warm affectionate woman, who was as comfortable in her apron in the kitchen as she was reading classical literature.

She had an uncanny understanding that her husband's outward lack of affection towards his children, grown up as they were, disguised a deep love for them, and this she was able to balance with pragmatism and sensitivity. Although to me she always seemed old, she had some wonderfully youthful ideas and revelled in the company of young people. And she treated my parents the same way as her two children.

Like my mother, *Nagymama* believed that there was a time and a place for everything. She taught me etiquette and, in a way, prepared me for polite adult society. She was a most subtle educator. She subtly placed two very heavy books under my arms. And they were heavy. But I only had to endure their weight a few times before my elbows were neatly tucked in to my body when I ate. She also taught me to eat the vegetables I disliked with the main course without any fuss. She knew I loved soup, so she made me eat my main course before I was allowed to eat my soup. It all worked well.

There was a certain order to things that had to be observed. The priority was my schoolwork. Before everything else, especially going outside to play, I had to finish all my homework. And worse, she tested me. Then I had to help in the kitchen with preparations as well as cleaning up. I was the official mortar and pestle cleaner polisher. Made of solid heavy copper, I had to climb on a stool to get it down from the top of the cupboard – a challenge for the non-sporty me – and once used, I had to wash it, then polish it again and put it back up. It always, always out shone all the other copper utensils. And I was allowed to lick the chocolate from the bowl when she baked some delicious chocolate cakes.

Although they rarely ventured out of the house, the Sarkadis took their adopted granddaughter, me, to the popular holiday place of Romai on the banks of the Danube River. I learned to play table tennis there and I nearly drowned there. But I shall never forget the view from my bed. It was a bright full moonlight that shone across a still Danube. There I learnt about the moon's cycle and to this day, I eagerly await and admire every full moon.

My adopted *Nagypapa* or grandfather never seemed to be anything other than older than anyone I knew. His hand was always cupped on his ear as if that would increase his hearing aid volume. He was always wearing the same plain camel woollen golf hat. In summer and winter, indoors and out, that hat was perched on his head at one or another angle. He even wore it to bed and on the odd occasion when I found him there, the hat was skewed, giving the serious and respectable old gentleman an unbecoming, dishevelled appearance.

Often while reading he fell asleep, and the hat would slide forward. The visor rested on his nose, while the back of the hat was caught between his head and the back of the armchair. As his body moved in rhythm with his breathing, so the visor would rise and fall. Periodically, he lifted his hat, replaced it in the same position as that which woke him, wiggled his moustache, and continued to snore.

One of his hobbies that he shared with me was creating small, colourful vases from used light bulbs. We would cut off the screw part. Then using a Bunsen burner, we melted the edge of the cut glass to smooth it, heat the area that was to be reformed and dented the bottom. When it cooled, we would pour paint into the glass, rotate it to form various colourful patterns. *Nagypapa* would then lift his hat, do a quarter turn, and return it to his head, visor over one ear. But none saw him in that undignified fashion.

Problems intrigued my Nagypapa. When he saw my thin wooden doll's furniture broken, he picked up his hat by the visor between thumb and forefinger and while holding it in mid-air, he scratched his bald head with his free fingers in a circular motion before replacing the hat by twisting it slightly from side to side. Once the hat settled comfortably on his head, he began to cut thin sheets of aluminium and form angle reinforcements for my toy furniture.

Although a retired engineer, he was often consulted on major projects. He sat at his large burgundy felt inlay framed mahogany partners' desk, which no one was allowed to touch. Not even *Nagymama* was allowed to dust it. When the phone rang, he adjusted his hearing aid, he leaned back, pushed up his hat above his forehead and listened. After a time, he pulled the hat back. That signalled the acceptance of the work offered to him.

As the only grandchild, I had the privilege of sitting opposite *Nagypapa* at his desk every day for the purpose of doing homework. Behind him, the wall was full of university degrees and accolades. I waited till he was engrossed in his technical drawings and when all I could see was top of his hat, I stopped doing my schoolwork. My eyes began to trace the bright patterns that adorned his certificates and decorations. The centrally hung Golden Diploma for 50 years of excellent service was especially ornate and repeatedly I meandered along the golden scrolls, until I felt his piercing stare from the narrow slit between his spectacles and the hat visor. Guilt made me return to my homework, but only until I sensed the lowering of the visor. Then once again, I resumed my golden journey on the wall behind my *Nagypapa*.

That and other rituals continued for many years. When we visited them about a decade after we left the country, my *Nagypapa* seemed to be the same man, perhaps a bit older, and his hand was still cupped on his ear. He was wearing the same plain camel woollen hat. He peered at me with the same glint in his eyes from between his spectacles and the visor, as he gave me two of the lightbulb vases we made together. Wrapped in cotton wool, together with two of *Nagymama's* cherished *Herend* pieces including a little vase with four animal feet, I carried them in a separate hand luggage all through Asia to Australia. The Sarkadi family truly loved me, and they too spoilt me with affection.

I had all the childhood illnesses except mumps which was caught by everyone at one of my birthday parties except my parents and me. When I was bedridden with chickenpox, I dug holes in the wall plaster because I liked the soft silky feel of the plaster. Otherwise, I was a good child.

I must have been six or seven years old when I had a very high fever, and I was hospitalised for a week. In hindsight, it must have been some unknown virus. I watched some frightening practices on other children in the ward, such as long tubes inserted through their mouths into their stomachs. Oh, the horror! I was so scared that my temperature dropped, and I escaped with only a couple of blood tests before I was sent home. The specialist doctors could offer no diagnosis other than I was a spoilt child and they recommended sometime in the country to toughen me up. But the immediate treatment was rest.

Since the lift rarely worked, I had to be carried on stairs. The fourteen-year-old Apor Gabi who played piano was one. However, I preferred being carried by Salamon Feri who was at least eighteen and lived on the ground floor. He was an engineering student, tall and very good looking. I felt sheer joy as Feri carried me down to the garden and then up the one flight of stairs to our flat, whenever he was home from university.

To counter being a spoilt child, that is to be toughened, I was sent to a farm in the country in *Budakeszi*. The Kacso family had five daughters, and I turned out to be their sixth. They lived in two rooms; one was the kitchen with hot and cold running water, and the other was the bedroom for all, accommodating eight people including me. And there was a toilet.

The toilet was a wooden outhouse a fair walk on the other side of the animal yard past the pigsty. It is amazing how quickly one can adapt to trudging through a rough dirt walk to get to a suffocating bug infested bottomless trench with a hole in the middle of a wooden seat. The stench was overpowering even with the wooden lid on, yet one acclimatised to that too. There was no roster for filling the outhouse with newspaper and often there was none. Once I dropped something into the wooden hole. There were tears, but no retrieval from the shit pit. And the memory of the outhouse stayed.

Since I was treated as one of the family, I did all the chores like everyone else, though I never had to kill a chicken, thank goodness. I fed the pigs and picked the vegetables from the garden. I always ate some carrots and shallots on the way to the kitchen. Once when we were peeling potatoes one of the girls dared me into a competition of who could spit farthest. Naïve that I was I tried to spit over the large pot of peeled, cut, and washed potatoes that was some distance from me. Unfortunately, I missed. We were all punished with extra work for my spitting into the pot of potatoes. But generally, there too I was spoilt with affection by everyone including the rather large extended family with numerous G-d parents, all of whom lived next door.

After two summers there, I was sent to another country home. This one was more upmarket with the toilet inside the house. Because the Erdos had two boys who were older, I had a room to myself. The whole family worked the farm. One of my main duties was to look after the two pet rabbits. They were beautiful, pure white with pink ears and very soft to cuddle. One had very red eyes and the other had very blue eyes. They were friendly pets and enjoyed the freedom of the house. I fed them and cleaned up after them.

One of my other duties was to milk a couple of goats and carry some milk up the top of the mountain to where an aunt lived. I may have spilled half the contents of the bucket as I climbed some very uneven terrain. The aunt was a very capable tiny woman who worked a huge loom, on which she wove very colourful rugs with very quick movements. She taught me how to weave on her loom and I looked forward to my daily contribution to her work every day for the short time I spent with the family.

Generally, my sleeps were restless there. I had nightmares about the white bunnies who stared at me with their bright coloured eyes. Did they know what I thought? I was terrified that part of our evening dinner would be one of them. But to my great relief, every morning the white bunnies greeted me. When I left, I missed the red and blue-eyed white fluffs.

The RTV where my mother worked had a holiday property, which was used for a camp for children for two or three weeks each summer. I was in tears at the camp too. I didn't fit into either of the two age groups and I was shifted back and forth a few times.

I had the most miserable time especially when the little frogs hopped on my face as I lay in a bed outside, and when I had to wade nearly waist high through the marshes on an excursion. Not even the excitement of stealing those lovely large sunflowers from the neighbouring farm fraught with delicious danger could make up for my unhappiness during those weeks. Most of the other children must have hated it there. Together we made up a song about being taken away from the camp by a very fast train and started to count down the days that were left. I promised my mother that I would never go there again. I didn't. We left Hungary.

I said that as a child I wanted for nothing. Well, that is not quite true. The truth is that I needed nothing and was never really discontented. But I always wanted a pair of sandals just like the other children wore in summer. Lace up ankle high boots were acceptable in winter, and I wore them also in summer with arch lift supports. In addition, I did some exercises supposedly to correct my flat feet. So, I walked around the dining table on my heels, on the outsides of my feet and on my toes every day for many years. I must have walked many hundreds of kilometres, but the arches did not lift. Once my parents reluctantly bought a pair of sandals on a trial basis. In their absence and against their wishes, I wore them for the better part of a day and dirtied them. Because they were not the correct fit, the sandals were to be returned. I received a scolding and no sandals.

I had very few toys, which occupied two small shelves of our cupboard. I had a small bear and two little dolls. They were so little that they fitted nicely into the miniature *polya*, which was a miniature of the kind of swaddle that was common practice for live babies in Hungary. My mother made clothes for my tiny dolls, and I loved to dress them. I had a small lounge room furniture from balsa wood which were neatly edged in blue and red floral patterns. When they were broken, *Nagypapa* fixed them with small aluminium angles.

There was another small toy to which I was attached. A little white plastic bear with moving legs and a weight attached to a string tied to its head. When placed on a flat surface such as a table with the weight hanging off the table, the bear waddled to the edge where he came to a complete halt. He never fell down. Clever little animal, still in very good condition after seventy years despite the fact that my three sons also played with it.

For my nineth birthday I received two precious presents. One was a fine red leather-bound diary with a small lock and key to keep my secrets private. In fact, others wrote in it, gems of wisdom, memorable messages on moral behaviour and shared experiences. The other present was an authentic fine porcelain white tea set with delicate pink roses. It was beautiful. I used it for real tea parties mostly with adults because I was afraid that children would break it.

I treasured my paper serviette collection. My cousin Anita and I exchanged precious napkins which ranged from ordinary everyday paper ones to fine beautifully coloured and designed thin tissue ones which were rare. Anita still had them stored in a cardboard box the last time I was in Budapest.

For my tenth birthday my parents gave me a lovely large doll who I named Kati. The morning after that birthday, I woke up early and with great enthusiasm I very carefully combed out Kati baba's beautiful blonde curly hair. It never curled back and remained stringy and tangled. She still wears the same scarf I put on her head that morning to hide the straggly hair that I created. A few weeks later I had to abandon my Kati baba and my other precious toys when we left Hungary. Sometime later my aunt Klari sent Kati baba to me. By then I was a grown-up little girl who worked a lot and had little time to play with dolls. But I still have her even though all her joints are loose.

I was also taken to the movies. Two movies that impacted on me as a child. First was *Holnap Mar Keso*, (or *Tomorrow is Too Late*), which was about a couple of teenagers at summer camp and was most moving. Yet I do not remember whether it had a *Romeo and Juliet* ending or not. No wonder when my first boyfriend came along, it was an invitation for total immersion in youthful romantic love.

The other was *Budapesti Tavasz* (or *Springtime in Budapest 1955*) about two Hungarian soldiers in 1942. It had scenes of soldiers lining up Jews along the shores of the Danube and shooting them into the river. Most realistic it was with images that remained with me.

My formal education under the communist system may have been regimented, but it was also of a very high standard. Morning sessions were 8-1 one week and afternoon sessions were 1-6 on alternate weeks. School cases were worn on the back for healthy balanced posture, and I carried the weight for a short distance only. It was fortunate that my school was literally around the corner in Csanadi Utca.

All girls wore a uniform that was much like a dressy apron that went over street clothes to protect them. They were navy blue with frills around the armholes, and on the front, there was a colourful embroidery of *'ABC'* with a pencil through the letters.

A light blue neck scarf was worn by all students of my age on special occasions, such as the 1st May march. I never did march. For some reason I always stood and stood still for hours in the warm sun. I hated it. That is probably why I cannot stand for any length of time in one spot. I had trouble standing still in school assemblies and even at my wedding ceremony which lasted only about 20 minutes.

My teachers were all extremely good pedagogues, and I was usually among the top students. With the beginning of my school career began my stationery fetish which remained with me to the present. I loved going to the shop on the corner of Csaki and Sziget Utca.

The first purchases at the beginning of each year were exercise books for the year, violet-coloured sheets of paper, white labels with red edges, a lead pencil, a few coloured pencils, a rubber, a small ruler, and a pencil case in first class.

Each one of our exercise books had to be covered in the violet paper and marked with our names and the subject on the label. I was meticulous about covering the books without any creases. I continued to cover all my books meticulously throughout my student days and was particularly careful later when it came to using transparent adhesive contact for the protection of my textbooks. Although I taught my sons how to cover their books, I seemed to have had the job for decades, with the strict instructions of "No bubbles, Mum!"

The elite students at school had what may be called double decker pencil cases. How I longed for one of those elegant wooden double decker cases, in which the top layer either pulled out or it swivelled around for access to the bottom layer. Mine was a single level plastic pencil case. I attended after school care at Sziget Utca where our staple diet was potato soup with a few small chunks of meat and received only the occasional seconds. Later we joked that it was horse meat. And sometimes it may well have been just that.

One day I found a double decker wooden pencil case on the playground. Without thinking I took it home. I didn't sleep that night. I was feverish in the morning. My mother was puzzled about my high temperature. When I told her, she said to take back the pencil case to school and tell the head teacher that I found it. I did that. Once I was relieved of the wooden case, I felt such a tremendous relief that my temperature dropped back to normal. Before or since that day, I have never taken anything that was not mine.

It was in first class in Pannonia Utca school that I met Kertai Juli who remained my best friend in Budapest. She was a very bright attractive girl who looked lovely in her favourite white spotted red dress with puffed sleeves, and in her double-breasted navy-blue coat with a white beret. We spent a lot of time together including at Christmas luncheons of the traditional *Halaszle* (or fish soup) and had much fun unwrapping the little gift packages. Amongst them at the last celebration were three pairs of soft woollen five fingered gloves. They were from the little Klein ladies for my parents and me.

At school Juli sat two seats in front of me and the nice Stern Anna who was another friend, sat next to me. Over forty of us were tightly squeezed into fixed wooden desks in pairs. We took turns in filling the inkwells each day and hence we took turns in having blue fingers full of ink by the end of those days.

Our teacher Ilonka *neni* (usually called aunt but more Miss in school) seemed like a kind grandmother who could be quite strict and was quite effective as a teacher. Her obsession was the position of the fingers on the nibbed pens. Each pen was to rest between three fingers and the pointer on top was to be slightly curved, not bent. Halfway through the year I received the low grade of three for writing, but by the end of the year Ilonka *neni* gave me a five. It is possible that it was for effort just so that my report card would be perfect fives. However, only in first grade did I receive all fives.

The following two years I spent in Csanadi Utca under the tutelage of two very stern but fair teachers. I thought Margit neni was a good teacher. Although I was not even popular, she made me leader for a year, and I had to mind the class when she left the classroom.

The instruction was that no one was allowed to leave the classroom. So, when a couple of the students needed to go to the toilet, I did not allow them to leave the classroom. Naturally my mother was called into the school. Of course, the next time I was in charge in the absence of the teacher, half the class exited.

Edith *neni*, my III/A teacher, seemed obsessed with oral testing. Those were rather intimidating at first, but eventually I got over most of the butterflies.

On one Mothers' Day I was to recite a poem and later sing a song. I was still so nervous during my solo performance that my palms were wet through to the wrapping of my nearly crushed small bunch of *nefelejcsem* or 'forget me nots' which I was clutching tighter than it was implied in the poem.

I stood in front of my school full of parents, teachers and students, sang my song and received the customary applause. What is strange is that every time I look back on all those occasions of performances as well as verbal examinations, I not only see myself *shwitzing* (perspiring), but I actually see myself standing in front of me, viewing myself from behind me. Curious. And I feel an incredible sympathy for me.

There was one performance of a musical at the end of one year. It was called *Erdei Dal* (or Forest Song). I am first on the right of the three flowers who sang. The directions were for identical costumes for all three flowers. My mother had an imagination. She followed the instructions with the exception of the thin wire she sewed into the edge of my petal skirt so that it could be bent into shape. After I was over my initial embarrassment of being different, I felt rather proud as a flower with my shapely petals.

Music was one thing and sport another. My mother always said that I was always a 'comfortable' child; perhaps a euphemism for 'lazy'? My lack of sporting ability may have started early with the terrible experience of falling off a swing. I was quite young when I did what my parents told me not to do. I sat on the temporary swing hung on a tree branch in the garden of our house. When the swing fell with a huge thud, I hurt my coccyx so much, it gave true meaning to the expression, "it took my breath away." I don't know how long I sat on the hard ground, wondering what to do to breath. I was relieved when my breath returned. I stood up, shook from the shock and felt weak but was relieved that no one saw me. I never told my parents about my breath-taking experience.

To extend my education to the body as well as the mind, I was enrolled at *Olympus*, a popular sports gymnasium of high standard with walls of bars, ropes, parallel bars, vault boxes, rings and much more equipment. The test came at the end of year exhibition, which just happened to be a week or so after I started at the well-equipped gymnasium. I was full of trepidations. No. I was scared stiff. But I climbed the wall bars, and I climbed two notches of the rope. Never got to the third notch. Never got on the vaulting box or the parallel bars.

Then suddenly from behind someone hoisted me onto the rings, and I just hung there. I have never been on the rings. I was unable to swing back and forth. No one hoisted my legs up into the rings or helped. I just hung there, limp, wondering how long before my hands slipped off the rings. Although my eyes were closed, I knew everyone was looking at me. It was not only a difficult position but also extremely frightening. After that embarrassing experience, I never attempted any gym equipment.

My weekends were different. Much of my Sundays seemed to belong to my father. When I was a little girl, he used to wrap me up in a doona and carried me around like sack of potatoes. He pretended to sell me at the market, but usually unsuccessfully. Later we listened to music, conducted some orchestras or sang together. He also showed me a couple of tricks such as spinning a ball only to transfer it to a flat surface. I could never do it well enough.

I never liked walking and still don't like it. One full moon lit night when we were walking down a long street I asked my father, "When will we be directly under the moon?" He said, "At the end of the street." Of course, time and distance were not measured out for me, but after what seemed a very long time, when we reached the end of the street, we were still not directly under the full moon. And I walked long distances on more than one occasion to test my father's theory without success.

I think my self-taught father was a wise man. He correctly predicted Hitler's rise to power and the Holocaust, and that China would be a dominant world power. And when I suggested the combination of a jet aeroplane with a helicopter, he did not rule it out. Little did we know that the Harrier existed already then. He always said that knowledge was power, but he had not yet lived in our technocracy and witness the control and the power of information. Perhaps it is better.

Every Sunday my father and I took the trolley bus to visit his mother. We always needed to wait for the trolley which seemed to take longer in the winter cold. Then my father looked at me as if to say, "We won't have to wait long," and he lit a cigarette. Immediately after the first puff, the trolley came into view. That action of his never failed.

At my grandmother's home, while she and my father talked, I placed some money for her between the sheets in her linen cupboard. Apparently at least one of her other sons also contributed to her collection between the sheets in the linen cupboard. I shudder to think how much money there must have been tucked away, but we never found out. And we never saw or heard of the lady spend on anything.

Then we left to meet one or both of my father's brothers in some Espresso, usually on the shore of the Danube or in *Zserbo*, which was similar to the Café *Sacher* in Wien. There I had hot chocolate in winter and chocolate ice cream in summer while the men talked for hours. On the whole I was very used to adult company, felt quite comfortable and was interested enough to listen to their discussions. Sunday morning meetings with my father continued into my late twenties in Sydney by which time my father took pleasure in being seen with me, and we rejoiced at hearing the spread of gossip that Mr Forbat was meeting a young woman.

On those Sundays when we arrived home, my mother waited for us with her delicious chicken soup and whatever else she cooked. Her brother Erno was also there and sometimes in the afternoon, he took me with his son Gabi to the *Vidampark*, Budapest's Amusement Park. There Gabi took great delight in crashing his Dodgem cars into mine. I was quite accustomed to his rituals of ruining every game in which cousin Anita and I took pleasure. However, being pushed over on the greasy car track was one of his finer accomplishments.

But I did spend many a splendid weekend with Anita. Her place was like another home away from home even if my bed consisted of cushions pushed together as did her bed at our place. It was not always comfortable when the cushions slid apart, and then I slept mainly on the hard parquet floor. The many splendid weekends at my cousins continued until one evening towards the end of December in 1956. Then my aunt Klari put my coat on me, and my Uncle Gyula plonked me on the back of his bicycle. He and I rode fast into the dark chilly winter night that marked my last day in Budapest.

Chapter Five

MIGRATION

*"Leaving home is a kind of freedom,
but the heart remembers where it belongs."*

Anon

The Hungarian Revolution broke out on 23rd October 1956, and without really understanding the seriousness of the situation, it was all very exciting for us children. The schools were shut down, so we stayed home.

We were experiencing some very unusual daily occurrences as the events unfolded. They included a gathering in front of the Parliament, and the radio station of Budapest was seized.

University students and rebels fought, and later they were joined by the army. Prisoners were set free, and borders were opened. None of that effected this child.

Our neighbours' the Sarkadis' apartment faced the street, and despite warnings to stay away from the windows, I would eagerly watch battles as men ran from doorway to doorway, shooting at I never knew what.

The arrival of the Soviet tanks was like watching a movie from the Sarkadis' window, and while they rumbled down our street, Russian troops advanced through underground passages to the city centre. As the revolt escalated, there were air raids, but we were never bombed.

I witnessed first-hand how the awful events were affecting ordinary people. While at work, one of my mother's colleagues was struck by a stray bullet. The hospitals were overloaded, and she was discharged prematurely. She and her daughter Judy stayed with us for many weeks while we nursed her until she recovered.

But those were dangerous times. The *AVO* or secret police were responsible for taking away the father of one of my friends. Soon afterwards, the rest of his family disappeared, never to be seen again. Such events became common.

It was dangerous to stand in line across the street to buy bread and knowing that there may be no bread left at the end of the queue. But I did and we welcomed the rare ration of butter or sugar. It may have seemed an adventurous time for a ten-year-old girl like me but not for my parents, though they never expressed any fears in front of me. I always felt safe despite hearing gunfire.

My father later told me that as early as 1938 he was preparing to emigrate to Australia when there was a mass exodus from Europe especially of Jews. In 1948 there was another wave of emigration when many left Hungary. Once more my father arranged for the necessary documents for all family members. But my mother remained resolute, and the families stayed in Budapest, believing that the events of the Holocaust could not happen again.

In 1956 there were many evenings when the extended family gathered to discuss leaving the country. My cousin Anita and I would quietly discuss our own plans that included riding on our own Vespas once we reached the New World. My parents who were forty-six years old at the time, with a ten-year-old daughter, with no knowledge of a foreign language other than German, were ambivalent about making the move.

One day in December, a couple of men from a country village knocked on our door. They said that they have been paid, that all arrangements have been made, and that they would return in three days to guide us across the border to Austria. They were sent by my cousin Marti in Toronto.

We later learned that my cousin Marti paid US $1,500.00 (a substantial amount then) to the two farmer brothers. The instructions they were given was to guide her sister Eva and her family safely to Vienna. They were given the addresses of the three uncles in case Eva's home was bombed. But the poor misguided brothers misunderstood the instructions, and they offered to take four families.

My father was one of the uncles. He saw this as the last opportunity to leave Hungary, despite the fact that by this time, much of the border was closed. He convinced my mother who agreed reluctantly to make the big move.

I was staying in Ujpest with my cousin Anita. Late in the evening my aunt Klari put my coat on me, my uncle Gyula plonked me on the back of his bicycle, and we rode fast in the dark cold winter night. We stopped a few times because when I sat on a cushion on the cross bar, or on the handlebar, or on the back wheel, I invariably slid off with or without the cushion. But I did not complain about the cold or the bicycle bars cutting into me. We were stopped once or twice by the military police during the curfew, but my uncle managed to explain away our need to be on the street. And I stayed quiet till we reached my home.

I had a very short sleep that night while my parents packed the barest necessities such as a change of underwear and toothbrushes. I was woken well before dawn and dressed in triple layer of clothes with a Doxa wristwatch on my arm. It was cold and eerie on the empty streets during dark hours in the curfew. We walked towards the *Keleti* (Eastern) train station as we listened to the echoes of our footsteps in the early morning silence.

After a few hours we arrived in *Gyor*. There were a lot of soldiers with guns, but that kind of scene was not unusual. We changed trains and after another few hours, we arrived in a border town, that was probably Sopron. There were soldiers milling around on the platform, but suddenly someone ushered us off the train on the wrong side of the platform and hurried us into a house thirty or forty meters from the train. From there we saw people being taken off the train, arrested and taken back to Budapest. But we were safe and warm in the farmhouse.

In time, there were about eight of us including a family with a boy of seven years of age. It was dark when we started on our journey. We were told not to speak. For many hours we walked across many fields. The first snowfall had already melted, and the mud was well above our ankles in the fields. Each step was heavier than the previous one. Once we stopped while a few of the men retraced our route, to try and find a lost shoe. No shoe was found.

When they returned, we continued our walk in the muddy fields until we rode on a horse-drawn hey cart for a short distance. I was so grateful. Then once more we were trudging in the mud in pitch black. Suddenly my mother pulled me to the ground.

The flares that lit up the whole area were shot up by the border guards. Although we heard voices we were not caught, and we resumed our mud fields walk in silence. The flares happened a few times.

Once we stopped because we were lost. The guides went ahead to reconnoitre but took far too long to come back. The men proposed that they look around to find the guides, but the decision was to wait till light. On my father's suggestion, we took refuge in a haystack where it was surprisingly warm, and I fell asleep.

When one of the guides returned, he walked with us close to a road that was the invisible mark of the Austro-Hungarian border. We walked the last twenty meters in silence and alone. With mixed feelings of joy and fear, the adults lit cigarettes and began to talk in whispers.

A small Volkswagen bus arrived, and real fear vanished when driver spoke in a foreign language. No one thought that they would ever be glad to hear the German language again. The bus made a short stop at a huge warm barn of a place run by the Red Cross. It had plenty of hot chocolate and chocolate bars were unlimited. Later when I was allowed to speak freely, I just ate my chocolates quietly.

It was still dark when my parents and I were driven to a coffee shop in the centre of Wien. We were the only customers, and the staff seemed acceptant of the fact that we gave them extra work as the frosty mud on our shoes thawed. It gradually dawned, and the streetlights were turned off, when a car arrived and drove the three of us to a family home.

It was a strange home, with dark brown furniture and some very pleasant smiling people. We were given a wonderful breakfast, a hot bath which was appreciated even more, and we literally fell into a bed covered with a very thick warm doona. And from then on, we were called *'fluchtlinges'* or refugees.

In the morning, we left the hospitality of the family and were deposited at the Hotel Wallenstein, a small three or four storey Hotel, with red and gold décor, which according to my mother was a *bordello* previously. Of course, at the time I had no idea what a *bordello* was, but I had a fine time with all the children, whose parents were waiting for papers to emigrate to various parts of the world. And I became a PEZ Collector.

We were there for a few days only, when we were joined by my cousin Marika Forbat who found us through the police registration and then stood in line with my father at the *Joint* (the American Jewish Joint Distribution or JDC) for assistance. Over the next few months, my father organised the required documents for immigration for all four of us through the Australian Embassy.

My mother's cousin Irene and her husband Walter Engel wrote personal letters to the Australian Immigration both in Canberra and in Wien, as the Immigration Policy required that each migrant be sponsored by an Australian citizen of standing, guaranteeing accommodation and work. Walter forwarded the applications and the waiting began.

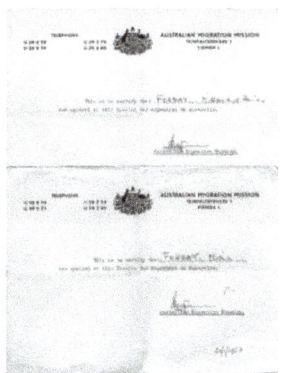

Application for Australian immigration

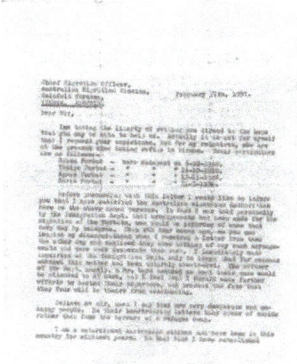

Letter of Sponsorship by Walter Engel 1957

After a few weeks, we left the hotel and rented a room in a boarding house. It was a light room with two single beds. My parents occupied one, and Marika and I shared the other. A bit cramped in the narrow bed, we had battles with the grey horse blanket. We were a family of four now and although we lived on 'spinat mit Spiegel eiern' (spinach with eggs, sunny side up), and shared one Wiener schnitzel between two, it didn't take long for our meagre 2,000 Forint to be spent.

My parents sold my father's signet ring, the *Doxa* watch and later my mother's fox fur collar. But that only lasted a short time too. Somehow even when both my parents were working, and Marika had a job for a while, we were always short of money. So, we moved again.

This time we moved to a *Lager* in Korneuburg, thirty minutes by train from Wien. Previously it was a military barracks, which was converted to house the Hungarian *fluchtlings*. The Lager was clean, and it was newly painted. It had new wooden double bunks, and new orange and yellow checked woollen blankets which were prickly but covered the new straw mattresses which were quite spikey. We could smell the freshness of the straw and got splinters in our hands as we climbed up into our bunks. We shared the large communal 'bathroom' and managed with icy cold water.

All the children were in 'school' in *Korneuburg Lager*. We were given English and History lessons. Of the history lessons I distinctly remember the screening of the Nuremberg Trials with the Archival clips which were photographed by the liberating American service men. Those horrific and nightmarish images have never been erased from my memory. But I clearly remember my young Anglican priest with who I was infatuated and who left me with his American accent.

My parents continued to commute to Wien to work. They never spared any expense on music. The memory of Franz Lehar's *The Land of Smiles* with its lush red and gold staging remains to this day with my cousin and me.

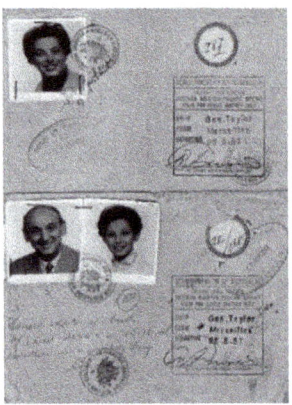

One Way Australian Assisted Passage Scheme Permit

By May we received notice of our passage. We were to spend a couple of weeks in another refugee camp in Salzburg. From there we had another outing, this time to the Austrian Alps. It was for the first time that I rode on a cable car and this one took us to the majestic snow-capped mountains of Semmering and Rax.

Then one day we packed our few belongings again. We were transported from the Salzburg *Lager* by bus and then by train to the Port of Marseilles. I remember little of that trip. By then I developed a temperature that soared to 42 degrees centigrade. While my parents were frantic, they fought a couple for a private compartment on the train and won, so that I could lie down for the overnight trip, all of which was and is a haze for me. When we arrived in Marseilles, my condition had not changed.

On 28th May 1957, we boarded the *General Harry Taylor*, a USA Navy Troop Transport with a most interesting and illustrious history. That time she was recommissioned to carry Hungarian refugees.

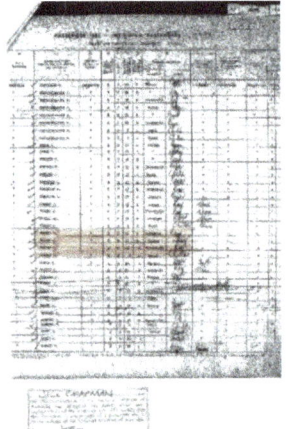

General Harry Taylor Log

We departed from Marseilles with about 1300 passengers of which about 300 were Jewish. One day a loud announcement started with the deafening *'Achtung, Achtung'* (attention). Not that I understood what was happening but later I was told that there was an anti-Semitic incident but one of the ship's officers quashed the hostilities.

Once on board *the General*, the nice young American doctor gave me a series of daily injections and by the second day I improved considerably. On many occasions, in his usual manner my father would tell stories about the expansive cabin on board our luxury liner. He would tell of the comfortable bed that was his despite the fact that 399 men occupied the other bunks in the same one large space. It was the same in the women's quarters. Four bunks of canvas stretched on steel frames which were folded up one above the other when not in use.

My mother and I had all four bunks in one corner, which gave us more privacy, but also more noise from the engine and the bulkhead which also amplified the sound of the ocean waves. There were a dozen or so wash basins and toilets and showers separating the two sections of 200 women. And always, but always, something was blocked. Hence the floor was usually flooded and there was a terrible stench due to lack of ventilation. But we adapted.

I liked the large grey oceanic machine and would have been happy to continue on board, even though there was not much to do. However, I found the room with the piano, where a very good-looking young man, called George Szigeti (later Segal, and a *2MBS FM* presenter in Sydney) played music beautifully for a group of young adults. I spent a lot of time there.

In June 1957, The General Harry Taylor was one of the first ships to sail through the Suez Canal after the 1956 Egyptian blockade. It was a very slow stop and start journey, with wreckage spread throughout the very narrow channel. We were docked in Aden for the large part of a day. While the ship refuelled, we stood on deck and threw coins into the ocean for the native children to dive underwater to retrieve them. Crossing the Indian Ocean, our voyage was quite uneventful. A few of the refugee passengers disembarked in Fremantle.

It was the *Great Australian Bite* that provided a great deal of entertainment for those not seasick and hence confined to their bunks. As a troop carrier, the dining furnishings were long grey mess-room tables with grey fold up seats attached. As the ship rolled, so did our meals. That meant that after taking a spoonful of food from our plate, the meal slid down to the other end of the table, and we had to wait for the ship to roll back again for our plate to return to take the next spoonful of food. For those of us who were well and could eat, that was quite hilarious till we held onto our plates. We docked for a day in Melbourne where more refuges disembarked.

At 7.00 am in the morning of 25th June 1957, the General Harry Taylor sailed into Sydney Harbour lead by a couple of Pilot boats. Half an hour later we were anchored in the middle of Port Jackson where we stayed all day.

Each person had to queue to go through a good many formalities of questions, forms, directions, medical examinations and visa distributions that took up much of the day. It was late afternoon, when the ship docked at Berth 20 in Pyrmont. The majority of *fruchtlings* were sent to camps such as Bonegilla or to various Boarding Houses in Sydney.

Berth 20 Pyrmont 1950

My family was picked up at the pier by one of my mother's cousins Litzi and her husband Ernst Desiatnik who took us to their home in Eastwood. Ernst served in the USA armed forces during World War II and was transported on the General Harry Taylor when she carried troops back to the United States. It is a small world indeed.

Our new address was 99 Victoria Street, Kings Cross, but we discovered that to call it Potts Point was more prestigious. It was a dark and dingy two room place, but we were free, and we were independent. In the years to come, my father would describe our palatial home, "We lived in a mansion. We had a pink room, a green room, and numerous other rooms, all of which were occupied by the neighbours."

(photo 2015)

In truth we lived in a basement flat of a Boarding House, in two small rooms with no windows except for an air hole, and a cockroach infested red kitchenette outside. To get to our flat one needed to descend via a dark, narrow, and high stepped staircase. The penny eating hot water boiler in the bathroom was two and a half floors above the ground floor. The seat-less, cracked toilet was on the other side of the garden.

Our landlady was a tall woman, who always wore the same faded pink dressing gown that matched her bedspread. Every week on the same day, I delivered the rent to the red hair rinsed, red rouge painted woman who always reeked of cigarettes and alcohol. She had countless male visitors all of who were cousins or some distant relations.

My father was happy before he actually landed in our new country and my mother was happy that a home of sorts awaited us in our new country. Her cousin Irene made sure that the flat and the bed linen were clean, and *Tante Olga* (aunt) filled the small fridge full of food for our arrival. Within three days my parents were working. And I went to school. We were very fortunate.

For me the attraction was the glorious city skyline. During the day the *AWA* tower resembling the Eifel Tower stood solitarily tall, as did the *Caltex* building. At night I spent much time watching the colourful neon lights on the horizon.

Even to the uninitiated newcomers, the *Cross* was an exciting place. Each day on my way to school, I stared at the giant flashing *Coca Cola* sign, which is still present and larger as a landmark. I marvelled at the acrobatic agility of the conductors while they performed their duty on the narrow platform of the open tram cars. I walked past the Fire Station that is still there and fully functioning. The Cross was the heart of the city and the hub of its social life.

We celebrated our first New Year's Eve there with thousands of people. Darlinghurst Street was closed off to cars and we danced on the streets till dawn. Even for a young ten years old it was safe, and it was fun. But like everything must, it too changed. Fifteen years later I did not feel safe and locked my car as I drove in a car through all of *Kings Cross*.

In the first few weeks, I concluded that five was significant in the fifties. My father earned an award wage of 15 pounds per week. My mother charged 15 Guineas for a lined dress. Our rent was 5 pounds per week, and I paid 5 pence on the green and cream double-decker bus. Oh, yes, and it cost 5 pence for half a dozen liquorice sticks.

It took a few months for my English to improve to the point where I was translating for my mother when she had customers, and when we were shopping. Although she and I attended evening classes at my school for English, my mother never mastered the language properly. However, she had no problem communicating in her broken English and had established a rather nice relationship with the Italian greengrocer who also had limited English. And she had no trouble speaking with the nice Australian lady next door. In her broken English she also managed to give a little lecture on modernity to the technician who fixed the ancient contraption of a radio.

My father too, managed to communicate with a few words of English, at times mixed with German. His fellow workers requested that he slow his work significantly to avoid higher productivity. Although he was not a drinker, he was inaugurated as a 'mate' when he joined his fellow workers in the Pub after they were paid on Thursdays.

Later, before he started his evening shift, my father walked the city in the mornings and tried to sell two garments made by my mother. Weeks passed before he persuaded someone to look at his wares, and finally he received his first order. And then the real toil began. So, my father did become a peddler after a fashion, though not quite like my image from my childhood.

Because my father worked at night, it was my uncle Gyula's friend who took my mother and me to the Kings Cross Theatre on the corner of Darlinghurst and Victoria Streets to see my first coloured feature film. What a memorable movie was *The Boy on a Dolphin*. I can still see Sophia Loren and Alan Ladd diving in the clear aqua Aegean Sea.

For the first few years, most of my weekends were spent with Aunt Irene and her family. In summer they spent a couple of months in Leura. In Blackheath I learnt to swim, and nearly drowned when my second Cousin Peter played one of his pranks on me. I learnt a lot of German which I used later in life. And so, even working daily with my parents after school, my happy childhood continued happily.

Not so my mother and if truth be known she was quite unhappy. She missed her brothers in Budapest. In November 1957 she wrote in a most understated manner:

"It is not easy at this age [she was 47 years old] and generally, to plant new roots. No new arrivals feel their best in the first year, and this is understandable. Relatively speaking, everyone is working and living well, perhaps not the most comfortably. It is very hard to start anew and there is no manna falling from the sky".

Later in December, she wrote: *"We do not go out [except to a movie sometimes] ... For two months before Xmas, I worked incredibly hard; I don't remember when I worked so much. I would not like to continue like this, but we will have to see. ... Agi as she says, is very 'happy', like her father; they are happy people."*

From the time we arrived my parents worked tirelessly. It was necessary, as the orders were increasing and so were the garments on my bed, which needed to be finished, invoiced, and packed before we could go to sleep. It was a natural state of affairs for me to work with my parents, and according to my mother, apparently my only complaint was the dishwashing.

A year after our arrival, the neighbour in our subterranean abode reported us to the police for using an electrically driven sewing machine, and we were forced to move. So, we moved to Bondi Junction to a flat above Mr Bayer's hardware store.

My new situation was that every day I walked down and up Vernon Street to travel on the 388 buses to Darlinghurst Public School. Later I walked up and down Hardy Street to Dover Heights Girls High School, until I caught the 666 School Special. I hated all the walking.

We lived modestly for many years. In the second year, we purchased a second-hand car for deliveries. It was a 1954 cream coloured Holden with burgundy leather upholstery. My father learned to drive relatively late in his life, so my mother always worried about his driving except when I sat next to him in the car. I never did understand how a twelve-year-old non driving passenger can assist a driver?

Gradually my parents made time for a visit to a museum or the Art Gallery. We even spent a weekend in the Blue Mountains. In time my mother settled into what she called a 'non-assimilated life', but very much integrated into the Australian rhythm. Despite calloused hands, one shabby suit in the early years after our arrival, and the long hours of hard work over many years, my father was always extremely happy in Australia from the moment he arrived, to the day he became ill and eventually died.

All through the years, amongst other things, I have tried to retain the lessons learnt from my parents together with the values which they instilled in me from early childhood, and what emigration has taught me in a short time span. Also, I am forever grateful to my parents for bringing me to this glorious country of Australia.

"When you move from one country to another you have to accept that there are some things that are better and some things that are worse, and there is nothing you can do about it."

Bill Bryson

Chapter Six

EDUCATION - SCHOOL

*"The beautiful thing about knowledge is
that no one can take it away from you."*

B B King

The 50th Dover Heights Girls High School reunion was interesting in the sense that some of the girls changed little while others I would not have recognized if I met them on the street. Many remembered a distinct dislike for school and some even hated it. The girls had some incredible stories to tell, and many have achieved great things. Sadly, Agnes Simon of the twins was one who passed away, as did most of the teachers. But Miss Butler who was a great maths teacher and Deputy Head had a jolly time. Talking to many of the ladies brought back memories, after which nostalgia lingered for days.

I liked school but I never excelled as a student. I never had any reservations about attending and I never hated school. Although I only did the barest minimum homework and rarely studied or read, my marks improved each year, and I passed the necessary requirements till towards the end of High School.

I must stress that I have learnt something important from every single teacher I have ever had the fortune to meet in Budapest, in Sydney in Darlinghurst Public School, in DHGH School, and at the University of New South Wales. What I learnt in a short time in school in Hungary I applied for many years in Australia, because the then communist system had a very high standard of education in every aspect. The basics of arithmetic including the multiplication table, reading including spelling and comprehension, and writing were important then, and continued to be when I arrived halfway through the year in June 1957 in Darlinghurst Public School where I progressed until I left in 1958.

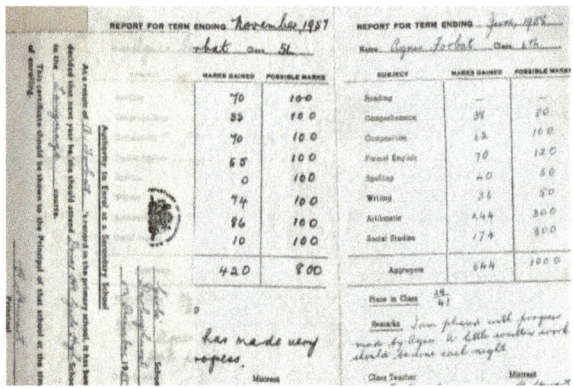

I crossed The Cross to get to my school. The first day is a memorable one for everyone. Rachel Spivak, a nice Polish girl was assigned to help me. Why would anyone assume that a Pole can translate English to a Hungarian? That still puzzles me.

They say that children can be cruel. Well, it was not the children. At morning break, this large frame charged at me. Her name was Miss Euroke, and she wore a floral nylon dress, with white flower ornamented hat on top of her blue rinsed hair. Head bent to peer above the false diamond studded pastel plastic spectacles, handbag swinging on one arm and a white gloved finger thrust forward, she shrieked, "No pants Miss!" In front of what seemed like hundreds of girls, in shocking embarrassment, I spilled milk on my one of only two sets of clothes. And then got into trouble for not finishing all my small bottle of milk. The next day, we purchased the navy pleated gabardine shapeless uniform, which was to barrel my form for the next seven years at least.

In fifth class writing style was still very important. Miss Lynch a slightly hunch backed schoolmarm distributed a guide page. It was a white sheet printed with thick black slanted parallel lines, to be placed under the leaf of our exercise books. By then, sloping running writing for me was a breeze and I became proficient without the guide sheet. Naturally in time, particularly after taking notes nearly verbatim in classes in high school and university, the even curves of my writing ran away and became almost illegible squiggles.

In the mistaken belief that I would understand the foreign language most people either mouthed words or just shouted at me. It is still beyond my comprehension why it is that those with poor language are treated as if they were deaf. In the first few months my lack of the English language was easily revealed. When we were to copy a poem from a small board, for lack of space Miss Lynch wrote "miss a line" to separate two verses. I copied it too and it became part of the poem.

There was no misunderstanding in the exchange of food. Although I did not like baked beans, banana or vegemite sandwiches, my Hungarian salami and the green capsicum sandwiches became a favourite among many of the students whether they were Australian or of European backgrounds. As my English improved, I came to understand and enjoy the *Lorna Doon* series on the Wireless and ferociously read the adventures of the *Secret Seven* and even *Biggles*.

In hindsight, through all the time spent working on the appearance of writing, it might have been more beneficial to teach the appreciation of literature and the value of the 'word'. But literary I was not, and I disliked comprehension from way back. In Budapest my mother would spend hours with me reading through passages and then asking the relevant questions. It did not help towards my learning to like language and its words. That came much later in my life.

The appearance of Miss Stewart the headmistress was that of a typical schoolmarm. She was small, thin, with wire framed spectacles and hair in a bun. But she was a good teacher and most accommodating, allowing me to freely use a dictionary. Also, within a few days, I was honorary gramophone winder for the girls marching into class. My Hungarian education was far more advanced and the change over from Metric to Imperial system came to me easily. Within three months, among other problems, I was coaching most of the class in arithmetic, as multiplying and dividing pounds, shillings, pence and such were difficult for the girls. But primary school passed relatively quickly.

 In High School the embroidered emblem of *Honour Before Honours* appeared on our hat bands and blazer pockets. It lent a certain amount of pride to the uniform and the institution, as did the school song:

There's a school to whom we sing, So let our praises to her ring; We to her will glory bring, Oh glory honour dignity. Dover Heights our song to thee, Dover Heights we glory thee; Dover Heights all praise to thee, Oh Glory, Honour, Dignity.

It was in my adult life when I discovered that the music was borrowed from a classical composition, but since I was never good with names, I don't remember from where it originated. Then there were the Monday morning assemblies of Psalm 23 followed by the Salutes: *I honour my G-d, I serve the Queen, and I salute the flag*. I felt that they reflected a certain amount of duty and respect as did the school uniform, both the summer grey and the winter navy. I liked the gloves and the hats. But it was always a problem not to squash the stylish summer straw hat and the winter navy felt hat. What I did hate was the prickly stocking and more so the daily walking up the Hardy Street hill in Dover Heights.

There were two streams in DHGH school. The 'A' stream of languages which included Latin, French, and German, and the 'B' stream of Home Sciences into which I was placed. Despite Miss Stewart's recommendation to enrol me in the language course, the Education Department ruled that I needed to learn English before I was allowed to take any language subjects in High School. And we never appealed their decision. Mistake!?!

My subjects in class IB were many and varied. English was compulsory and I chose Mathematics I and II which placed me in the 'A' stream in second and third year. However, I was to continue with the Home Sciences which meant cooking and sewing. The full year of 'home economics' included cleaning with a variety of detergents and a greater variety of cloths all of which were to be washed after the lesson. It seemed an awful bother to me who always used one wet and one dry cloth that did all jobs well. I also learnt never ever to make or even taste junket that we made in cooking class.

Each week we were given a list of ingredients to take to the following week's cooking class. One week we were to make Devonshire Tea. So, I went to our continental Delicatessen and asked for Devonshire tea. Despite having many different teas, I did not understand why the shop did not have Devonshire tea. Neither did other shops. Of course, I later learnt why. To this day I thoroughly enjoy fresh scones with jam and cream. And any tea.

Needlework was three years of battling with my teacher. Since I was working with my mother for years I had much more knowledge than the other students and some that was contrary to the teaching of Mrs Wilson. I designed a summer dress that was a little different from the fashionable nylon floral. It was a green spotted white cotton dress with a full-length zipper down the front. Although she disapproved, I made it and wore it at the fashion parade. We had to make patterns for blouses, cut them out of printed tissue paper and stick them together to create small three-dimensional body models. I did get high marks for my collection of near perfect paper models that stood like little soldiers in my cardboard box. Anything to do with patterned paper like paper serviettes was a pleasure with which to play, as it was reminiscent of my childhood in Budapest.

Bookkeeping, Shorthand and Typing were my other subjects. We learned to type with ten fingers but blind; our two hands were covered with a black cloth so that we could not see our hands and the keys. I did well with over 100 words per minute and received my Pitman certificates for both typing and shorthand. I could have become a secretary. Alas, by the time I got to university I forgot much shorthand, though I frequently used the shorthand symbols for 'the,' 'a,' 'as well as' and such. It is true that if you don't use it then you lose it.

Regrettably the subject of Art was only one year during which we practised many different techniques of art and craft work. Any more would not have made me into any kind of artist, for talent I had none then and still have none. Painting I was never good at, although I faithfully followed instructions for attempting the different methods of art; drawing with a candle and painting over it comes to mind. I guess I received marks for effort rather than for ability.

But I learnt to appreciate it all and to criticise it all. As an adult on one visit to the NSW Gallery, with considerable confidence and perhaps quite loudly I stated that a small Arthur Streeton was "not a good painting". And I still hold that view of that particular painting. In hindsight, possibly it was an unfinished work.

The history of art was interesting but too brief. It is no wonder that I always confused the Ionic and Corinthian Greek columns, and the Pantheon with the Parthenon until I visited the ruins of the latter in Athens.

The visits to galleries were most informative. Especially striking was the view of the bronze nude sculpture as one entered Gallery of NSW. Titled *The Dancer* by Sir Edgar Bertram Mackennel, she stood 168cm tall, slightly larger than life, well-proportioned, attractively shaped into a position that alluded to movement. She was most impressive.

When the gallery issued limited editions of copies of her that were one third of the size of the original, I purchased one. My husband always liked nudes, and *the Dancer* was very shapely. She continues to shine in our living room in her 'naked glory.'

The Dancer

I was fascinated by the Heidelberg school of Australian artists such as Condor, Roberts, McCubbin and others who painted impressionist landscapes. I didn't know then how realistically they captured the Australian scene, how I would come to appreciate their representations of our arid land and how I would come to "love a sunburnt country" of Dorothea MacKellar. In contrast there were the more modern surreal painting such as the one titled *The Christmas Tree* in which there was nothing that resembled any kind of tree. I have never been a friend of cubism, or any art form that leans towards the schizophrenic. I always confused Monet and Manet but was drawn also to the European school of impressionists, probably because I was a romantic from way back.

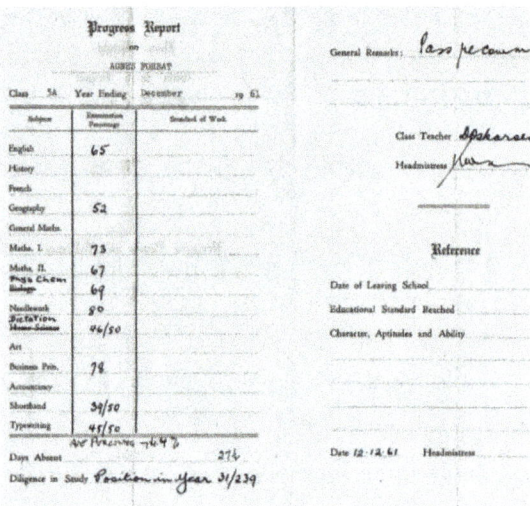

Because I was a city girl who knew nothing about animals and plants, biology and botany were out of my league with froggy dissections and Latin names. The alternative was combined Physics and Chemistry although I wanted to escape the Periodic Table of Elements from the first time when I laid eyes on those overwhelming symbols. I got by over the five years, and I still remember many of the symbols. Oxygen and water are the easy ones to remember. For me Hg is hard to forget from when it was challenging to try to catch the little silver balls of liquid Mercury as they rolled around the kitchen floor. I used a thermometer for humans to measure the temperature of boiling water.

Maths was something else. And every day we started with an analysis of the date, to find out whether or not it was factorial, that is divisible by other than one and itself. Our first teacher was the young Miss White who was probably (1961) just out of Teachers' College.

She was in tears on many occasions. Although I was never a part of the group that caused incidents, I certainly was never part of the prevention of her being bullied either. But she did teach the proofs for equations and long division well, which later was reinforced by Miss Butler. And the date factorializing continues to this day. I asked my sons repeatedly through their school years and on occasions even now.

Miss Cole was a slim attractive woman and good teacher who must have been as organised at home as she was in the classroom. I had an image of her stylish clothes hanging in her wardrobe like soldiers with invisible weekday tags on them. They must have been forever in the same order because we could tell the day of the week by the dress she wore.

I empathised with her exactitude as I loved to draw accurate graphs, and to very finely colour in diagrams especially in my geography books of which I was rather proud. I still have my treasured rather used 36 Staedtler coloured pencils as well as my very first compass set. Over the years I collected a good many pens favouring Parker who introduced a slim and very smooth feeling biro in many pastel colours as well as black after the US space program began. I have retained my fetish for stationery from a young age. Even today I like to browse in a store where I may purchase writing material I don't need.

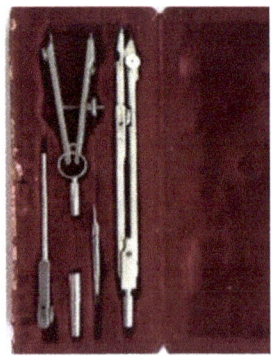

Our geography teacher Mrs Finney was a tall imposing woman. She stood out from other teachers with her thick and very colourful glass frames, resembling those of Barry Humphries' *Dame Edna Average* character. I don't remember her teaching method as much as I remember our altercation over assignments and test papers. I requested them back. I wanted to see the comments and my marks. Besides I collected them. She thought I was impudent, and emphatically stated no one received them back. When I asked what happened to them, she informed me that they were kept for seven years after which they were destroyed.

I don't know what happened to me, but I insisted that I wanted them back. The result was that I was sent to the principal and never received back any of my papers. Several years later when I was at university already, I discovered Mrs Finney lived opposite to us in Rose Bay. When we met, we never mentioned our confrontation. But of course, she remembered me by name.

In senior High School that is in 4th and 5th year, just before the introduction of the Wyndham Scheme which added an extra year to high school, I continued with the compulsory English, Maths I and II, and combined Phys Chem. For a sixth subject I selected Accountancy which was mostly bookkeeping because I thought it easy. It was and I did very well in it. It also became a very useful tool later in my working life.

Although I did like Geography and took great pride in my geography book, I changed to Modern History which I thought would be more useful though I knew not for what. In two years, we tediously read through chapter by chapter, from cover to cover, two volumes of history books. During each period each student read a paragraph from the text. We rote learned events, dates, names, and other relevant information from the Industrial Revolution of 1850 to the end of WWII in 1945 and then regurgitated some facts in the examinations. Dull it may have been but strangely enough, it certainly added to my general knowledge.

(1963)

Words had little meaning until Mrs Lloyd-Jones started to teach essays and poetry, both of which were short, concise and dense in meaning. Addison and Steele were interesting, but it was Francis Bacon's *'Of Revenge'* that had attraction for me. I read it so many times, that I knew the whole essay verbatim by the time I was examined on it. It began with, *Revenge is a kind of wild justice; which the more man's nature runs to, the more ought law to weed it out.*

Then there was Samuel Taylor Coleridge's *'Ancient Mariner's "Water, water, everywhere, nor any drop to drink,"* together with his romantic friend William Wordsworth and his famous sonnet composed *'Upon Westminster Bridge.'* It was most moving.

Earth has not anything to show more fair: Dull would he be of soul who could pass by A sight so touching in its majesty:

And it finished with the exclamatory couplet,

Dear G-d! The very houses seem asleep;
And all that mighty heart is lying still.

Physical Education was something else. I have always stated that I was never a sporty person. I hated walking to school. I still don't like walking and avoid it as much as possible. In the 1960s Dover Heights Girls High School did not have a gym and the Assembly Hall doubled as such. At the beginning of each PE lesson, we shifted over a thousand chairs and out came the sports equipment which were shifted back at the end. Our PE teacher Miss Singleton realised early that I was a lost cause especially at the vault box. I don't know how we managed to save face, both hers and mine, but over the years I never jumped the vault box.

Most of the time I tried very hard to opt out of sports, however escaping swimming eluded me as it was compulsory. Our names were marked off the list getting on the school bus at school, getting off the bus at Bondi Baths, getting into the change rooms and getting into the water. Afterwards, the same marking off process was reversed. In short, I failed to get out of swimming.

But one year, I did add a win to my name. I was very proud when I took second place in one swimming race. Even if there were only two entrants in the heat.

I learnt to swim what was called 'overarm' now freestyle, and later taught myself breaststroke and backstroke. The trick was to properly coordinate the breaths with the movement of the limbs. Never very proficient but sufficiently competent to do some short laps and better still, to feel confident in the water and enjoy it. Except once in the sea. How I came to be swimming in the ocean in Wollongong I shall never know, but I almost drowned. The waves were far too powerful, and I never learned about undercurrents.

At a very early age I did play soccer and was goalkeeper most of the time. I had a lot of scraped knees. Of course, I played table tennis and later shuttle cock, so tennis and squash followed easily. Later still I took enough golf lessons to master the game, but never really played. Similarly, I took enough skiing lessons and managed to move up, that is down to level four. Once I mastered any sport, I did not feel the need to excel further or compete, and that probably applied to most tasks in my life.

The winter sports problem at school was solved. After a couple of seasons of tennis, I took dancing classes. Ballroom dancing that is. The Arthur Murray dancing school was in the city, and it not only took a longer time to get there by bus, but it was indoors, and it didn't involve a change out of uniform, and it was musical. I learnt all the Latin American dance steps, which kept me in good stead not only in my youth but all through the years.

And *MUSIKA* was always different. I simply gravitated to it. Mrs Desmond was a great music teacher. She made us listen to a huge variety of classical music and she had a large repertoire of songs that she taught us. I still sing Offenbach's Barcarolle from *The Tales of Hoffman*. My sons used to wonder where I learned the lyrics,

"Shed oh moon thy beauteous rays, upon the river gleaming, Murmurs borne by zephyr winds, shall lull us to rest. Night shall pass with morning pass, an end to all our dreaming,"

And some others like,

"Wring out the old, wring in the new, Wring out the false, wring in the true. Hope in the heart, youthful and ..."

I always looked forward to her music lessons and in fact anything musical.

Together with Miss Graham as directors, Mrs Desmond conducted the two Gilbert and Sullivan performances in which I appeared as principal. There were long hours of rehearsals of my principal roles as Pish Tush, a Noble Lord in *The Mikado* and as the Captain Corcoran in *HMS Pinafore*. She was most patient, cooperated well with Miss Graham and that partnership achieved the most successful of amateur productions that could have competed with any of the professional opera companies I have seen around the world.

The Mikado 1961 (First from right)

I remember little of the year 1963. Though that final year at Dover Heights Girls' High School was somewhat turbulent, it must have been an exciting one. It began unexpectedly with my being elected as one of the eighteen Senior Prefects, through no achievement of my own. Of course, I enjoyed the status, but it came with responsibilities. Quite a feather in my cap, for I was not particularly popular, and I never excelled in anything while the other prefects excelled both academically and athletically.

HMS Pinafore 1962 (Second from left)

I was preoccupied. I was preoccupied with thinking about my boyfriend and spent much of my time with him. As I stated earlier, I was not only not an excellent student, but always managed to get away with the least amount of work. Then suddenly no more. At the Trial Leaving examinations, I failed five out of six subjects. I only passed Accountancy, came second last in my class and almost the same in the whole year of about 200 students.

Mr Roth confronted me, "Do you intend to sit for the Matriculation at all?" his voice echoing from the top of the stairwell while half of school's students filed past, that time in perfect silence just so that they could hear me being humiliated. "Yes, sir" I replied. Of course, I intended to matriculate because in my family it was understood that I would need to matriculate to get to university. "Then you had better start studying."

My parents knew about the boyfriend's constant presence. However disappointed they were with my results, they expected me to have a university education as they were firm believers in the adage that *One thing that no-one can take away from you is your knowledge*. To that end they decided to engage tutors for me. I was coached intensively for two months at the Power Coaching College in Phillip Street particularly in English and Maths. Since my mind was rarely on schoolwork, I recall nothing I was taught of the lessons from my regular visits to the Heritage terrace building, which was as interesting, as quaint and as old as was my kindly tutor. Yet I must have learnt something, perhaps just enough.

On the eve of the published results, we stood outside the Herald building in Castlereagh Street waiting for the first prints of the papers. The minimum Leaving Certificate requirement was four B's including English. The minimum requirement for Matriculation was six B's including English. I received six B's including English and hence was qualified to enter university. Our traditional graduation ceremony from Dover Heights Girls' High School took place in the Sydney Town Hall. For the occasion all the girls were very splendidly attired traditionally in white dresses, with white socked white shoes and white gloves.

"The roots of education are bitter, but the fruit is sweet."

Aristotle

Chapter Seven
EDUCATION - UNIVERSITY

"Education is the key that unlocks the golden door to freedom."

George Washington Carver

I do believe that one's education is a kind of work in progress, that is an ongoing process without an end. And I seemed to have been at university for ever so long.

My very first day at the University of New South Wales (UNSW) ended in disappointment. Because I always loved machines, I decided to study Mechanical Engineering. My application and that of another female student was initially discouraged and eventually enrolment was refused. The reasons given were that we would be outnumbered by the male students and that females were not meant to become engineers. Like sheep we accepted the verdict and enrolled in Bachelor of Arts degree. After all, for me the aim was to "get an education". In hindsight, it was a great shame that we did not contest the decision. Perhaps not. However, the important thing was that I was a student to get a university education.

I enrolled in four subjects, Psychology, Philosophy, Scientific Thought and Mathematics. The large lecture hall for Mathematics 1 was housed in the main building which was of dark red brick. I was not prepared for what seemed like a foreign language and I battled with calculus in particular. School maths did not prepare me for it. When I was very behind the class, my cousin's engineer husband Paul tried to explain some of the material and could not comprehend why I, who he thought was an intelligent person, was struggling with what he thought were basic concepts. Of course, he knew that there was a boyfriend on the scene but was totally unaware of the fact that I spent most of my time in his lectures at his university and not at mine.

My very last university examination was where my very first Psychology 1 lecture was in room 101 on Western Campus which was on the other side of Anzac Parade, and a long distance to walk in less than five minutes to other lectures on the top campus. 101 was a huge barn of a hall with what seemed like hundreds of eager students at single desks. The man who walked in was not very tall or very imposing for a lecturer. However, his soothing voice and articulate delivery immediately revealed a man of knowledge and integrity.

In his introduction, Mr Jarvis stated that if any of the students enrolled in Psych 1 to solve their personal problems or to psychoanalyse themselves, then they should leave. The sound of chairs scraping the wooden floor echoed the massive exodus, but a large number remained. By the end of the year, that number had dwindled again considerably. I believe Mr Jarvis was right to discourage individuals to dabble in playing therapists of the self or others. It was and is highly dangerous with little knowledge, just as the short courses for Life Coaching are hidden with risks for the same reason.

Philosophy was only interesting when the lecturer, not very young, not very attractive and a habitual pipe smoker told us about his private life. One story was how his child, or children slept in the same room as he and his wife, and thus they were privy to their parents' sexual acts. "And why not?" said he. I don't remember any of the "Logic" he taught but his philosophy surpassed that of the great Philosophers.

At the end of that year, I achieved a most unique position at the University of NSW for which probably there was no previous precedent. I failed 4 out of 4 subjects. Well, not exactly, I got a deferred in Scientific Thought, but did not attend the deferred exam on Saturday. The night before I gave an engagement dinner party for my friend Rosemary. By morning, I developed a high temperature, and I was bedridden. It was from sheer guilt. In short, I failed the full year.

I tried to explain my dismal failure, justify and excuse such results, but to no avail. It seemed perfectly natural to me, that since I was spending all my time at Sydney University, I couldn't possibly pass any of my exams at NSW University.

Disappointed as he was, my father gave me a choice. I could go out to work and earn my living, or I could return to the university, study, obtain some decent results and a degree of some sort. Naturally, I decided to take advantage of the offer for a second chance and returned to UNSW. Not that I was afraid of work as such, but I remembered what my mother said about a person needing an education as well as a trade. Besides that, all my friends and acquaintances in my social circle were university students. False pride? Perhaps.

When I repeated year one, I replaced Mathematics with Sociology which was not particularly interesting, but it encompassed society to complement Psychology which referred to the individual, Scientific Thought and Philosophy. Why philosophy I don't know, but in the end, I was conceded a pass in it. However, I did like Scientific Thought which later was renamed most appropriately History and Philosophy of Science or HPS. Professor Thornton was a great lecturer who was most enthusiastic about his subject and was good at imparting a liking for it all. He opened my eyes to the wonders of the history of science and left me with a desire to learn about the world. My friend Barbara remembers him similarly.

HPS included a lot of astronomy, which I tried to impart to my sons. For instance, I still remind them when there is a full moon and to make sure that they look at it with their children. Also to watch the planets when they are visiting the Southern Hemisphere and even try to trace their paths, although in this digital age, I am not sure that they can leave their iPhone camera apertures open long enough, if at all.

Further when their children ask about the appearance of a bright 'evening star' every night, they can tell them with confidence that it is also referred to as the 'morning star.' And as I told them they can say that it is not only not a star but the planet Venus who is loyal to our Earth for she is visible from Earth every day, whereas the other planets visit at different intervals. As for the visible bright star which is a star, it is very likely Sirius. And so on.

At the end of first year second time, I gained sufficient credits to receive a Commonwealth Scholarship. My parents were rather proud of me and that seemed to vindicate me. Strangely even then, it was believed that any education was unnecessary for women. Further, in many discussions there was general agreement that a Bachelor of Arts was not very practical.

So, I changed to Bachelor of Social Work (BSocWk) which was not only more practical, but it led to a profession that dealt with people. BSocWk was a four-year course. I continued with Psychology, Sociology, one year of Public Health and Social Medicine, and three years of Social Work theory and practice.

A well-established educator, Professor Parker reminded me of Miss Payne the headmistress at DHGHS. She was our lecturer for Social Work and Perlman was her bible which we inherited. It was divided into the four "P's" namely the Problem, the Person (or client), the Process (or social work practice) and Place (or agency) and I was constantly conscious of those 'p's during my practice. However, I did deviate a few times. Part of the Process of social work was to guide the client through therapy to arrive at their own decisions to resolve their problems. However, there were occasions when I instinctively told clients 'What to do." But no harm was done.

The course also called for four placements which were exceptional practical experiences. My supervisors were great teachers and most memorable. Miss Daphne Cahill was my first supervisor at my first placement at Prince Henry Hospital (PHH), sister to Prince of Wales Hospital (POW.) PHH was a teaching hospital of UNSW situated in Little Bay, right next to Long Bay Gaol and had the only infectious ward which still housed lepers then. It is no longer and has been replaced by private residential accommodations mostly for Senior citizens.

Miss Cahill established the Social Work department in the hospital and was protective of her position as it was her life. She was a good supervisor. A single woman who must have been attractive in her younger days and had an attraction for the Rehabilitation Director. My first client was her favourite patient Monsieur Gebert who was a nice old gentleman with advanced diabetes among other ailments, lived on his own and needed support. My biggest problem occurred on a home visit when he offered me a cup of tea and I had no idea how to refuse him. There was nothing clean in his place. Thank goodness I only visited him a few times and learned to say no. The cup of tea problem haunted me throughout my career in other homes.

My second placement was in the Psychiatric department in the Royal Prince Alfred Hospital (RPAH) with Miss Margaret Topham, who was the first Social Worker to establish a private Social Work practice in Sydney. She was a very imposing woman, a strict supervisor and left me with a statement that still rings in my ear. In one of our supervisory sessions, she told me that I may appear as rather confident, "but deep down" I was "an emotionally insecure little girl." Well, I was stunned. I still see myself sitting in silence on the opposite side of her desk while she towered over it and me.

I am still not sure of its relevance to my supervision, but I did consider it unbecoming and certainly unprofessional from an educator. However, since I did not agree with her and still do not agree, my psyche remained intact. It remained in my memory purely to remind me how not to treat students. And I never did.

I learned a lot about the large organisation of the Red Cross which had a Social Work department all of whose members were regular blood donors. Naturally I became a regular donor of a litre of blood for a number of years and on each occasion, I was happy to drink the orange juice to replenish the fluids.

My supervisor there was a married lady who may well have had some marital problems. Her heart was neither in her work nor in her supervisory sessions with me. Still, it was an interesting placement where I found out about the Red Cross, and its great work for and with families whose members were in the Darwin theatre of war during World War II. One such was the veteran Mr X who moved out from his home and although his wage was garnished to support his family, they needed extra financial and other assistance. So, I inherited my multi-problem family.

My final placement was in Bondi at Scarba Children's Home which was under the auspices of the Benevolent Society. The original building must have been a grand home once on lovely grounds and still stands as part of Heritage listing, although the larger part of the property has been developed considerably. When I was a student there, Scarba offered a daily cooked lunch for the staff in the dining room where I ate my first typically Australian meal of lamb chops. It was delicious.

There I met a little girl. Together with all the other Scarba children, she stood in line for most activities as well as for the hair brushing. The children all seemed to be blonde, all looked the same and smelled the same, as did the babies who I helped to feed on occasions due to staff shortage. The little girl was four years old and a member of my multi-problem family X who followed me for a number of years to other agencies.

Mrs. X was physically and/or mentally unwell. She was looked after by her 16-year-old daughter, who also looked after four younger children and a boy of 14 still at school, while two other small children were with foster families. I found Mrs. X in bed on all home visits to Green Valley, where I parked my car two blocks away as I did not want anyone to see me arrive in a luxury Chrysler in the Housing Commission settlement.

Mrs. Colby was an intelligent and a most empathic Social Work supervisor. She explained how all the problems in most multi-problem families sadly were handed down from generation to generation and that I should not be discouraged if I cannot help the X family. Further that I should not be surprised if the 16 years old girl fell pregnant.

Sure enough, a few months later we found out that the 16 years old was pregnant and that was another problem with which I had to deal. Mrs Colby stressed that if I succeeded in helping one member of such a family, then that would be a real achievement. To interview the teenage boy was a challenge and on each home visit I spent considerable time following him from bus stop to sportsground to Milk Bar, to try to establish some kind of rapport with which to work. A ten-minute interview was a great feat. For some time, I lost contact with him and the family.

While we worked with the families of some of the children at Scarba, my fellow student and I were asked to do some research and report some recommendations for improvements for the Home. So, our results clearly outlined the needs of small children in care and the detrimental effects of institutionalisation, focusing on the importance of parent-child interaction and fostering. We documented some short- and long-term goals especially for the development of relationship between staff and children. One of our long-term objectives was to establish living accommodations for retired person on the grounds of Scarba and for the retirees to engage with the children. The former had little activities and much time, and the latter needed extra carers and attention. It was most gratifying when some years later I discovered that even that long-term recommendation was implemented by the Benevolent Society.

My undergraduate years in the 1960s were quite uneventful after my first-year failure debacle except for Foundation Days. One year it was decided that we organise a large contingent of students to cross the Harbour Bridge very early in the morning with ten and twenty-pound notes and insist that they were the smallest currency in our possession. At that time the toll was two shillings only and because change was scarce, after a short time the traffic stopped for a long time. Another year we organised a kidnapping of the stars of the very popular *Mavis Bramston Show*. We picked up Barry Creyton, Carol Raye, and Gordon Chater, and held them in three separate locations for a full day. They were most gracious, and the publicity was successful for them as well as for the university. These events were arranged with the cooperation of the actors and the police of course. And we the students enjoyed our one day in the year which ended in the annual Foundation Ball.

Generally, I enjoyed my university life with little work. After I spent much time with my boyfriend at the other university, I spent much time in the Roundhouse or Union at UNSW having coffee and watching fellow students play cards. Most of them were exempt from conscription to fight in Vietnam till the completion of their degree course. I did join the Jewish youth group where I met some very wonderful people who became long standing friends. I was elected to the committee but most of my time was spent typing for the magazine.

I owe my degree to Dr Tony Vinson who was then the head of the School of Social Work, who later became Minister for Corrective Services and was a social justice reformer. As a result of visiting Third World countries, he gained valuable practical lessons which he imparted to his students such as "change must be planned; that change must be slow; and that change must be from within, by the people themselves". Due to his generosity to give me extra time to write my overdue essays, I was granted my degree.

In 1968 my proud parents were present at my graduation ceremony. I wore a white dress under my black graduation cloak under my black mortarboard with its annoying dangling tassels. And I carried my Bachelor of Social Work degree in my white gloved hand.

I practiced as a professional Social Worker for over six years until I was married and took over my parents' business. During that time, I enrolled in a Master in Social Work at Sydney University and in 1971 received a gold lettered Certificate of accreditation for Part I. Sadly, together with all my high school books, university notes and documents, it too drowned in the 1999 hailstorm.

One day at the end of 1983 I woke up and asked, "Is that all there is?" Make no mistake, I was not unhappy. I was settled happily in a marriage with three lovely children who were at school, a solid business and a very satisfactory social life. While I continued to do the usual daily activities mostly in service of others, something was missing in my life.

My continued association with UNSW began, but only part time. I owe much to Helen Milfull who gave me permission to re-enrol on a number of occasions. On the day of my first return to enrol at UNSW, I was not found. The young person at Unisearch House apologetically said, "Our records don't go back that far." Microfilms were obsolete and I guess I have not been uploaded yet.

A few years later I actually applied for a degree of Masters in Social Work and was interviewed by Prof. John Lawrence, the then acting Head of the department. "Did you publish anything?" Remember the university edict of 'publish or perish'? "No, I did not publish anything." I was informed in no uncertain terms, that on the basis of my past records, I was "not academic material." That resonated with previous words that were not good for the ego.

But I did continue to study for the pleasure of it all. I did numerous General Studies subjects and felt elated as I grew. Well, I grew mentally. There was an added element in my life and once more my mind was active. Although it was all quite demanding on my time and on my concentration, it was therapy and pure enjoyment.

I then enrolled in Australian Welfare History. The course examined the question of class in a different perspective from social stratification of my undergraduate sociology studies. It was more the hegemonic ideology of the dominant class or socialism. Having lived in a Communist country, I believed that the assignments and the examinations would prove to be easy.

Not so. I attempted to make a case for the marked difference between the theory and the practice of socialism, but Ms Wilson would have none of it and was adamant when she stated that "this is not a place for your soap box." Her main point was that academia required a different form of argument. After my initial anger at near failure, I conceded to a lesson which I learnt well. And gained a memorable mere pass.

And I moved to Contemporary History and Global Problems without any difficulty. I am not sure what drove me towards the Theory of Ancient Philosophy of Technology and later to Modern Philosophy of Technology, but I am very glad that I did those subjects. The course was structured around Dr Graham Pont's paper titled, *From Biotechnics to Total Art: Towards An Encyclopaedic Curriculum for the Technological Society*, based on the ancient meaning of techne (art, skill, craft, etc – "know–how" as distinct from "know that"). It was very much grounded in ancient Greek theories and supposed practices of education with specific attention to dance as an expression and music as the rational bases for the harmonic ordering of nature and man. Towards this understanding, his main texts were Lewis Mumford and Robert Pirsig's *Zen and The Art of Motorcycle Maintenance* (1974). And what an education one may gain from riding a motorcycle on tour intertwined with Socrates.

All of Asia was foreign to me and much still is. And so, I studied some history of the Philippines, Vietnam and China. India was part of the course too, but neither the lecturer nor his text arrived in time for the beginning of the semester. I did not do well on the question of Confucianism in the "traditional" Vietnamese society facilitating Marxism in the 20th century. But I passed and I did much better with a mark verging on distinction on an assignment on the role of Ho Chi Minh in the emergence of the Vietnamese Anti-colonial movement before 1946.

As my grades were steadily cruising at Credit levels, I was free to look into any area. So, I thought about exploring creative writing to discover the remote possibility of some latent ability in that field. But I refused to adhere to the required feminist perspective, so I changed to a Factual Writing course that offered a variety of registers. There too I incurred a hiccup or perhaps another lesson in education and added it to how not to teach.

At some stage in the course, I requested some information from a Dr Egan about writing and publishing my autobiography. The conversation was along the following lines. "Are you somebody?" she asked. I was stunned. "Excuse me?" I asked. "Are you someone famous?" she asked. I wondered if only the famous could write their autobiography. She never helped me, and I decided to write one after a fashion anyway. So, it won't be a best seller.

But I had some wonderful lecturers and subjects in which I engrossed myself. One was Personal Development Programs in Schools which in my old days was called Personal Development, Health and Physical Education or PDH and PE. I revelled in the contents for it focused on real life experiences that can be and should be taught formally in school. And I believed that I did that in my teaching practice.

My practical teaching experience as a student left a lot to be desired. On a couple of occasions, I returned to my old school of Dover Heights Girls High. First, I had the strange experience of returning as a professional Social Worker about a student. Second was my student teacher placement. One memorable experience was when one of the fourth-year students threatened to jump out the third-floor window as a prank or simply to test me. Some of the boys stopped him and so the situation was defused. What was hard to believe or just bad luck, that at every single one of my Teaching Practice assessments, something went wrong. Usually with the technical equipment. Suffice to say I achieved a Satisfactory grade and so I graduated.

In 1989 I received my Diploma of Education with Merit from the University of New South Wales. My family was there to witness it. I felt such pride in the presence of my husband and my three sons in their uniforms. They may not remember, but I remember it well.

I continued to study. I was a mature age student for many years. I was motivated and involved in my subjects including the ones in which I was not that proficient. And lecturers appreciated motivated mature students.

The required Statistics was not my forte, but I was eager to learn. Even in high school I needed to understand the 'why' not just the 'what.' Dr Jin Putai knew his material and was an eager teacher, but the students in the class were as confused as I was. So, I asked questions. My method was to ask if I interpreted the explanations correctly. That clarified concepts, the students appreciated it, and the rest of the sessions went smoothly with my intermittent interpretations.

That must have been the reason why one day Dr Putai asked if I would be interested in tutoring. What must have sounded like a hesitant consent, was actually suppressed excitement. I am most grateful to him for giving me the chance to teach.

I graduated with a Masters in Education in 1996 at the UNSW, making my position as Tutor to first year Bachelor of Education students in Department of Education official. To some extent, it cemented my teaching position which I continued to enjoy for a decade or more. In a way I felt that I did not deserve the position of Tutor but felt proud and welcomed the challenge. And if truth be told, I was thrilled.

So it was that for many years while I was teaching, I continued to study other subjects majoring in English and Film. My real interest started with the subject of 'The Rise of the Novel' and specifically with *Heart of Darkness*. An amazing achievement by Dr Bruce Johnson to hold the attention of his students for a full hour's lecture on the single opening paragraph of Joseph Conrad's famous novel. An authority on jazz music and a jazz musician himself, he also introduced me to 2MBS FM, a volunteer run 24-hour classical music radio station now called *Fine Music*, to which I have been listening ever since.

Dr Christine Alexander immersed herself in the Juvenilia of the Brontes for some time as she became a world authority on the subject. Hence when we visited the Brontes' Haworth home in Yorkshire, I felt close to the world of the Brontes. And each time I watched such films as *Devotion* (1946) which was also extraordinarily well researched, I felt I lived a fragment of the lives of the Brontes with them.

Spectatorship and Critical Theory were a new and most challenging dimension of academic study of film for me. It was Walter Benjamin's life, and his essay titled, *"The Work of Art in the Age of Mechanical Reproduction"* on the loss of the "aura" that I found fascinating. But I must confess that I excelled in Censorship and Responsibility in the Performing Arts. I already had an introduction to the banned Mary McCarthy's *The Group* when as a teenager we all read the deflowering scene on page 72. During my research in the State and Federal Archives I also enjoyed reading some fascinating behind-the-scenes documents not relevant to my topic.

Teaching, Reading and Filming Literature taught by philosopher Dr Jim Gribble was of particular attraction. What stayed with me was the significance of "these words in these places" in literary criticism. I also became a footnote reference in one of his articles for the Teachers' magazine. And the enormously gifted Orson Welles, the *'wunder kind'* or wonder child still looms large for me as a mighty talent. Much can be said for Shakespeare on stage and on screen, and I did say much about *Kiss Me Kate* (1948), the musical film production of *The Taming of the Shrew* as one filmic representation of the Bard's work.

I continued to study and in 2003 I gained another degree, a Bachelor of Arts with Hons in Film Studies. It was on filmic representation of Second Generation of Holocaust Survivors and not quite complete for 1st Class level in Honours. Despite that, I was encouraged to work towards a doctorate. I was to have enrolled in a Masters by Research program which was a prerequisite for a PhD. I deferred.

An interesting lesson was the expansiveness of a thesis. It can be effectively applied for many years. One can take parts of it for publication on associated topics, produce a number of papers and presentations on related topics and/or extend it into a book. I used my Honours Thesis to present at a couple of Jewish Studies conferences on Second Generation and one paper was published in the Australian Association of Jewish Studies magazine. I was also able to extend aspects of my thesis to Humour Studies. My interest in Humour Studies was sparked by Dr Jessica Milner Davis. I am grateful for her encouragement and the opportunities she provided for being a presenter at the Humour Colloquium in 2003 and 2005. I do believe that she may have handed me one of my degrees while she was Vice Chancellor.

It must be remembered that the total aim of the exercise was to enjoy the whole experience of learning and education. And teaching was most enjoyable. However, the main problem which I faced for years persisted. If I had problems to propose a topic area for a Masters degree, which I did have, I also had problems to design a topic for a PhD. That was the dilemma for me who lacked the imagination or ability to formulate a topic area that was new, unique and original. And of course, life did get in the way. Also, there was always just a little procrastination, if not lack of talent. Perhaps I was not academic material after all.

My association with UNSW continued over many years, including the number of times I returned to her. I still feel a great attachment to her. While I sought an education, she provided. While I searched for knowledge, members of the teaching staff were always ready to assist and significantly influenced my appreciation of their specific subject if not my thinking altogether. Many are entitled to my expressions of gratitude. They all have left an indelible mark with me, and I will continue to remember them with affection and deep appreciation. And I developed a true fondness for the students who were part of my education as a tutor.

In those last few years there, our relationship became entwined in a complex way. I was enrolled in an upper-level undergraduate subject in one school, I was a postgraduate degree program student in another school, and I was a casual staff member tutoring in a third school at the University of New South Wales, all at the same time. And so ended my formal education, but not my informal one. Life is also an excellent educator. I have learned much, and I am still learning. However, I must admit that my education has been a privileged one in every respect.

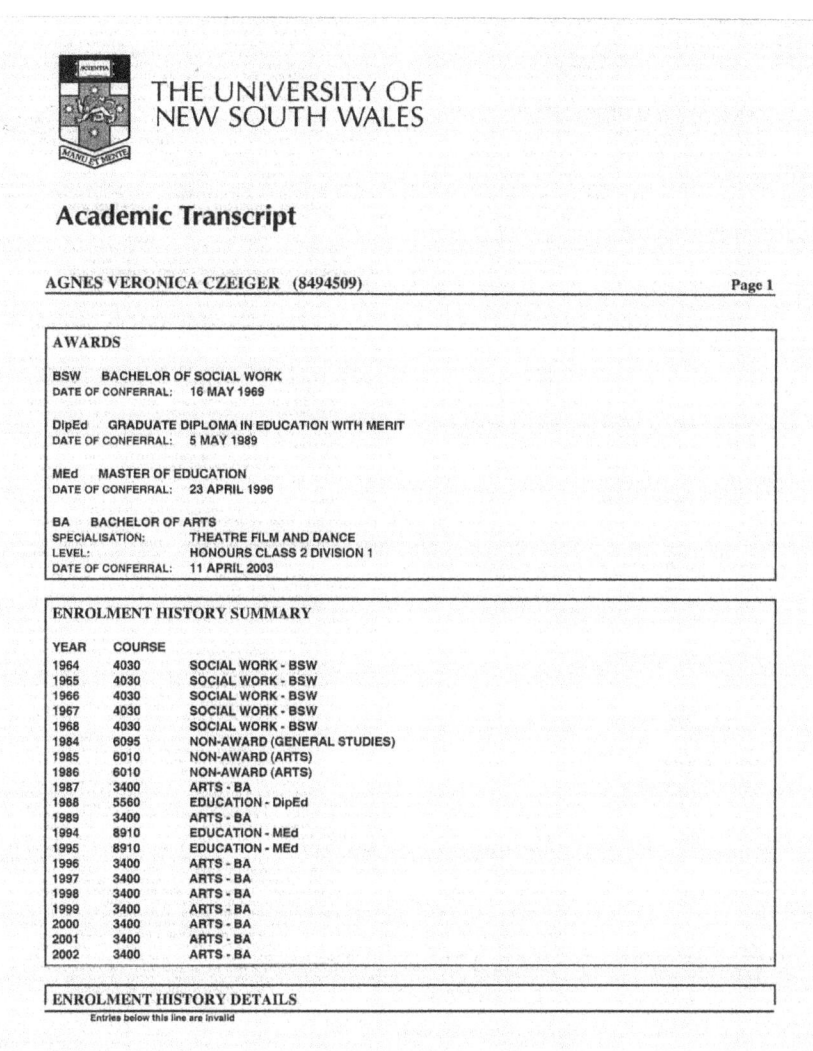

"Teach me, and I will learn."

William Shakespeare

The only thing that interferes with my learning is my education.

Albert Einstein

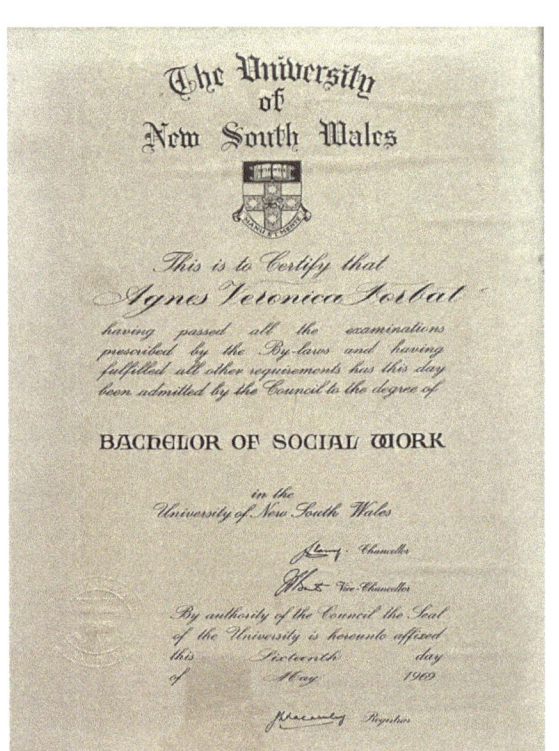
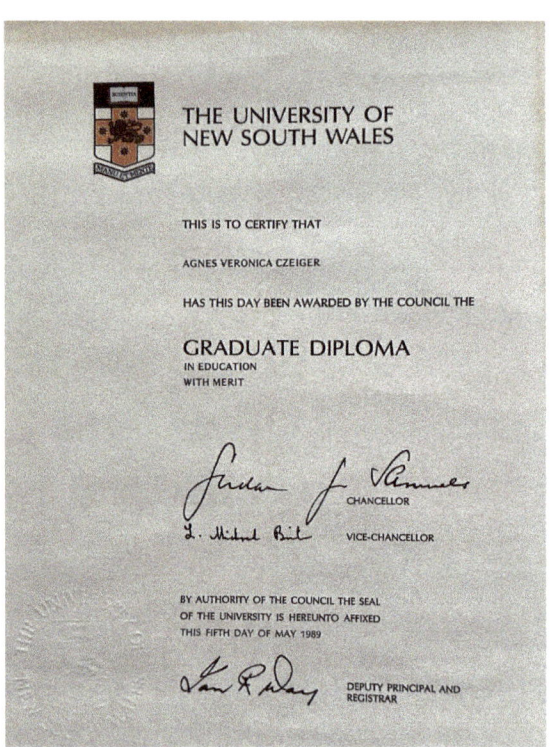
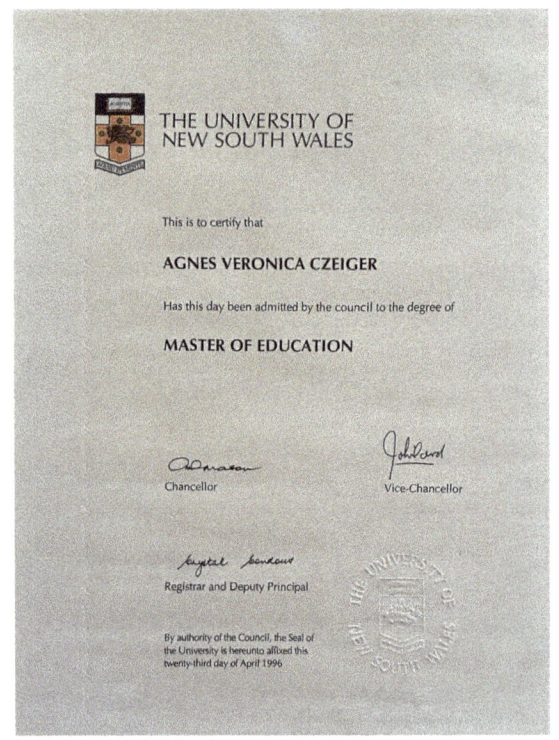
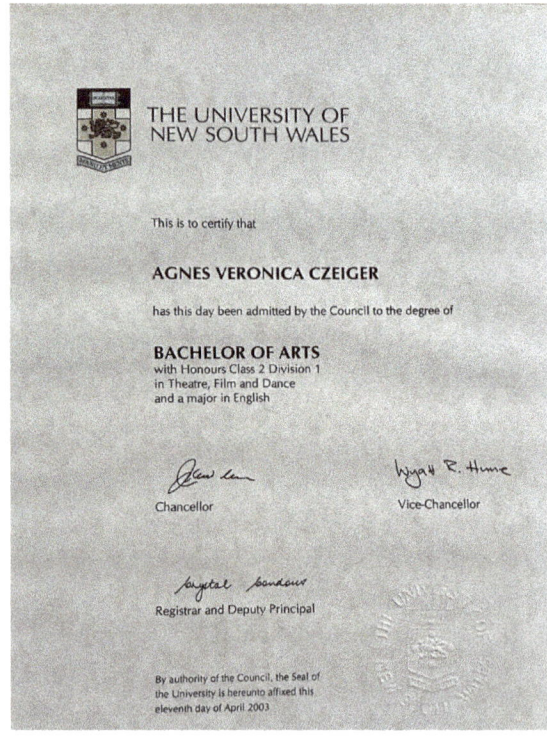

Chapter Eight

RELIGION

> *"Religion is the opium of the people."*
>
> Karl Marx (trans)

Religion was absent from my early childhood. It was limited to the occasional little old lady making the sign of the cross on her body as we passed a church while travelling on a tram and my mother's best friend placing her hand on my head to bless me. I knew not the difference between those practices. Under Communism all religious practices were simply discouraged. I later found out that there was a synagogue even in our street.

None of our family or friends spoke outright about religion. Only in outdoor spaces such as parks were the adults free to speak about religion and politics. The word *Zsido* or Jew was mentioned, but I had no idea what it meant to be Jewish. It took many years after we arrived in Australia, that I began to formulate my conception about Judaism and Jewishness. However, basically religion was not significant in my relationships as I was 'a-religious,' if one can coin that word.

When I was enrolled in Darlinghurst Public School, my religion was required for the record. My mother must have felt safe in our new country, and I was recorded as belonging to the Jewish faith. Much later when we received a copy of my birth certificate, I discovered that I was born *Reformatus* or Reformist which we perceived as a kind of non-descript traditional religion for the non-observant, as distinct from Protestant or any other religion. But in Australia I started attending Jewish scripture classes in school and in sixth class with a couple of other Jewish students, I learnt about the High Holydays and a little history attached.

In Dover Heights High School there was one period a week when the young trainee Rabbis tried to instil in us some knowledge and feel for the religion. Yet of that indescribable bond between the Jewish people that draws them to one another, there was never a word spoken. In second year, I had one contrary encounter when of all people, the Rabbi's daughter called me something anti-Jewish to which I took offense, and I never spoke to her after that. Apparently, I was not religious enough for her.

My mother was well versed in her Jewish religion through her mother. She asked me if I wanted her to keep the *Shabbat* or the Sabbath or a *Kosher* kitchen according to strict Jewish dietary laws, or just the Friday night candle lighting and High Holydays. I did not feel the need for any of those rituals. Yet there are some rituals that one inherits unintentionally, and I still have separate dishes for *fleischig* or meaty and for *milchig* or milky and boiling water.

My parents believed in interpreting their religion for themselves. When I was quite young, they started their own ritual of which I was very fond, and it continued while they were alive. On *Yom Kippur* or Day of Atonement, my mother would light the appropriate *mecses* or candles and send my father to *Shul* or Synagogue to say *Kaddish* or mourners' prayer for all the relatives who passed away especially the Holocaust victims.

When he returned from Shul, instead of fasting the whole day as is customary, the three of us sat and had round table discussions while sipping coffee or hot chocolate and ate some *Kuglof*, that delicious cake filled with chocolate on the inside. I tried to continue the ritual after my parents died, but my husband Harry would rather fast. I still have my tea and cake in the middle of Yom Kippur though I miss the round table discussions.

There were a number of Jewish groups between ages 13 – 16 and above 21 years of age in Sydney. So, with the encouragement of Mr Simons, we established Central Seniors, a socio-cultural group for 16 to 21-year-old youths attached to Central Synagogue. Starting with Saturday night dances, he gathered a core group of young people who set up a committee, painted the club room, ran the weekly Sunday meetings, and organised functions.

I became part of the core group, and we were active in the community. We organised social functions such as a day's outing to Sutherland National Park, as well as cultural events with guest speakers, where we learnt more about the history and the traditions of the Jewish people. We also raised funds, collected JNF Blue Boxes, and transported senior members of B'nai B'rith from their home to luncheon or card meetings or wherever they wished to go. Hence my association with Central Synagogue where I met my first boyfriend, where I danced a lot, where later I was married, and where my sons had their *Bar Mitzvahs* or initiations into manhood at 13 years of age.

1974

1992

Once at university, I joined the Jewish students. At first the group was attached to Sydney University's SUJSU, until we created our own student union called NSW University Jewish Students' Union or NUJSU, in which I occupied all the committee positions at one time or another. I was one of the first NUJSU Presidents and my end of year gift was dated 1967. A spoon is a spoon is a spoon. But this one is for the memorabilia collection.

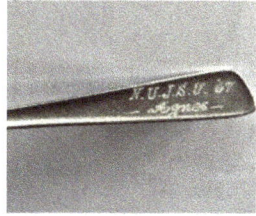

In June of that same year, when the Six Day War of Israel broke out, we were present in the Maccabean Hall in Darlinghurst which was the centre of the Jewish organisations in Sydney. We watched anxiously the progress of the war, marked the map of the Middle East as the Israeli Defence Forces captured the Golan Heights from Syria, the West Bank from Jordan, the Gaza and the whole Sinai Peninsular from Egypt. The atmosphere was so charged that some students volunteered to fight with the Israeli forces, despite the fact that they applied for and were granted deferment of their Australian Conscription to fight in Vietnam.

I can recall one specific instance of a student who requested and was granted an exemption on the grounds of homosexuality. He later moved to Israel, married and had a family. And like all Israeli citizens, he was conscripted into the Israeli Defence Force. We all volunteered to help, but only a few were accepted to assist in the war effort but only as truck drivers in Israel. Besides, the war was over very quickly. The rest of us did what was necessary, whether it was administrative or fundraising. And we all rejoiced at the totally unexpected victorious outcome.

For a number of years three of us, Nick L, Norbert S (who I called Bubbles for some reason and there were bubbles sketched next to his name in the magazine) and I edited NUJSU monthly magazine called *Forum*. I was elected probably because I could type of which I did a lot. My typed stencils were attached to the rolls on the Gestetner printer to Roneo and the duplicated pages were collated. When the machine broke down before the required numbers were printed, I was forced to learn a little mechanics to repair it as needed.

The whole process may have been time consuming, but it was enjoyable and educational. The magazine was quite a substantial production with articles of interest about the university and Judaism, with editorials, poems, cartoons, crosswords, and with announcement of functions. Not to speak of the fact that my name appeared at the bottom of some articles.

I joined the Hillel Graduates where I met some more nice Jewish students. After I married, we supported most if not all of the Jewish organisations in Sydney and Israel. What remained are the questions how little I knew about Judaism and what it meant to be Jewish. My knowledge originated from scripture classes in school and there weren't that many of those. Besides there were much more interesting past times in school.

Well, there may have been fifteen commandments originally until coming down Mt Sinai Moses dropped one of the tablets that contained five of them, according to Mel Brooks. However, there are actually 613 Commandments in the *Torah* or the Hebrew Bible or the Old Testament which contains the five books of Moses of laws and traditions.

The *Talmud*, often confused with the Torah or Bible, contains the history of the Jewish religion and is the book of "learning." It is what is studied, debated, interpreted, and commented on by the learned scholars. Hence the infinite Commentaries. That is one of the most significant differences between Judaism and other religions. Jewish texts are questioned, debated and interpretations are recorded for the ages, whereas in Catholicism for example, the laws are dogmatic Doctrines that are to be obeyed without question or pause.

Another major difference is that Judaism is monotheist with the singular G-d, as distinct from the Trilogy of G-d the Father, the Son, and the Holy Ghost of Christianity. There has been debate and denial about the Jewish heritage of G-d's son Jesus who was born to Jewish parents. The young carpenter became a reformist in his early twenties. He was considered more of a prophet by the Jews and by some even a false prophet at that. Some called him a Rabbi, others a rebel. My cousin has always called him a 'troublemaker' who caused nothing but problems for thousands of years, as proved by all the religious wars of the past.

On one occasion in Budapest, my mother's friend Gal Kati took me to the synagogue in Csaki Utca, now Hegedus-Gyula Utca, the street where we lived. I remember walking through narrow doorway and down some steps to a small grey dimly lit place, where there was a distinct drone of a few men chanting something incomprehensible to me. Naturally Kati said some prayers, naturally she blessed me, and we left. And I left it at that since we were not religious. Years later in Sydney someone tried to convince me that there was no such place in that street. However, I was convinced that I was in such a place.

Not so long ago my cousin Anita in Budapest sent me an article which proved that the synagogue was not only there, but that the place of worship was recently renovated with bright blue glass dome, and that my memory served me well. Kati would have been pleased as this must have been her synagogue.

The synagogue was built for the Lipótváros prayer circle in 1911 according to plans by Béla Vajda. In the wave of synagogues built at the end of the nineteenth century, the buildings were alternately accessible and restrained or disguised in character. One of these was the Hegedűs Gyula Street Synagogue which was adapted from the shop front of a residential house. In 1927 Lipót Baumhorn, one of the most famous Hungarian architects of synagogues, expanded the temple by adding a courtyard.

On 8th September 2016, the Israeli violinist Eyal Shiloach played with the Klezmer orchestra in the Csaki Utca Synagogue. The sensational violinist who was discovered by Isac Stern (and may have been taught by him) can be found on UTube.

But there is something that is present in all Jews. There is no specific expression for this bond or binding force that is present in all Jews other than faith and spiritualism. It is what united the Jewish people over the thousands of years and unites them today. Of course, there was the Holocaust and then there is the land of Israel that is within that union with its heritage and legacy. But I am referring to *Yiddishkeit* or Jewishness that has no appropriate words to describe it. It is just part of being Jewish and hence the Jewish being.

Harry's family were much more observant than my family. Hence after I became engaged every *Shabbat* or Sabbath night was spent at his mother's house. Every Friday night, Harry's mother Lilly, lit the candles and cooked a delicious meal and did the same for each of the High Holydays. The numbers grew with Fedor's marriage, the birth of our children and the tradition continued while she was alive. After her passing, my sister-in-law Liz and I continued for many years. So, the family was together on Friday nights. *Pesach* or Passover was celebrated at Fedor's home and the breaking of the Fast on *Yom Kippur*, or the Day of Atonement was held at our home until Uncle's passing. After that we had *Pesach* and later Monika set a lovely table for *Seder* night.

Pesach was a considerably big event as all the family and some close friends were invited to Fedor's home, so the numbers may have exceeded 30 in some years. It was also especially lively as both Uncle Julius and Ron had birthdays around that date and both birthdays were celebrated. By 2011 all my sons were married as was the only girl Natalie, and some had children themselves. Uncle had an unexpectedly jolly time opening his presents on his 90th birthday while surrounded by his family and the five grandchildren.

It was now time for the great grandchildren to have *Bar Mitzvahs* and Natalie was leading the way. Her three sons just finished with their rites of passage, and they were great events. My three sons with their families were invited to the Services as well as to the celebrations even though the youngest son had his *Bar Mitzvah* in Israel earlier. Our only grandson Ethan had his recently and the *Bat Mitzvah* will come. Tradition!

Lady Maleficent's Blog – August 27, 2016

For some time, I read the Wentworth Courier, not because I am a conscientious community member, (although I am not unconscientious) but because I like my weekly Sudoku and there are some articles of interest. It is also nice to view some beautiful properties that are on the market in the Eastern suburbs. At the end of August 2016, there was an article about a Rabbi receiving a plaque on Bondi Beach, "honouring his service to the community". He and his wife provide meals for people in need through "Our Big Kitchen". He is also active in a number of organisations.

On being the first recipients of this award, one of his responses stated that the plaque represents, "children, family and the community". Mayor Sally Betts spoke of the Rabbi in admiration, and that he was an "iconic resident" in the community.

This man is part of a people, towards whom non-Jewish people feel hatred, and part of a people whom terrorists want to blow up. He is one of a small group of people inhabiting the globe, who have contributed so much to humanity and whose tiny nation, the Arab Muslims want to "wipe off the face of the earth". Why?

In 2019 an anniversary celebration dinner in Bowral in the Southern Highlands the conversation turned to the current state of the world. Everyone agreed that we are living through an era of great turmoil especially in the Middle East. One person said,

"I am of two minds about Israel." I asked why. The reply was, "Because Israel is practising genocide against the Palestinians."

Suddenly I was enraged. Antisemitism at our dinner table? This was the first time in my life that I spoke up. I am not an activist, more like a pacifist. I am not a Zionist. I am not a political animal. I am merely a secular Jew, who never asks a person his or her religion.

After a short time, very calmly I asked, "Do you know the meaning of genocide?"

The answer was in the negative. I then asked, "Do you know anything about the Holocaust?"

Again, the answer was in the negative. I then entered into a rapidly flowing tirade of a totally unprepared lecture in simple terms for the benefit of this frighteningly stupid simple person who most would consider merely ill-informed.

So, I started. Genocide is indiscriminate mass slaughter of a people. It began with tribal man for his survival and has continued to date in parts of the world not merely for survival, but for power and control. The Holocaust was a genocide but because it was unprecedented in history, and it is a unique classification of the term.

In fact, it is called the Holocaust because it was a mass destruction that was a systematic and mechanized annihilation of a people, most specifically the Jewish people and for no other reason but that they were Jews. The Holocaust existed and it cannot be denied.

It is an incomprehensible state of affairs that today antisemitism is rampant on the European continent where millions were exterminated of which six million Jews were gassed and their bodies incinerated in specially built ovens, for no other reason but that they were Jews. It is even more incomprehensible that antisemitism is present in this distant land of Australia, a country which always supported the victims.

There are some facts that may not be well known to the general population of the world. After thousands of years of exile, pogroms and persecution resulted in the Holocaust, the Jewish people fought and founded the State of Israel, which was legitimately and legally granted Independent Nationhood in 1948. Yet the fighting continued ever since.

Israel is a very small piece of land which is surrounded by the Mediterranean Sea on one side and the very large Arab lands on all the other sides. The aim of all Muslim Arab nations is to sweep the little Jewish State into the sea.

It is a huge problem that the Palestinian people live in a buffer zone between Israel and her enemies. Where are the wealthy Arab nations and why don't they come the aid of the poor Palestinians? I do not wish to enter into the debate that they aren't Palestinians. What is very sad and incomprehensible is that the Palestinian people use their children as shields.

Part of the daily life of the Israelis is the unprovoked unexpected bombings that leave numerous casualties of injured and dead civilians. Those daily bombings are rarely in the media, but when one Palestinian is injured, it is reported worldwide. We know about that lifestyle because phone conversations with the people living in Israel were often interrupted when the alarm was sounded, and the populace needed to seek shelter in bunkers which for years have been compulsory in all buildings.

There are over a million Arab Israeli citizens who are treated the same as are all Jewish Israeli citizens. They are contributing members of the Jewish State, educated and employed, free to practice their religion, and they serve in the Israeli Defence Force. They would not relinquish their citizenship or their freedom. What the Muslim regime offers for the suicide bombers besides the virgins in their next life, is a return to primitive and barbaric life, oppression of women and female children in this life, as well as a life of terror and death for all non-Muslims.

We also know that much of the Palestinian social infrastructure such as schools and hospitals were established by the Israeli government. Further that thousands cross the border daily into Israel for paid employment. It is disastrous that some of those schools and hospitals are used for storage of ammunition by Muslim terrorists.

Much more tragic is the fact that Palestinian children are used as human shields. These are the poor Palestinians who gain the sympathy of the world. And when attacked, the small Israel retaliates to defend herself as did David against Goliath, the world condemns her. Yet despite her size, not only has Israel built a modern nation out of desert sand, but she has also overshadowed all her neighbours of hundreds of millions and has been a leader in the world in every field, particularly science and technology. This was confirmed by the Jewish Nobel Prize winners and the percentage of inventions which is totally out of proportion with the ratio of percentage of the general Jewish and non-Jewish population. It is such achievements that cause jealousy and envy, adding to and resulting in further antisemitism.

Jews have always had to fight to survive. It is because knowledge is the only possession that cannot be taken away from them that Jews had to be learned, besides the fact that they were excluded from most professions and occupations. Hence, they have been educated and successful in many fields in recent history too. Further it must be stated clearly that despite the groundless fears, there is no Jewish conspiracy. Jews do not want to dominate the world. In truth, all they want is to live their lives in peace in Israel and everywhere.

I am no student of religion, but it is a fact that the Torah and the Talmud or bible and book of laws of the over 5780 years old Jewish religion is based on what today we know as the Ten Commandments. No Rabbi will preach killing of any kind, and Orthodox Jews in Israel can refuse to fight in the Defence Force.

On the other hand, the tenets of the Quran of the mere 600 years old Islamic religion are to "kill all Infidels", that is all non-Muslims but especially Jews. No, not all Muslims are terrorists, but all terrorists are Muslim. And the new Mantra of Jew Hate is "From the River to the Sea" was added to "Kill all Jews."

My father specifically selected Australia because of its freedom from political and religious persecution, and because it was the country furthest from Europe where Jews were and still are hated. But the tyranny of distance has permeated that evil even into this far away land that my father and I came to love.

Covert antisemitism is timeless even in Australia. In the sixties a Sydney high society lady was heard in a radio interview to say that she is not prejudiced at all as, "Some of my best friends are Jewish." When there was a Warsaw Ghetto memorial celebration in the Sydney Town Hall, all parked cars in the surrounding area had their fuel tanks filled with tissue paper. The media constantly reports about 'a Jewish doctor' or 'Jewish lawyer', but never about a 'Christian doctor' or 'Catholic lawyer'. Today, we have more overt antisemitism on the streets where there are frequent demonstrations against Israel in countries all over the world, student demonstrations and sit ins on campuses, as well as university staff boycotting Israeli universities. That in academia, the highest seat of learning. Shame on humanity.

The above is most simplistic and excludes much; and even the most knowledgeable are never totally informed. But it is a fact that Israel is not practicing genocide against the Palestinians. Israel is fighting for survival, for her very existence because the world cannot tolerate the existence of Jews. 'Jew Hate' has become part of language.

So how does one combat the enemy of hatred for Jews and Israel, and with what weapons? In the past my solution to most problems has been 'education'. But we have failed in that field, and it is well known that humans cannot learn from history, especially when such events as the Holocaust are being denied and removed from school syllabus. And recently the world witnessed a Holocaust on 7th October 2023 in Israel.

I fear for Israel. I fear for humanity. The question of peace in the Middle East is a continuing debate. However, a teacher who became the fourth Prime Minister of Israel, Golda Meir said it perfectly,

> *"We will only have peace with the Arabs when they love their children more than they hate us Jews."*

For those who need to understand the Jewish people and some of their history, I highly recommended what I think is essential and should be compulsory Reading:

Inga Clendinnen: *Reading the Holocaust.*
Primo Levi: *If This Is A Man.*
Ruth Wajnryb: *The Silence; How Tragedy Shapes Talk.*
Elie Wiesel: *Memoirs*
There is more, much more but the above are crucial especially the first three.

Because my thesis was on *Visual Representation of Second Generation of Holocaust Survivors in Australia*, I needed to do considerable research into the Holocaust itself. It is only by immersing oneself in the subject that one can gain true understanding of what happened to those millions who died or were there and survived the Holocaust. And perhaps even then not, as it is impossible to believe the unbelievable. My thesis illustrated some understanding of the impact of the Holocaust on the Direct Descendants of the Survivors or my generation, an impact that is fading in the subsequent generations fortuitously but unfortunately understanding the Holocaust itself is fading also. However, Jews have a legacy of *Tikkun Olam* or repairing the world. If only they would let us.

Despite all said and done about being Jewish, for a very long time we had a Christmas tree in Australia. She was small, about two feet tall, very artificial but lasting. At first, she was my Christmas tree. Each year we decorated her, adding more baubles to her and crowned her with a *Magen David* or Star of David. Each year we folded up her branches carefully and packed her away in cotton wool till the following year.

We celebrated with her it mattered not what. It was jovial and a time of present giving which for me originated in Hungary. Later she was used by the boys to decorate at the end of the year and together with Chanukah, once again the time was for present giving. Also, she was used by the factory staff when work stopped, the place was decorated, and lunch was set up on one of the cutting tables which was headed by my very decorated little Christmas tree.

For the last few years Christmas was spent at the home of my oldest son Richard whose non- Jewish non-religious wife celebrates with a real Christmas tree, shellfish, an English style Christmas lunch including her very delicious pudding and lots of presents. Alexandra takes great care to start her Christmas pudding early and bastes it frequently in English style which is with lots of the right drinks. It always turns out to be delightful, probably because it is loaded with alcohol. And the children love their presents. They spend considerable time wrapping them and very little time unwrapping them. After all what is Christmas if not for giving presents.

At the same time, we also have been members of the Southern Highland Jewish Community or SHJC since we arrived in Bowral. The old guard is no longer but there is a solid core who meet regularly and preserve the group for those who wish to maintain a Jewish identity. Although there is no Rabbi or Synagogue, there is a religious coordinator who informs us of relevant history and customs. So, some basic rituals and traditions are observed, and prayers said on *Shabbat* or Sabbath nights and on High Holydays. And we always have a table full of tasty cuisine to satisfy.

One year our granddaughter Rebekah was present to wave the *Lulaf* at *Sukkot* or harvest festivities at our place. For a number of years, Channukah was celebrated by the group at our home in Bowral. We usually had a large gathering for this happy festive occasion. The candle lighting of the *Chanukiahs or Menorah* lamps or Candelabras is especially fun and not only for the children. Irrespective of the day of Channukah, we light all eight candles. In another year our grandson Ethan lit some candles. And so, the tradition continues.

"God has no religion."

Mahatma Gandhi

Chapter Nine
WORK

"Goodness and hard work are rewarded with respect."

Luther Campbell

My parents and I landed in Sydney, Australia on 25th June 1957, literally with only the clothes on our backs. It might be said that within a week my working life began. I went to school on the third day and my mother began making dresses for ladies within a week. From then on, for over six years, I was working with her after I finished my homework.

It might also be said that my parents' business began in our rented two-bedroom furnished basement flat in the boarding house in Kings Cross. Our first investment was a full-length mirror for five pounds which was one third of my father's weekly wage. It was needed for fittings of our customers. A few months later, my mother made two sample skirts; one a straight black barathea with a satin ribbon pocket trim and the other a lilac weave textured straight skirt with a pocket.

Those two skirts were neatly wrapped in tissue paper and packed in a grey cardboard box. While working the night shift, during the day my father carried them from shop to shop in the city of Sydney. After many weeks, a German speaking shop owner opened the box and found that the merchandise was just right for her shop, and she ordered three of each of the styles. By Christmas, my parents were delivering a couple of dozen skirts to each of a number of city shops. I finished most of the black satin ribbons. But whether it was tacking, finishing, or hemming, or sewing buttons, or ironing, or writing invoices or packing, I did it all. Both my parents trained me well, my mother in clothes production and my father in administration.

The next investment was a one by two meters board which was placed on top of our small one-meter diameter round dining table. If the fabric lay was not too high, I was cutting the skirts even when the board wobbled. Through the Engels, we obtained a motor to convert the foot pedal driven Singer sewing machine. That was when my mother taught me to use a sewing machine. Later I was testing all the machines before we bought them.

My parents and I worked literally day and night every day as the business machine gained momentum. My mother had little time but attended parent teacher meetings. When she did, she wore the very masculine English style raincoat which we received from the Joint in Vienna and ankle high shoes with toes and heels cut out as worn by factory workers in Europe. That is how she appeared at my school while other mothers wore dressy dresses, hats, and gloves. I was most embarrassed, but my mother had no feelings of shame, since she went from work.

That is also how she appeared one day in city of Sydney department store of David Jones on the sixth floor which was for exclusive imported clothes. I was in school uniform, so I fitted in nicely. My mother was feeling the fabric of a lovely navy silk Italian blouse when one of the staff told her she should not touch it as she could not afford it.

Remember the scene in the film *Pretty Girl* when she tried to shop and was refused service? So, without saying a word, my mother opened her purse and over 200 pounds fell out of it. That was at a time when the average weekly wage was about 15 pounds. Well, the reception we received changed immediately. Suddenly chairs were provided and afternoon tea. And I became the owner of the elegant silk blouse.

When I spoke about working with my parents at the tender age ten and a half years, it was suggested that that was forced child labour which was and is illegal. In retrospect I did not consider it as such and still do not. It was not only not forced upon me, but there were no questions asked and there were no discussions. It was the most natural thing that I helped my parents. Later, I discovered that most immigrant children felt the same as they helped and worked in their parents' businesses from a young age.

My mother continued making dresses for private customers. She also designed and cut skirts for mass production which was made up by registered Home Workers who were mostly new immigrants. She was making visits to supervise the quality of the production of the home workers. I used to accompany her even late at night and I still have a vivid image of the revolving light beam of the Macquarie Lighthouse on Old South Head Road in Vaucluse as we sat waiting for the tram.

In the first half of 1958, when the neighbour who lived in the other basement flat reported us to the police for using a motor driven sewing machine, we were forced to move. For this purpose, my parents borrowed a second lot of 650 pounds from Jewish Welfare which they also repaid within a year. The money was used to finance the move, construct a professional cutting table, the purchase of a second small round blade cutting machine, a second sewing machine, and other living necessities.

Our new accommodation was one floor above Mr Bayer's Hardware Store in 356 Oxford Street, Bondi Junction. In 1958, Forbat Styles Pty Ltd was registered as a company and I recorded the business development in *"The Forbat Story."* (2017) As the business grew, so did the height of the fabric lays and I also learned to cut with straight electric blades. But I spent considerable time laying some fabrics for skirts that were cut one piece at a time, to match the checks or stripes perfectly. I continued to work in the factory after school with my parents till I went to university, when I worked on all my holidays, weekends and whenever it was necessary.

My Social Work career began as a university student and covered medical, psychiatric, community and family work. I spent many years working in hospitals and at least one of my sons was under the impression that I was a nurse. Obviously, I was good at Band Aiding and did not faint at the sight of a bloody wound.

On a very warm October morning I sat for my last examination towards my Bachelor of Social Work degree at UNSW. Intermittently I looked up from my paper and watched the water droplets trickle down the back of the student sitting in front of me. I did finish the questions on time despite the heat. And then I had an empty feeling as if I had nothing to do for the rest of the day, the month, and the year. Not true. To qualify for my degree, I needed to write another six essays which were required for the completion of my course.

But that day I felt free. Instead of writing any essays, I drove to Prince Henry Hospital, where I was a student previously and informed Miss Cahill (seated in centre) that I have finished my exams. She offered me a two-week locum position. I accepted and started work as a Social Worker the next day. I stayed for over eighteen months. She also gave me her pet ward to look after. Not easy.

Ward 4 was the Intensive Care and Neurological ward which housed the paraplegic and quadriplegic patients. At some stage I also came to be involved in research. I waded through hundreds of records that studied circumcision. The result was a positive outcome of reduced incidence of infections in paralysed males.

The Honorary neurosurgeon Professor Gonsky was a great teacher. He was probably the only doctor who respected Social Workers and treated them as professionals not merely as 'hospital bed clearers.' At least once a week he held his ward rounds which consisted of representatives of all the practitioners. The large group that followed him included the Registrar, the Residents, a number of medical students, nursing Sisters, Nurses, nursing students, Physio Therapists, Occupational Therapists, Pathologists, Pharmacists, all their students as well as Social Workers and their students.

On one of the ward-rounds Prof G lifted the skull flap of a young man. I excused myself and found myself sliding down the wall to the ground in the hallway. The sight of the pulsating open brain was a bit too much. Yet not enough to pass out.

At one stage I was sent to a Social Work conference in Tasmania. It was my first conference and a great experience even if it was only a few days in freezing weather.

After I resigned from PHH, I felt lost without work. I phoned the Royal Prince Alfred Hospital (RPAH) which was Sydney University's teaching hospital and discovered that the Helen Morris I met at the Hobart conference, was in charge of the Social Work Department. Without any references, I started work on the following Monday.

RPAH was bigger than PHH and so was the Social Work Department. I was assigned to a number of general wards and in the end covered most of the hospital. My X family followed me there too. However, I do remember being effective on occasions and some of the cases were unforgettable.

Casualty sent us a lady who attended on Fridays with bruises that resulted from 'falling.' It was typical of Australian men who received their wages on Thursdays, to visit the pub with the mates, then go home drunk and beat the little woman. I saw this lady weekly for some time. One Friday I became very angry and did the unethical in Social Work practice. I advised her.

I told her that next time he came home drunk, she should hit him over the head with a frying pan. The following week she arrived without any bruises and a smile on her face. She did hit him over the head but only hard enough to knock him out. After that, I only saw her again once, smiling.

Then there was my alcoholic lady who came for a small cash allowance regularly every two or three days. No, she swore, she would spend the few dollars on food and not on drink. When I asked her if she drank, she denied it with a smile and we both new that she already had an alcoholic breakfast early that morning.

She begged me to talk to the doctors to operate on her to alleviate her stomach pain. That was a real problem, for she already had numerous operations and she had very little stomach left. She persisted in asking for another surgery. Based on her history, I prepared a report. After a number of conferences with the specialists she had her surgery. Sadly, she died. I was shocked that my report may have carried so much weight, but then again it was a medical decision. However, I do believe that a little of the guilt has settled at the back of my mind and there it has remained.

I used to dread Fridays. Every Friday just before five, some crisis arose. On one such occasion, a large family arrived from the country with one member needing surgery after the weekend. They were minus accommodation, minus a meal and minus money. Panic set in, but within a short time I found a hostel that served them dinner, I gave them some petty cash and left the hospital just after five to follow up on Monday.

On another Friday a young lady arrived alone from the country. She was in tears because she was pregnant and didn't know what to do. She was far too advanced for a termination so alternate solutions were needed. I managed to arrange accommodations with a family where she was to board and help with two small children. During the following months I worked with her to prepare for delivering and adopting out her baby, all of which was a most painful experience and was expected to stay with her for the rest of her life. But she did have my support and that of the family where she stayed.

Thus, I had a good introduction to King George V which was the Gynaecological and Obstetric ward. There I had patients whose problems were mostly unwanted pregnancies. Those ranged from the very young innocent teenage girl who arrived at Casualty with a stomach-ache and promptly gave birth to a baby without knowing she was pregnant, to teenagers with unwanted pregnancies, as well as an older woman who did not want to have another child to add to her six children.

For those with unwanted pregnancies I arranged the necessary legally required medical and psychiatric certificates for termination of their pregnancies which were followed with some counselling. I also did many obstetric Outpatient Clinics on Friday mornings during which I drank coffee incessantly and smoked at least one packet of cigarettes. Those were stressful three- or four-hour clinics of dozens of interviews, and regrettably due to lack of time, I could never do any decent work with the ladies. However, I did arrange for follow up with sessions afterwards.

Rachel Forster was another hospital that received staff from RPAH. An all-women's hospital, it changed roles to include men when it became a specialist hospital for orthopaedic surgeries, a Rheumatoid Arthritis clinic, and had a large number of Occupational and Physiotherapists and Social Workers. It also became Australia's first bone bank though the hip replacements were metal. It was Dr Harry Tyer who looked more like a jokey than a surgeon and who performed elective orthopaedic surgeries. One of his first patients was a most delighted 82-year-old lady who was free from pain and walked the day after her hip replacement was performed. It was a pleasure to see her almost dance. At the Outpatient clinics we worked with a number of different treatments for arthritis ranging from analgesic medications to brass bracelets and gold injections, some of which worked for some of the patients. But in the end, it was surgery that was the most successful treatment.

During my working at RPAH, I had the wonderful experience with a couple of Social Work students. Supervising them, in fact teaching them was the most enjoyable and rewarding experience of my working career. During our sessions we discussed the reasons for their choice of profession and the pressures it made on their total person.

For working with personal problems was demanding, it could be stressful and invariably even the best counsellors could take their clients' troubles home with them as it were. I regretted not having more students, but I did give some lectures to medical and nursing students also. There is something most gratifying in seeing students develop and have an "Aha" response to something that they learnt from me.

One morning not long ago, I was buttering my toast when the aroma of the almost burnt offering brought back memories of days passed. Goulburn Base Hospital served a large surrounding district and RPAH rostered Social Workers for three- or four-months while they were accommodated in the nurses' quarters. A couple of incidents still stand out such as delivering Meals on Wheels, cleaning up the small house of the disabled Mrs. D's and choking on the dust while sweeping her floor. Attending AA meetings was an eye opener to say the least and found all of the alcoholic people terribly friendly.

Visiting the hospital ward in Goulburn Gaol was another interesting experience. I was called in to see a patient who supposedly attempted suicide by swallowing numerous lethal objects. The hardened criminal's Xray film was filled with large needles, nails, open safety pins, razor blades and other such items. Astonishingly, he remained totally unharmed. He really wanted a stint in the hospital as a respite from his routine life in the gaol. That was not quite a *kosher* experience for a nice Jewish girl.

Then there was my most important lesson from the meeting of my prized patient, the good looking intelligent young man of nineteen or twenty. I am not sure why he came to see me. Immediately after meeting he declared that I could do nothing to help him, that many have tried in the past as he has done the rounds of therapists, and no one could do anything for him. When I suggested that he add me to the list, he decided to stay awhile.

After about twenty minutes something happened that neither of us expected. He was surprised that someone could so well understand him. We were not only on the same wavelength, but it was as if our minds met. It was a shocking experience for me, and I never allowed myself to reach that point ever again, whether it was empathy or not. I don't remember seeing him again.

At the end of each day, I followed the same routine in the better part of that Goulburn winter in 1972. Before getting into my cold bed in my cold room, I turned on the small two bar electrical heater, and at the end of the long cold corridor in the bathroom, started the hot water in the ancient deep bathtub which took ages to fill and was tepid by the time I got into it. After my bath I boiled the kettle for tea, placed two white square slices into the old toaster and selected my choice of apricot or strawberry jam. Then I settled down to a simple tasty snack late in the evening in a cosy warm room.

This also after the odd evenings out on the town with Eric and Tom, my two resident doctors from Sydney. Doing the town in Goulburn meant either going to see a film at the only movie theatre or having dinner at the restaurant of the only Motel. To top that, we were actually invited to a private restaurant that was the diner for all the doctors who ruled the town and who entertained important personages. There was a rumour that the hospital held a room empty for a prominent member of the Parliament for when he was under the influence of alcohol and needed to sleep it off before returning to Canberra.

The year after my Goulburn stay, I decided to go overseas. I stayed with my cousin in Toronto for a few months during which I helped open a ladies' fashion shop with her for her and was present on her buying trips including the sales exhibitions at the York Hotel downtown. It was a great experience, but the aim was to find a husband. I organized accommodation, had two job offers and a certain amount of cash. I qualified to emigrate to Canada and was also accepted for a post graduate course at Toronto University.

It was not to be. Sadly, my parents became ill, and I had to stay in Sydney. And work I did again in my parents' Forbat manufacturing business. I replaced my father for many months and liaised between my mother and the production staff. Shortly after that I met and became engaged to Harry.

I obtained a position in Community Health which led to a Psychiatric Outpatient center, established in a church hall in Randwick. Callan Park was to be closed, and the aim of the center was to keep patients out of hospital, and at home as well as active in the community. And so, the 'Day Centre' was established.

It was an experiment set up by the American psychiatrist Dr Richard Lambert. It was the first of its kind in Australia based on an American model, and a most successful venture with a team that worked well together for at least seven months while I was Team Leader. During that time, we hospitalized only one male patient who was suicidal and possibly homicidal according to the diagnosis of Dr Yvonne who was our consultant psychiatrist and who became our friend to this day.

The work was quite taxing and eventually I applied for my position to be part time only but continued to do the full-time load within the shorter hours. As the work became too much and I felt an obligation to my parents and their business, I resigned reluctantly just before my wedding. Regrettably, the Day Centre closed soon after.

When in 1975, both my parents became ill, I continued liaising between my mother and the factory team, particularly for the last year prior to her death. My parents' partner Ernie Friedlander was in charge of the day to day running of the business for over a year. Early in that year my mother died, and my father became totally incapacitated. I inherited the whole of the two thirds business. After I carried out my father's will Ernie and Leah Friedlander became 50% partners with Harry and me.

The transition was quite smooth. As I grew up in the business, I was familiar with most of it. However, although I was one of the bosses, a fully grown woman, most of the staff looked at me as Mr and Mrs Forbat's daughter. But I was my parents' daughter only for a while until I proved myself, even as I had to learn to grade patterns as well as other more specialized tasks. Among other roles I took on the accounts and paid wages.

Later I worked full-time, looked after production and was involved also in the design of the sample ranges, certainly at the final critical stages of fitting the sample garments. As I became involved in all aspects of the business, the staff began to understand that I was also in charge. I became Mrs Czeiger or Mrs C, and I do believe that in time I earned their respect. Harry remained Harry forever. He took on the responsibilities of the business, applied himself completely, and enthusiastically to manufacturing ladies' fashion. Leah and I filled in wherever required.

On one of the overseas fashion research trips to Canada I spotted a pair of pull-on slacks with an elastic waist that was smooth without any gathering or separate waist band. My mother experimented with the construction of flat elastic band before, but after the Toronto trip, we improved the process, patented it and the venture resulted in a production of over 750,000 slacks and as many skirts, as well as in winning an Award. At some point I actually had to model the Forbat Line.

Harry was always an innovator and thought that his uncle could make a better living by having his own business. Uncle's Childrenswear was established in 1978, when Ili Rose of Independent Properties Real Estate designed a range of clothes for children aged 3 – 10 years. I also worked in it in every capacity from administrative to delivering garments. "Uncles" was successful, and the workload increased. Even when I was in the last stages of my pregnancy with Rony, I stood for hours and helped lay fabric with Lilly.

I remember the time-consuming stripe laying very well. So, for quite a while I worked in the two factories. And our son Richard modelled "Uncles" clothes for promotion.

In the early 1980s many of the 600 small country shops supported their family farms and they had great difficulties keeping up with their creditors. I spent many hours for many years on the phone listening to all the rural problems while trying to collect outstanding debts. It was a matter of business was slow; people didn't have any money; if they paid us, they could not afford to pay their rent and then they would have to close their shop. So, we always arrived at some agreement for periodic payment. At other times I transported goods from one of our Attraction Sportswear shops to another.

After Ernie and Leah returned from their 1984 overseas business trip, Ernie proposed a separation of the partners, which was an amicable one. The personal relationship between the Ernie and Leah and Harry and I, still continues to this day.

Since the business never had capital injected into it, it had no cash funds to pay out the Friedlander partners. Hence, we were forced to arrange for a Bank loan, the story of which is documented in detail in *The Forbat Story*. Suffice to say that despite my constant worry about the large debt, we continued to work, and our company continued to be profitable.

Around that time, large Shopping Centres such as Westfield became the vogue, and they approached Forbat with offers Harry could not refuse. Within a couple of years, we opened a dozen shops named "Casual Corner" along the East Coast of Australia, from Coffs Harbour to Noosa. We spent some time shop hopping especially during school holidays.

Two of our Casual Corner Shops along the East Coast of Australia 1989

Even while we were officially in Voluntary Provisional Liquidation and a Scheme of Arrangements was in place on the advice of our accountants, we continued to operate and our creditors all but one continued trade with us on a cash basis. In the early 1990s we purchased 'Think Big', a label for larger size fashion for a very reasonable amount and it became a great success.

The 1990s were also profitable with acquisition of customers such as the retail chain of Noni B and Wombat, Amway and Damart. We manufactured corporate uniforms for the Lions Club as well as the white suits for the relatively newly established White Lady Funerals. We sponsored Fashion Parades such as "Miss Large and Lovely" and "Miss Big and Beautiful" raising funds for charities such as MS. And we took on the production of labels of upper end of the market such as *'Ita's Collection,'* *Mela* and *Mary Gualtier*i, all of which were manufactured until *forbat* ceased operations.

The hailstorm of April 1999 destroyed everything. The roof, all the glass in the front and back of the building, all office furniture, computers, machines, cutting tables, all fabrics and readymade garments including those packed in plastic bags had to be replaced. The ice balls were the size of a tennis ball, and the sky was visible through the holes in the roof. The water was ankle deep. The staff, my sons, friends and even the bank manager were extremely helpful with the clean-up for over a week. Fortunately, most of the cut garments were at the subcontractors and we were well insured including for loss of profit. For over six months we operated from the car park, then a rented factory space until everything was replaced, and we could return to our factory by the end of the year.

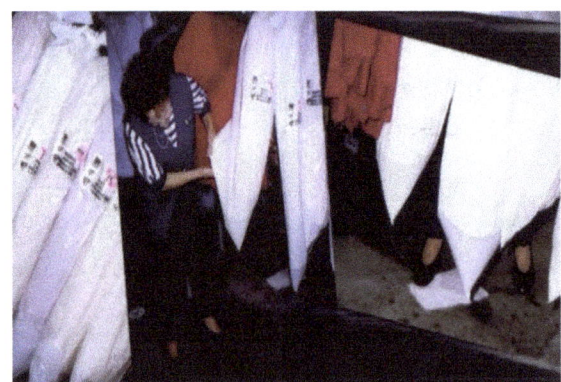

Manufacturing was becoming an increasingly difficult business, and we planned to wind down with the view of closing down. All the staff especially those that were with Forbat for a long time, some for over 30 years were fully compensated. Some found new jobs and some retired. We were no longer caught in the assembly line which kept moving whether or not the humans could keep up with it, much like in Charles Chaplin's *Modern Times*. We were no longer part of the mechanical production or the "machine" to which my mother always referred. On 31st October 2001 we delivered the last of our orders, closed the doors and I officially retired.

We rented out the factory space. When the tenant moved, enterprising Harry decided to turn the premises into small spaces for art studios and working artists. *'May Street Studios'* was established, and I managed the books. When the building was sold, Ron's wife, also an artist, continued to manage the *May Street Studios*. I then looked after the books of what became *Space 4 Studios* in Tempe.

In 2005 Ron opened *Flywheels Motorcycle Engineering* in Alexandria and I worked for him as his receptionist, his data entry person, and his bookkeeper. When he expanded into selling Kawasaki bikes and kept stock for most of the popular motorcycle brands, the inventory entries of three to five thousand parts of an average bike became quite time consuming. Besides studying and teaching, I often worked into the middle of the night, reminiscent of the *Forbat* era when I always took some work home. I also worked on the accounting books of Harry's building projects for several years. And somehow, I am still doing some accounting work besides writing this my past.

I have often wondered how I could have done all that work when I was younger and for so many years. I looked after the needs of three boys and a husband, house and home, worked in our manufacturing business, studied and worked some more. But I did do it.

Perhaps the best part of my working life was the teaching. Dr Putai Jin must have seen in me a potential to teach small group seminars. From 1996 I was a part-time Tutor of first year Bachelor of Education students at the University of New South Wales. I was teaching Sociology of Education and Philosophy of Education as well as marking all my students' essays.

I did spend considerable extra time teaching students how to write essays and particularly to avoid plagiarism. Asian students who comprised a high percentage of the student population had a different educational training background. They were taught to rote learn, to repeat or regurgitate material supplied to them and never to question teachers. Hence, they needed to learn how not merely to copy and paste, but how to present arguments in essays and especially to acknowledge their sources.

I am not sure that I considered it work. Although it did require time and effort for preparation, and complete focus for the duration, I enjoyed it thoroughly. It was most satisfying. Interestingly the student assessment of me as a teacher was surprisingly high, providing evidence that I must have been a pretty good teacher. That was good for the ego. It still is. I missed my university tutoring after 2006, but I am ever so grateful for having had those unforgettable years on which to look back with pleasure. When I do, just as when I think of my children, I smile to myself. And I have been doing much of that of late.

"That which does not kill us makes us stronger."

Friedrich Nietzsche.

Chapter Ten
BOYFRIENDS

"Blessed is he who expects nothing, for he shall never be disappointed."

Alexander Pope

I was in love once and once only. I had a few boyfriends, but I had many more male friends with who I had Platonic relationships. I was engaged to be married three times, and each engagement was broken directly or indirectly by me. I was a bridesmaid three times and eventually I was a bride when I married my husband, Harry.

The night before my wedding I discarded all photographs of all of my boyfriends. It was a big mistake. Huge!! I waited so long to get married and was so happy to start the 'new chapter' in my life, that I never thought I would miss my photos, though there are a few odd ones. I certainly never thought that I would need them as proof when my children asked after my boyfriends. So, if I have regrets, then one of them is the loss of those photographs.

My attraction to young men began at the very young age of about seven. The first was the eighteen years old Salamon Feri who was tall, dark, and handsome and lived on the ground floor of our apartment block. The second was the very cute fourteen years old tall, dark, and handsome Apor Gabi on the second floor. The third one was the tall, dark, and handsome Anglican priest in the lager in Korneuburg who taught us children. He must have been in his early twenties while I was just ten years old. I looked forward to school, learnt my basic English very well and I must have borrowed his American accent which pops up now and then even after so many decades. I was especially good at *I, you, he, she, it, we, you, they*.

My English was fluent when four years after our arrival in Australia, I received an invitation to the end of year School Ball at Sydney Grammar School from the nice red-headed Richard. So, I accepted reluctantly, for I knew nothing about the protocols. My mother quickly made a lovely satin dress, and we bought a matching purse and my first high heeled shoes. Actually, the heels were quite low. When I arrived at the Great Hall in Big School, I not only fitted in, I received my first prize trophy for the Barn Dance.

I was fifteen when my mother urged me to invite myself to a party held in the home of my then best friend Nina. I was one of the youngest there, until the sixteen years old Leah floated in, followed by an entourage of four or five young men. For a moment all activity stopped to greet her.

That party was wonderful. It was a happy celebration of I don't remember what, so there were lots to eat and to drink. I met the twenty-three-year-old chemical engineer whose wavey hair was similar to that of my father in his youth. At ten o'clock I phoned my parents who wanted to know that I was safe and told them that I was staying till midnight because I was having a delightful time with a young man called Mr B. I phoned them several times that night to inform them of the deferred time of my arrival home, that they need not worry and not to call hospitals or the police. And I insisted on that same phone ritual from my sons when they started to go out at night on their own while they lived at home. Of course, I was rarely successful. They say boys are different.

Shortly after yet another phone call to my parents at three in the morning, Mr B drove me home. He was the perfect gentleman, and he even opened doors for me. Thus, he set a high standard for my future friends and gave me confidence while I was still a young teenager.

The following year I spent a lot of time on the school production of *HMS Pinafore* by Gilbert and Sullivan. I don't remember how we came to hear about the Synagogue dances, but my new best friend Rosemary and I went to one.

It was in the summer of 1962 that I met Joe at a Saturday night dance held in the Goodman Hall at the Central Synagogue in Bondi Junction. I spoke with him briefly and may have danced with him briefly, as I did with some others.

The following week I received an invitation to a 21st birthday party in a private home of Len who was a stranger to me. It turned out that he was a close friend of Joe who asked him to invite me. That night was the beginning of our beautiful friendship. No, it was more than that. Much more.

On our first date, Joe took me to dinner at the *Milano* restaurant which was rather elegant. He too opened doors for me. We dined, wined, and we danced. And I felt 'at home.'

Later we drove to the northern end of Bondi Beach, where we watched and listened to the breaking ocean waves washing over the two bronze mermaids seated on the rocks. Ben Buckler became our favourite parking spot. It was all very romantic and what I felt must have been love.

Joe was everything girls dream about; tall, good-looing, intelligent, pleasant, and romantic almost in the manner of courtly love. He left Sydney a few days later for the outback. Letters arrived with the most picturesque descriptions both in prose and poetry of the stark arid desert of the 'back of beyond,' the back of Bourke, of the oppressive heat, and the "naked glory" of the cook who served him burger in a hot tin shed.

He wrote that he missed me and of course, he wrote about love. On his return among other things, he presented me with a poem written on the back of a Boomerang which I had safely stored somewhere until the hailstorm in 1999.

And of course, I can still recite the two stanzas.

This is the mystic Boomerang of love,
Which swoops and swerves like a soft breasted dove.
It offers a symbol of the grace and skill,
With which a lover must make his kill.

And when he makes his mighty conquest,
Love must take the spiritual test,
Of which poets for centuries wrote and sang,
And which is contained in this Boomerang.

I fell in love with Joe. Very much in love. I spent all my spare time being with him or just thinking about him. And because I could not concentrate on anything else, I spent precious little time studying. At the Trial Leaving I failed all but one subject. I did matriculate with the barest minimum requirement of six Bs and in due course enrolled at the University of New South Wales. Joe was at Sydney University studying Arts Law at that time.

My happiness knew no bounds. I was light-headed. I was floating on air. My whole life revolved around Joe. After that glorious first year with him, I was prepared to settle down to spend the rest of my life with him once we obtained our degrees. I spent most of my time with Joe at Sydney University. One day I stood in front of the blackboard in an empty lecture room and drew up a budget for our future together. It was tight but manageable and it all seemed as if we were to be together forever.

Joe was on my mind constantly. At some stage Joe left for Israel. We missed each other and the letters we exchanged were of little comfort to me. Also, with time our relationship suffered from some pressures. Mainly it was sex and Joe's father.

My virginity was a problem. I was saving it for my husband for my wedding night. I was a good girl, and Joe never made any great demands, almost as if he understood and he respected me. He found solutions to our sexual abstinence, and we broke up for that reason at least once. Just as an aside, it was sometime after my relationship with Joe ended, that I lost my virginity. It was well planned and seamlessly executed. I started to take birth control pills well in advance and made a date just for that specific purpose. The nice young man I selected took me to a quiet dinner accompanied by a ceremonious toast, after which the incident took place as smoothly as that of Dottie in Mary McCarthy's *The Group*. Whenever we passed the "The Shore Motel" in Sydney's North Shore, I announced that that was the very place where I lost my virginity, to which my passenger, usually my sons, chanted in unison, "Too much information, Mum."

Jo's father had a strong influence on all members of his family. He must have realised that our relationship was serious. He told me that I was "an attractive and intelligent young woman who had a long and happy future ahead" of her. I was not quite twenty years of age. Further that I should not be in a hurry to settle down. My response was silent nods of agreement. It was quite clear to me that he did not want me to marry Joe, but he did not use those words specifically. I don't think he liked me. Perhaps it was our different backgrounds, mine was Hungarian and his was Polish. There were always hostilities between those two nations in the past. However, I neither raised the history, nor intended to come between father and son. Obviously, his father wanted us to part.

Very likely Joe's divided loyalty between his father and me, played a major role in our four years on and off relationship, although most people treated us as a couple. In the off periods I often saw some of my friends and even attempted somewhat more serious relationships. There were a few young men who I dated. One was a keen surfer whose car reeked of the ocean. Body and board surfer, the back seat of his car was full of wet towels and the sea odour permeated my nostrils for days.

Some I dated only because our parents were friends, and they persisted that we meet. I must admit that they were all very nice people. One young man had a hole in the floor of his car causing a draught which tore through me on every date in the cold of winter. There was a very nice very tall young man who also liked to dance. The problem was that as he held me, his belt buckle was rubbing painfully against my breasts.

Another nice young man was Peter who was an engineering student a couple of years ahead of me at University of NSW. Just to please our parents, we went on a date. Although it backfired, we had a pleasant evening dining, dancing and drinking a single bottle of wine between us. Despite phoning my parents, I arrived home somewhat later than expected and was smiling in the hope to minimize my guilt. As I put my key in the door, my father opened the door from the inside.

When he saw me, he promptly slapped my face. I was shocked. He had never come close to hitting me in my whole life. Later as she examined the five-finger print on my face, my mother explained that my father was afraid that I was drunk. His father was an alcoholic, but that was never discussed in the family.

I dated a literary friend with who I attended the theatre and saw some wonderful plays. I had a mathematician friend, with who I went fishing from five in the morning. I always wondered why fish wake up that early. With another friend I went to concerts, with yet another I played squash, and so on. I went to an annual Medical Ball with a doctor all the way from Sydney to Newcastle, just for the one-night event.

Most of my friends were university students who could not afford the expensive tickets to functions as charity Balls, or Chequers Nightclub or such places. So, we went Dutch, which meant we each paid for ourselves. That had the added advantage of my not being obligated to my friends either financially or otherwise.

I loved the whole affair of going to Balls, of the preparation, the formal gowns, the matching accessories, of the corsages, of being driven, the decorated Halls, the waltzes, and the elegant formality of the whole event. Whenever ball gowns are mentioned, I think of my lovely youth and how I danced through it.

Gold Jersey 1964

Cerise Crepe 1965

Embossed Swiss Satin 1967

There were a few good friends of who I think very warmly. Gary was busy studying Law and was not involved with anyone at the time. We were together a lot when my Joe relationship was off. He liked much the same things as I did. He was charming and most affectionate. Also, he was always there when I needed a partner. And vice versa.

We met many years later when we were both married, and he would have been happy to see me again. Alone. Propositions are very good for married egos also.

Another good friend was David. I was delighted when he invited me to his mother's wedding, and I certainly felt very elegant in my navy silk ensemble. But I was included by most in family affairs as all parents liked me and the feelings were mutual.

He and others may have liked to have a different relationship, but it was not to be. The reasons varied from friend to friend, but on the whole, something was always missing. Joe was missing.

Then there was my wonderful dancing partner for all the years of my youth. Lee was a wonderful dancer friend. He preferred Latin American dancing as I did. And we seemed to have been in a physical synchrony as we moved to all the music. It was a unique association. Even while we were seriously involved with our respective partners, we always managed to enjoy dancing together at parties for a good number of years.

Since my parents worked so hard they finally booked a holiday that was more than just an extended weekend break. They booked what sounded like a luxury cruise. The P & O's *Australis* made a number of stops as it sailed around New Zealand and the Fijian islands. A great contrast to our migrant voyage in the grey steel of the *General Harry Taylor*.

There was a Sydney University student who entertained me until I met George, a nice young engineer from Melbourne of Greek origin. He was very attentive and caring. We spent all our time together on the ship and on the islands without both of our parents.

A week or ten days after our meeting he proposed marriage. Savu Savu became even more delightful. A most romantic and memorable gift for the sixteen years old me from one in his mid-twenties. I may have been mature, but certainly not ready for marriage. And he wasn't Joe who was at home.

It was December 1966, nearly ten years after our arrival in Australia and I just finished my second-year university examinations. During the holidays I was to work in the factory at *Forbat Styles*, but my parents convinced me to go with them on their overseas business trip. I protested about being away for two and a half months. It seemed an impossible time for me to be away from Joe, much like an eternity.

My parents' argument was based on their 'meant theory.' If Joe and I were meant to be together then he would wait for me to return. If he would not wait for me, then it would be better to know sooner than later. In short, my overseas trip with my parents was a test. I was relatively confident in my state of unofficial engagement to marry Joe. I simply did not want to be separated from him for such a long period. Eventually I consented.

In those days it was quite a special occurrence to go overseas and quite a luxury to travel on one of the new 727 Jet planes. Most new immigrants were eager to visit their relatives 'back home,' so they borrowed the fare for their trip. That was never the case with my parents. My father either had the money for his purchase, or he did not purchase.

On the evening before our flight, we had a dinner party for family and close friends. Those invited included my cousin Marika, my mother's cousin Irene and her husband Walter Engel, my parents' best friends Kati and Andi Gal, the Friedlanders since by then Ernie was a partner, and of course, Joe who was part of the family for four years.

My parents and I flew to Los Angeles and New York in the States and then to Europe. London, Paris, and Rome were the stops for fashion and Budapest was a private trip where we spent a few weeks with our relatives. The big event was my new cousin Sylvia who we have not met yet. She was born a few months after we left Hungary. Also, my destructive little cousin Gabor grew into a nice young man of nineteen. He and I took a walk on a mild clear winter night and as the icicles on the barren tree branches started to melt into water droplets, the romantic scene made me long even more for my Joe.

In the meantime, my cousin Anita introduced me to some of her university friends. Over drinks they were chatting away in Hungarian, and they were talking about me, the *csaj* or chick from Australia. I was amused to hear all about what they actually thought of me. They even wanted to date me. I had to force myself not to smile, until eventually I could not hold back. When I commented in perfect Hungarian, they were surprised indeed and we all had a good laugh. I wrote many letters to Joe during my time away but posted none of them except for the customary tourist postcards.

Our plane landed in Sydney at six in the morning in February 1967. To this day we take a flight that lands in Sydney at six in the morning. I was extremely excited and impatient to make the call of my arrival. When Joe came over to our place at six in the evening, he was a different person from who I left behind. Whatever was said I never remembered. Somehow, I understood that he wanted to end our relationship. When he left, I just sat and cried.

Once my mother said that I would cry where no one saw me. And yes, for a long time I did cry because I was totally devastated. Was this the suffering of *the slings and arrows of outrageous fortune*? I bore the pains and wounds of my dying love, and I whole heartedly believed that I would never love again. But in time I realised that my life did continue without Joe. I did learn that there is a great difference between 'being in love' and 'loving.' Of course, being in love is fleeting. It is love that lasts. I have been teaching that ever since.

And the boyfriends continued. There was George the doctor with lovely parents also. We had some very nice times together whether out to dinner or a concert. It didn't matter that there may have been interruptions by calls from a hospital for him to deliver a baby or whatever the reason. In *La Traviata* we missed the dying scene.

I always had the feeling that George would have brought down the moon for me, if I only asked him. Figuratively speaking of course. One would think that any girl would be grateful for such a man. I became afraid of what I might do to him. So, I broke up with him.

A very short romantic interlude with the Norwegian ski jumper Tom in the snow fields left me with a wonderful memory for always. I wrote about it shortly after the event. And as I revisit it, the memories return with the images of my Viking man in the snow country.

My friend Anita and I stayed in Peer Gynt, the northernmost lodge in Perisher Valley. In the morning, we awoke to the echoing yodels of Dieter, the son of the owner of the Chalet. He appeared as a small orange speck near the top of the mountain and gradually grew larger as he professionally executed a wide downhill spiral trail.

"I think I can master the yodelling by this afternoon," I said to Anita, "but that zigzagging might take a few years." It was my first time on skis. Anita started towards Dieter's ski class. "I'm right behind you," I said as I clicked my heels into the ski bindings. Unfortunately, my skis were pointing in the opposite direction, and I began sliding down an icy road. As I gathered speed, so did my fear. I panicked. I placed the points of my stocks in front of me. They slowed my speed but jabbed me in the chest and threw me off balance. Once I was rolling on the ice, I was no longer afraid of falling, only of pain.

It was sometime before I joined the class and missed the most important part of the first lesson; that of falling correctly and standing up on skis unaided. The second half of the lesson was spent in repetitious procedure of an exhilarating ten seconds of snowploughing downhill followed by the physically torturing ten minutes of sidestepping uphill, intermingled with numerous falls.

When we were offered transportation to the Valley and the T-Bars, we accepted eagerly. Some 20 beginners on skis clung to two chains attached to a Snowcat. As it started with an unexpected jolt, all collided with each other or with each other's skis or the ground. This occurred several times till the Cat dropped us at the base of the Pommer Lift where most collapsed in two heaps.

The Pommer looked easy, and the instructions were simple. "Place the bar between the legs, bend the knees, hold onto the rope and do not sit down." Well, the first thing I did was sit down. On the way up the mountain, I realized that I was crouching and that no muscles came to my rescue to help me straighten up. Nearing the top, I needed a plan of action to get off. So, I just keeled over and lay there for a while, wet and cold and hurting.

I managed to scramble a short distance to the top of Number 1 T-Bar and started to snow plough downhill. As I gathered speed, my fear increased. This was no mere slope, and I had no control over my skis. My eyes were closed tight when I smashed into a ski class. The shrieking and swearing were interrupted by the instructor's, "Welcome!" He helped me to my feet saying, "Good of you to drop in." A roar of laughter from the group, a quick private lesson in public for me and once more I began my descent to the Valley by snowploughing. The Hotel commonly known as "The Man" was a hospitable haven for my body that was weary, numb from cold sweat and pain.

Every day was exciting despite the familiar routine. Each morning greeted us with yodelling, ski antics, followed by a skiing lesson after breakfast. The rest of the day was spent in the snow field skiing. As a diet lunch, we consumed ample portions of Gluhwein and chips, Smiths Crisp that is. Once re-energised, we resumed riding the T-Bars up and skiing down until late afternoon when the shadow of the setting sun lay a dark cover over the whole valley. Then, from the top of Number 1 T-Bar, we traversed across the mountain side and within minutes we were warming ourselves in front of the fireplace in Peer Gynt.

It was towards the end of the first week in the snow country that I met him. Typically, Anita was sitting with two men, immersed in conversation with one of them. He was considerably older than she, but age was no barrier in the relationship that was developing between them under the guise of flirtation. The other, a younger man must have been watching me watch them, because he came towards me and extended his hand.

"My name is Tom ... Would you like something to drink?" he asked. I looked at him, nodded and placed my hand in his. It was a warm confident grip that he held until I pulled away as a hot flush engulfed me. I bowed my head, not believing the man's attraction and good looks. 'Adonis,' I thought and looked at him again just to confirm the reality of a G-d.

Tom ushered me to a table saying something to the effect that his friend was occupied with a young lady. I was about to reply that 'that's no lady, that's my friend,' but thought better. How would he interpret that? Instead, I said, "Thank you" after he pulled out a chair for me on which to sit. 'A gentleman G-d,' I thought. I had great difficulty focusing, heard only snippets of his dialogue and was totally oblivious to the presence of others.

The Gluhwein was welcome; at least I could hold onto something. I took a sip, then put down the glass. Picked it up, took another sip, held the glass in one hand and then moved it to the other hand. I lifted the glass to my lips, took a sip, then replaced it on the table, twisted it a few times, lifted it again and held in both hands. Then I repeated the glass dance. I never found out whether or not Tom noticed my preoccupation with the glass, but it did not matter.

After lunch we were to ski together. I declined with some pretext, but they insisted on spending time together and we agreed to meet in the evening. The rest of the afternoon I skied alone, and I was glad. It gave me time to think, to recollect and enjoy my new feelings. As I was pulled up by the T-Bar, I tried to remember what I found out about Tom. He was from Norway originally, he was a ski jumper, and he was a married man with an eight-year-old son. Married. I released my grip on the rope and fell off.

It was dark when they arrived. Tom and I stood looking at each other. He combed his fingers through his thick blonde hair and white flakes fell on his shoulders. "There will be a fine, fresh layer of snow tomorrow," he said. "I know," I smiled as I replied, "and it will cover a multitude of sins." It must have been ski-land slogan, because every man I met told me the same when propositioning me. "And every virgin is reborn again," added Tom. We laughed and hand in hand walked into the dining room.

Dinner was fine. The music was fine. The conversation was fine. And the dancing was fine. Then we moved into the lounge room where the fire radiated a warmth till late in the night, and the brandy emitted a fine bouquet. We were watching the flickering flames when Tom asked, "Have you ever skied at night?" I had to laugh as I saw this vision of me tumbling down the other side of a mountain. Then I managed to say, "No. I have trouble skiing during daylight." But Tom was serious and took me by the hand. Silently we gathered our gear and with my gloved hand in his, he led me out into the night. It was a magnificent scene.

Tom and I skied holding hands. I began to glide freely and felt as if I had been born on skis. Then Tom skied off into the distance. In the light of the moon, he was a dark silhouette gracefully dancing in a white desert. He came close and I was overwhelmed. "If this is your life, I love it!" I exclaimed and heard my voice echo in the silence. Tom stayed long enough to reply, "I love you," and skied off again. I felt as if I were floating on a white ocean. It was exhilarating. I let my body fall. I was flat on my back in the snow, and I opened my eyes.

It was magic. Nothing existed but the glittering stars sprayed on an infinite deep blue sky. They appeared so close that I felt if I stretched out my arms, I could touch them. I held out my arms, closed my eyes and whispered, "I must be dreaming." The snow crystals crunch was followed by the reply, "This is real," as I was embraced and kissed.

I can still see that fine-looking specimen in Peer Gynt after a good dinner, standing in front of a glowing log fire, warming my brandy in his hands. He was beautiful. Later we went for a walk and then on those moonlit nights he ploughed the Skidoo, spraying the snow high into the air and steered it to draw geometric shapes until it tipped over and we rolled off into a laughing heap. And there is the image of the two of us dancing in the pure white snow and leaving behind our footprints as we walked towards some distant light. Oh, the beauty of it all and the memories. Sweet memories!

I liked skiing and especially enjoyed traversing across a snow-covered mountain side and did so to Peer Gynt daily. But there were also the unfortunate experiences of damaged limbs in the snow, such as the torn ligament one year which weakened the ankle for the following year.

On the third day of the long weekend my friends and I decided not to wait any longer, and we braved the bad weather. So, we put on our skis. I clipped on the hired skis and faced the snowstorm for a short time. Heading back to the Sundeck Lodge for lunch I skied into a snow-covered bush. X marked the spot on the postcard I was to send to my parents. I heard the crack of the breaking bones and when I fell, I just lay there trembling in the freezing snow not daring to move. Lesson learnt. No one should ski in a blizzard especially with hired skis with bindings that did not release.

Fortunately, it was a clean spiral fracture of the tibia and fibula from knee to ankle, but it prevented me from skiing for a couple of years. To this day the fracture makes itself known in certain inclement weather and that calf is some four centimetres wider than the other one.

Everyone was most attentive and helpful. Michael N was at my side when the Medics skied me down the hill to the Ambulance. Michael was at my bedside in Cooma hospital after they set my leg in plaster up to my hip.

My inability to drive with a full plaster cast coincided with my inability to drive without a licence. I was late for my appointment in Goulburn, and I was speeding on the wrong side of the road over a double dividing line at a T intersection. That cost me nine points totalling twelve points out of the ten for the year. That led to six months loss of my driver's licence.

As luck would have it, I could not get into my car to drive for some sixteen plastered weeks of that six months period anyway. My friends, especially Michael and 'Bubbles' drove me around to functions and dinners. Wonderful friends. Bubbles was the first and only person I knew who picked up the phone and ordered a ZX sports car.

I was the one who severed my ties completely with Joe. I was the one who broke off with my official fiancée Danny. The notice of that engagement appeared in the Jewish News, and I had a diamond ring on my finger as proof. He had a similar European background, and we had quite a few acquaintances in common. His nature was most agreeable. He was a very easy-going person, perhaps too easy. So much so that I came to be convinced that in the long term I would over-power him in most of life's situations.

My timing was inopportune as it was shortly after his father died. I further embarrassed him when I bargained at the Chevra Kadisha about the cost of his father's funeral. That was not the thing to do. I returned the engagement ring when I decided not to postpone the inevitable.

Sometime after I was twenty-two years old, I concluded that I will not find the right man for me. And because I wanted a family, I seriously considered having a child and raising him/her without a husband. Financially it was quite feasible as I had the earning capacity of a professional, and my father could fill the role of father figure. I thought it could work, provided my parents agreed. They did agree reluctantly though they continued to worry about their only child. They feared I would remain single, let alone with a child.

But along came the Shrimp, an unfortunate nickname because he was shorter than all my previous young men. Not tall but an impressive man, very cultured, very charming and an Ear Nose Throat surgeon. He too had a European background with parents of Polish origin. He also played the piano very well and we enjoyed music together.

I don't remember how we met or details of how our times were spent. My cousin Marika met him like a number of my other contenders and to this day she recalls how she watched the surgical procedure he performed on her roast chicken when she invited him to dinner. He and I were very comfortable in each other's company and would have satisfied each other's needs perfectly well. I would have been very happy as the wife of a doctor knowing full well the demands of that profession and he needed a woman who would have been a worthy wife of a successful surgeon.

One Saturday evening the man formally asked my father for my hand in marriage. This was unexpected and I thought I might need a few minutes to decide for myself first. But my parents approved of him as they approved of all my friends, and my father agreed. I am not sure that I was as happy as I should have been as we left for an anniversary celebration, at which uncharacteristically I was either deserted or worse, ignored all night.

I was most disappointed in him and told him so the next day when we met. I was not convinced that I should have broken our engagement but had considered it seriously. Further because he sank greatly in my estimation, I suggested to him that he may need to reconsider his decision for such a life changing move. What I really meant was, "go home and talk to your mother." and that holiday back home would give him time to rethink.

He left the next day for what I thought would be a couple of weeks, but he returned within a few days. He phoned me at work and told me that "there was no reason why we should meet because we don't have anything to discuss." Oh. Well, it took a few seconds for me to say good-bye and hang up. After that I just sat at my desk in silence for a time.

The scene was very different on my return home after completing my work for the rest of that day. I suppose I was in a state of delayed shock of another breakup of a meaningful relationship, and I started to cry. I could not stop. My mother was very good. For a long time, she held and rocked her twenty-six-year-old daughter as if she were a small injured little girl. Then she undressed me, put me under a nice warm shower, dried me, dressed me in a night gown and put me to bed.

I was fine next morning, and I thought I was fine a few weeks later until early one Monday morning when I was driving to Goulburn. While I wondered how many thousands of nights I had to wait to find a suitable husband, the radio was playing Rimsky-Korsakov's *Scheherazade*. My tears flowed from the recurring haunting melody of the violin solo and blurred my vision. By the time I arrived at the Base Hospital I was all cried out, ready for work. I also gave up the idea of becoming a single mother because every child needs a father.

In 1973 I decided to go overseas husband hunting. My first stop was Toronto in Canada where my cousin Marti and her family welcomed me. Initially I stayed for a few weeks but after my trip to Europe I returned and stayed for some three months, during which time I met and went out with the son of Marti's friend, the nice urologist.

He was tall, dark, and very good-looking. He wore a double-breasted navy blazer with gold buttons and smoked a pipe with a pleasant sweet-smelling tobacco. He was intelligent, cultured, liked classical music, had an easy calm manner, and had a rather subtle sense of wit. I thought he was the epitome of the perfect partner, and I had a lovely time with him. I loved Toronto. I fulfilled all the requirements to settle there.

Unfortunately, my parents became ill, and once in Sydney, I remained. Over the years my cousin Marti told me that he was living with his nurse already when I saw him. Years later she told me that he married his nurse and more. In a way it was fortunate that I did not return for him, though I still love Toronto.

So, when at twenty-seven I made the decision to marry 'the first thing that comes along,' who was not a gambler, or an alcoholic or a criminal, Harry Czeiger came along. During our engagement I filled half an exercise book with what could be termed as love letters. When I read them later, I thought it a lot of sentimental drivel. I was not in love with Harry. Rather, as my cousin so very astutely pointed out many years later, I was in love with the idea of love. And more to the point, I was in love with the idea of marriage. And Harry was not in love with me either though there were strong elements of romance in our relationship.

What Harry and I had was a genuine deep affection, respect for one another and more, all of which seemed to have stood the test of time. It was a much more solid basis for a loving marriage than the fleeting 'being in love', and I felt "at home." We were engaged on 13th April 1974, and four months later we married. We are still married. That is how my great expectations ended.

25th August 1974

Chapter Eleven
WHEN HARRY MET AGNES

"Love looks not with the eyes, but with the mind."

William Shakespeare

The story of how Harry and I met is quite familiar to all our family and most of our friends. It has been told many times with little variation and what by now are clichés. With the passing of the years, many may have forgotten our splendid tale, which has always been received with a combination of astonishment and good humour. So, I would like to record it for the benefit of those who are memorially challenged like my husband, for the younger generation and the amusement of anyone who is interested.

In 1973 I went overseas husband hunting. I arrived home to inform my parents of my intention to return to Toronto and temporarily settle there. That was in October. I had fulfilled all the Canadian immigration requirements; accommodation, the minimum amount of cash, a couple of job offers, and post-graduate enrolment guaranteed at University of Toronto by a Professor Schlesinger. I also had a charming urologist as a good marriage prospect. My parents simply asked me to stay a while and enjoy the opening of the Sydney Opera House. Many years earlier my father promised that we would have the best seats at the opening of The Opera House. In order to accelerate its completion, he even bought numerous lottery tickets in the course of that decade of construction of the great white shark fins or sails. And he bought the best tickets for the opening.

In late September an official government letter arrived requesting that my father relinquish his precious two centre seats in the Dress Circle. Apparently, the whole of the front row was reserved for Her Majesty, Queen Elizabeth II and her official party. My father and I attended that unique Gala opening performance on Saturday, 22nd October 1973 and sat in the fourth row in the stalls. My father and I, and later Harry and I have occupied those seats for decades.

The exhilaration of that night lasted but a few days before my parents were scheduled for surgery. For the rest of the year, I was looking after them while they recovered after a fashion and later Harry was to be several towers of strength and support for me in the years that followed. Although I was working, I was also the go between my mother and my parents' manufacturing business. Early in the new year my aunt and uncle were visiting from Hungary, and I was their sole guide for a couple of months because sadly my parents were not well enough to share their unique experience.

After many weeks of turmoil and as both my parents began to recover slowly, I met a few new young men. For instance, there was this nice dentist who insisted that we go sailing with his friends. Being an over cautious person, I was reticent about the small boat in Sydney Harbour. But I agreed and had one of the best times in my life. By the afternoon, I was steering the sleek twenty-three-foot *Endeavour* alone, and thoroughly enjoying sailing in Port Jackson, while the poor dentist lay in the cabin for most of the day suffering from the rolling waves of Sydney Heads.

There were others too. When pestered about an introduction to one more nice young man, I did not hesitate because it was not far to go; just two flights up. More particularly because I made a decision. At twenty-seven years of age and both my parents ill, I informed my parents that I was ready to marry 'the first thing that came along.'

I gave up my ideals of marrying the near perfect doctor. I gave up all whatever secret little dreams I may have had, although I never had any illusions of a knight in shining armour on a white stallion. I never rode a horse. But I gave up the hunt and I was prepared to compromise. I was prepared to marry "the first thing that came along, provided he was not a criminal, not a gambler or an alcoholic. And along came Harry." Those were my exact words then and now they are a cliché.

Unbeknownst to me, Harry was in Toronto at the same time as I was. He was in the same area as I was, and he was visiting his cousin at the time when I was visiting my cousin. However, he had no intention of moving there. Later he said that if he would have settled anywhere, it would have been New York which was just one of the many cities in the world where "the girls were madly in love with [him]". And I think that he still believes that.

At the time when I thought that I had nothing to lose by yet another introduction to some strange young man, Harry had recently broken his relationship with a Judy. Later I learnt what a very generous person this Harry was. He bought her a wardrobe full of clothes and weekly groceries. A few days previously they had a disagreement over the dog that did not want to be locked up and followed her everywhere. When Harry asked Judy to choose between them, the dog won, and Harry was free to play the field again. I met him when he was planning to fill the vacancy.

To this day Harry recites his three life goals as if to justify our meeting. The first one was to marry by the age of twenty-seven, the second was to become a millionaire by thirty-five and the third was to retire by the age of forty-five." As he was twenty-six and nearing his deadline, he too thought that he had nothing to lose by an introduction to some strange young woman.

On Sunday afternoon 10th February 1974 I farewelled my Hungarian relatives. The week that followed was eventful and memorable to say the least. On Monday I had my hair cut. One might think that a haircut was not some monumental event; this one was. For years I suffered at hairdressers who pulled, tugged, and yanked at my naturally not just curly but frizzy long hair. Then at the end of hours of the same torturous process each time, I carried this bird nest on my head for a week; no washing, no brushing, just lifting of the large, teased rolls into place with the pointed end of a comb and lots of hair spray. And all that time, I had considerable itchy scalp.

For over a decade I took the crowning bouffant to bed every night. What women go through for what someone dictates as fashion or for beauty! Why I went through it when it did not make me more beautiful? Obviously because I was husband hunting. So, I had my hair cut by this chic Afro-American character at the exclusive *Lloyd Lomas Salon* in Double Bay. True, I did become much more lightheaded. However, by the time he finished with the prescribed three stage shaping design for my page-boy style, which required considerable lengthy labour for its management, many months, and many hundreds of dollars later, the frizzy look came into vogue. Then all I had to do was wash my hair and pay no further attention or further money. Bless Barbara Streisand.

On Thursday afternoon of 14th February 1974, I met Harry for the first time. Gary Davies lived on the third floor of our building and worked for the development company *Progress and Properties* where Harry was employed as a construction manager. Gary was our *Shadchen* or matchmaker who organized what today is the dreaded 'blind date'. The invitation was for both my parents but my mother was unwell, so it was my father and I.

We had a most pleasant afternoon. There was coffee and cakes, and a considerable amount of joke telling on all sides. I remember that Harry seemed to have a good sense of humour, thoroughly enjoyed his own jokes and was quite conversant in many areas. Harry only remembers the jokes and that I put an ashtray in front of him. He also remembers that much of the time I interrupted his jokes by punching him in the arm as I intercepted his punch line. By the time he reached his "*Izidor*" joke, we were on friendly enough terms. It was Harry's outstanding joke. I cannot tell jokes but having heard numerous and various short or long versions of it over the years, this is the gist of it.

Two friends are travelling, wanting to see as much of the world as they can fit into a short time. When they arrive in Spain, Izidor suggests to Moshe that they go in different directions and at the end of the day come together at the 'Café Espana' to share and compare their experiences. That evening when they meet, they tell each other of their adventures of the day. Izidor tells Moshe that the parts of Spain he saw were wonderful but that the highlight of the day was the Bullfight. He tells of the huge arena; the overwhelming masses, being propelled by the power of the pushing crowd, being shoved into a large space with some Spaniards and thinking "when in Rome, ...". So he goes along with what they do.

I think this is the long version. However, it has become part of our past, and although Harry lacks memory for detail, I remember it well.

He tells of the spectacle of coloured costumes and hats being thrown into the air at the entrance of the first set of bullfighters and the roar of the crowd shouting "Matador". The Matador waved a red cape, did a few dance steps and when the animal tired, he stuck a sword in it and slew it. Then the crowd roared "Bravo". When the second set of bullfighters entered, there was another spectacle of colours, hats, and the crowd shouting "Picador". The Picador waved, and danced, and slew, and the crowd roared. As a third set of bullfighters enters, another spectacle of colours and hats and the crowd shouted "Toreador". There was more waving, dancing, slaying and roaring. And he was so enthralled with the atmosphere of the spectacle and the hats, that he was pushed into the arena, and the crowd roared.

At this point, I impulsively punched Harry's upper arm and said, *triumphantly shouted, "Izidor"* much to his surprise. And much to my surprise, that was not the punch line. It was to go on, and on; and over the years as Harry's ability to embellish increased, it was to go on even further.

For Izidor, this was the triumph of his life. He was so taken with the moment that he did not realise what was happening. When he came face to face with an enormous bull, he got scared. Very scared. But the cheering crowd urged him on and being in a kind of trance, he went with the flow. Having seen what the others did before him, he waved his red cape and ran around the arena until the cheering stopped. He too stopped, looked back and saw the bull falling to the ground. So, he jabbed and stabbed, slit and sliced, and killed the bull.

Harry then sat back in his chair with increasing pleasure and a laughter that escalated with the length of his narrative.

Moshe was amazed. He said that it was an astonishing story. However, he was bothered. If he would have been in Izidor's place, when he saw the bull, he would have s..t in his pants. To this Izidor replied, "What do you think the bull slipped on?"

And his audience burst out laughing despite the not altogether unexpected punchline which they had to decipher after a fashion, because amidst Harry's obvious laughing enjoyment, his words were rather garbled. In the following years when Harry told this and other jokes, his overt pleasure in the telling grew to the point of incomprehensibility and many times he was unable to deliver the ending at all. At those times I would fill in for him.

Harry's appearance was also outstanding, in the sense of standing out. He wore a body hugging yellow floral embroidered silk shirt with buttons open from neck to waist, skin-tight cream and brown small checked bell-bottomed pants held by a wide leather belt with a large sparkling buckle. He had yellow gold rings on his fingers on both of his hands, a chunky yellow gold bracelet, a necklace with a large *Chai* (Life) pendant and a gold watch. I later learned that the bracelet was engraved with the words 'Mother loves you' in Hungarian. This was at a time when we were not accustomed to bejewelled males. He looked gay and not just happy.

At the end of the evening as I was leaving, Harry followed me to the stairwell. As I started down the stairs, he asked, "How about dinner?" I thanked him and suggested coffee, but he persisted with the dinner invitation. He said that he was asking me to go out to dinner with him, not for coffee. I asked, "Are you sure you want to invest in me as much as dinner, when coffee will do?" Harry said, "No. It's dinner or nothing."

I remembered that I had nothing to lose, and we did spend a pleasant afternoon, Harry looked nice enough and seemed safe. I had wrestled for my supper so many times in the past that it was refreshing to think I would be going out with a guy who was unlikely to pounce on me. So, I accepted the dinner invitation. I later learnt that he distinctly hated my pink striped bell-bottomed slacks and that he liked my placing an ashtray in front of him when he lit a cigarette. But what motivated his invitation to dinner was that he liked my father. So much for first impressions. And so much for love at first sight.

For our first date on the following Saturday, Harry arrived punctually, but two minutes before the appointed time. I was ready but short of exactly two minutes. He was and still is punctual, whereas I was and still am chronically late. And over the years, the short two minutes have expanded as much as I have. Consequently, he spent a few minutes waiting for me; his impatience increases with the increasing of the years, and so does the loud signalling that he is waiting. The intent is to make me hurry. The result is not just annoying, but invariably makes everything go wrong and take twice as long as it would take without the familiar dog whistle or the engine revving.

He and my parents chatted for a while about I know not what and then we left for Hunters Lodge in Double Bay. It was the Hungarian restaurant where years before we celebrated occasions such as my cousin's engagement. Then it was early days for the family business where the owner George Fisher's mother was in the kitchen and his wife worked there too, and the cottage had a distinctly hunters' décor with huge antlers hanging on the walls.

That night, on the first floor of Hunters Lodge our party of eight dined, wined and danced; all very continental. This was a restaurant Harry visited frequently; there was even a dish on the menu called "Harry's Steak Diane". He was very friendly with both George Fisher and the band leader Rony Fabre. Apparently, everyone wondered about who was Harry's new dish.

We were joined by his brother Fedor and the long-standing girlfriend, almost fiancé, Vivian, as well as Fedor's business partner and wife, and another couple. The food and wine were fine, the conversation and the company were fine, and the music was fine. But what was better than fine was the way Harry held me while we danced. With his open palm on the middle of my back, above my waist, close and firm but not too tight, I felt secure and 'at home' as it were. Probably the only thing that Harry remembers is that we danced very close. The way he tells it is that the reason for our closeness was that I wanted to 'feel his manhood'. The truth of the matter is I liked to dance, and we had a wonderful time. To prolong the evening, we drove through the city, across the Harbour Bridge, parked under the northern pylon, watched the city skyline, talked till early morning.

Grotto Capri April 1974

The next day was another memorable event. Harry and I went for a drive and started to get to know each other. We sat under a large old oak tree in the Botanical Gardens which I later learnt was one of Harry's favourite haunts. Harry leant against the trunk and my head rested in his lap. Harry still tends to do things suddenly and unexpectedly. Suddenly he said, "I want love and affection, understanding, respect and trust, support, honesty, ………. in my marriage." And he listed a dozen or so necessary and sufficient conditions or qualities he required in a wife.

At the end of his list, without hesitation, I said, "I qualify," and continued with my list. "I want love and affection, respect and trust, understanding and support, honesty, ……." and continued with a whole host of additional characteristics required from a husband such as, "caring, consideration, equality, and partnership", in my marriage. Harry said he can cope with all that.

I treated it as a light-hearted game of say cards, where the parties call out one suit, but may mean another. Fedor was better at it than his brother. When he played the game on his very first date with his wife-to-be at our first wedding anniversary celebration, he called a spade a spade and no one noticed that he meant it, except my very observant cousin. He was seriously talking marriage.

After that glorious sunny Sunday afternoon, the way I felt I decided that unlike in my past experiences, I will neither assess nor analyse, and that I will enjoy the relationship mentally and physically without any emotional attachment. So, we embarked on our future dates and enjoyed our growing relationship.

February was a full and happy month. Harry pursued me and I offered every opportunity for him to do so. He called me at work every day and he brought me little presents. Some were not so little such as the gold ring from a designer collection. Harry continued to build for Progress and Properties, and I had a full load as Team Leader in the Psychiatric Community Day Centre, as well as having extra work of total housekeeping for my parents, and liaising between the factory and my mother while nursing her. However, the weekends were occupied with carefree activity.

One was a lovely day trip to the Blue Mountains. A few days later Harry presented me with a little booklet of photos of us taken at the Three Sisters. Despite the fact that he was wearing another one of those tight-fitting embroidered yellow shirts and I was wearing the hated slacks, but, in another colour, we looked good together.

Opposite our photo he wrote,

"Let us always remember each other, with love and affection in confidence and understanding."

On one page he wrote a poem about "love is" and as if it were a foregone conclusion on his part, ended with a somewhat disarming signature statement,

"To my darling future wife – Agnes".

Blue Mountains, February 1974

Was he for real? Was he serious? I took it at face value, as perhaps humorous, although distinctly premature. However, I did enjoy the obviously romantic. At the time it was a great relief in my life. And still I had nothing to lose.

Harry continued to pursue me. He phoned frequently during the day and evening too. We talked for hours about nothing in particular, and everything in general. I still have the comfortable armchair in which I sat for hours talking with him at home.

One Sunday morning he phoned to say, that he is taking the dog for a walk. "Is it alright if I come over?" Of course, it was all right. I hung up, seemingly just turned around when Harry was whistling outside my window. Fedor's Doberman raced Harry down from his home in Murriverie Road, Bondi, up Hardy Street, Dover Heights and down to my home Chaleyer Street, Rose Bay, in fact three suburbs in a record five minutes. The dog then proceeded to dislodge a sapling tree to which he was tied in front of our house, in about the same time.

It was a spring like autumn. It was flowers and chocolates. We were young but old enough. I thought Harry and I were dating seriously, yet without any physical intimacy. Harry rejected every one of my propositions. In all my youth with the previous candidates, it was always the reverse. This was new as I was the one to proposition and I was rejected. I thought we were mature enough. There was no element of fear involved. I had no doubt about my appeal. It was not just a matter of annoyance and curiosity. I wanted a complete relationship irrespective of its outcome in the future. I wanted to have fun in every aspect of the word.

When Harry refused to have a sexual relationship with me till we were engaged, I was not sure what to believe. Was I right about his sexual preference in the first place? Was I so unattractive for him? Was I wasting my time in a relationship that was not going to satisfy me even for a short time? Was he truly so moral? Was he an old-fashioned young man? Any of the above was possible. For the first time in my life, I wished that I were respected a little less. Or not respected at all. I decided to give him another couple of weeks, but only because I enjoyed being with him. Also, there was no one else on the scene. And anyway, I was too busy to look for someone else.

Then I discovered that my serious boyfriend who respected me so much, was actually corresponding with other girlfriends. He was writing love letters to two girls in different parts of the world. I was always a one guy gal. I never have played second fiddle to any females whether they were an American department store manageress or an Israeli army officer. I issued an ultimatum. It was them or me.

Harry's story is that I moved from friend to friend, complained about him and cried buckets of tears from jealousy and a broken heart. Not true. Discussions took place with friends mainly because everyone was eager for me to marry. However, it was a matter of principle. When I was young, I played a fine violin, but always, always refused to play second fiddle for any man. Harry sent a telegram to each of his girlfriends, ending their relationship. A telegram yet? They must have been nice ladies, apparently not vindictive, for they were never heard from again. Or perhaps just not all that keen? So, Harry and I continued dating seriously for about eight weeks.

It was a warm day when we drove to the Botanical Gardens. We spread the notorious grey horse blanket, which was a repository for many untold stories, some of which Harry did tell. Common knowledge was Harry's sore back, and he assumed his usual horizontal position, flat on his back on the blanket. I was sitting and talking as usual. It was all very wonderful really; the two of us, content. Looking towards the Sydney Opera House, I was squinting into the setting sun and its shimmering rays across the bay, as I reminisced aloud about a full moon reflecting its rays across the Danube in Hungary.

Sometime in my childhood when I was eight or nine years old, I spent a holiday with the Sarkadis. I said, "This reminds me very much of the rising moon in Romai. I learned to play table tennis there. I beat many adults, but I still had to go to bed early. From my bed I saw the bright full moon, with its white light shining across the Danube on clear nights."

That required some further explanation that the Sarkadis were not really my grandparents but adopted and so on. As I continued my reminiscing about my childhood in the old country, Harry startled me with the question, "When do you want to get married?"

Now, under normal circumstances, this was not an abnormal question. On the contrary. Any girl in her right mind would have been delighted, even thrilled to be asked; especially one nearly 28 years old. And I should have jumped at the chance and answered something like "today" or "tomorrow".

But I have been asked three times before and I have been engaged three times before. Also, a few months before meeting Harry, I returned from a relatively long overseas trip, which had the primary purpose of husband hunting. And I was twenty-seven which is the cut-off age before a girl remains a spinster. Thus, I did not take the matter lightly.

My very first reaction was laughter. Of course. He was joking. I said, "That's not funny." I continued with my reminiscing about the Danube, when he repeated the question. This time I was very definite about his no sense of humour, and I explained to him how I felt. I said something to the effect that, "There are not many subjects that I would not joke about. Marriage may not be a sacred subject, but it is no laughing matter either. Marriage is a very serious matter." Harry said that he was serious for all the reasons that he has stated early in our relationship, and he repeated the question. I said that "I need to think about it." He replied, "How many minutes do you need?"

I repeated that "Marriage is a serious business and I never joke about it." Harry said that he didn't either and that he was quite serious. When I asked, "How serious?" he said that he was very serious and that I should name the date. Now I was willing to consider it seriously. After all, I thought to myself I had nothing to lose. Also, that I could always go back to Canada to continue my husband hunting. So, a few minutes later on 12th April 1974, I accepted his casual proposal casually. It was Good Friday.

Harry was very excited. He kissed me, jumped up and immediately started to fold the grey blanket, which could now add a very tame tale to its stock of wild and memorable events. He forgot about his back pain and about a lot of other things too. Just as today everything has to be done in a hurry, we had to tell somebody in a hurry. "We must tell my mother and uncle," he said. We must tell his family, but to tell my parents could wait till tomorrow. "Ah, there's the rub!" thought I. He gave some reason for this little delay, and I accepted it. After all, we were engaged.

Harry was so excited that he not only forgot about his back pain, but he forgot the day of the week. To be sure that there was enough to eat, we arrived at his home with a Kentucky dinner box for the whole family. It was Friday and the table was laid for the Shabbat dinner which Harry's mother cooked every week. That was a loud signal that something happened. Mother and Uncle looked surprised to say the least but also pleased that we were engaged.

I, on the other hand, would warn my parents that although this Harry planned to propose marriage formally, it may not eventuate. They should not be surprised, and I will not be too disappointed because I had a very nice time in the relationship for about two months. When I arrived at my home, both my parents were waiting with intense curiosity and anticipation. I told them of the events of the afternoon and the evening, adding my reservations and assured them that they had nothing to worry about. In other words, considering my past experiences, I was quite in control of my emotions, and if he didn't show, probably I would not miss the chewed fingernailed guy. I even had a good night's sleep.

However, Harry was true to his word. Next evening, he arrived five minutes early with a nice little gift box for me. He looked impressive dressed in a dark suit; a far cry from his normal attire which may have added some concern for some people. The little box he carried indicated some knowledge of social etiquette which was a definite plus. Harry then proceeded to formally ask my father for my hand in marriage.

He started by saying, "Mr. Forbat, we really don't need your permission to marry. We are both over 21. But". In other words, it would make the whole affair much more wonderful with their consent. While probably feeling some form of *de ja' vue*, my father agreed naturally, and both my parents were genuinely pleased and happy for me. They have taken an instant liking to Harry on the few occasions when they saw him in passing.

Harry had everything worked out in his mind and in practice. He had already ordered an emerald cut diamond, which was to be picked up the next day and placed into a setting of my choice. Wedding details and all other arrangements were to be discussed at a later date, after the two families have met and came to know each other.

I happily received my engagement present of four golden baubles; a small hat, a colourful traffic light, a teapot and a pearly drum, all of which were added to the other meaningful charms from my parents, and which are still dangling on my bracelet. By now they increased in number and make an awfully loud jingle when worn. Much to Harry's dismay, I rarely wear it because of the noise. But on that Saturday night of the 13th April 1974, I carried Harry's little golden gifts with me as we celebrated our engagement with Fedor and Vivian.

We dined and wined and danced at Hunters' Lodge again. We looked a fine couple. And our delight in our engaged state was not disrupted by Vivian's jealousy, who after all was a lady in waiting for much longer than I to be formally attached. A week later, waving a baguette cut diamond ring just over one carat, we enjoyed a delicious dirty weekend away in the Blue Mountains. It was a good Good Friday after all when I accepted his proposal.

The months before our wedding were busy with work, organising and worrying. Harry spent the week in Canberra completing a project of 32 Town Houses in Weetangera and driving back to Sydney for the weekends. My workload at the Day Centre was becoming increasingly heavy next to tending to my mother as well as being the go-between her and the factory. To help her, I changed to part time work. That resulted in having to fit the same amount of professional work into half the time.

The nicest part of the engagement was the planning of the wedding and our home. It seemed so simple to make a list and discuss it with the relevant parties. I cannot understand why such affairs cannot be a pleasant and exciting experiences, except when the finances are a problem.

I made all the necessary arrangements. Booked the Synagogue, caterers and hire cars. I selected cerise colour scheme with white orchids for flower arrangements, material and styles for the dresses for the mothers and bridesmaids. All were in consultation with and approval by Harry and our parents. I thoroughly enjoyed the whole business of organisation except for the fact that my mother's condition was deteriorating, and we were not sure whether or not the reception would take place.

My Chaleyer Street unit was easier to refurbish than the O'Donnell Street house which belonged to Harry's family and required considerable renovations. We received $5,000.00 from my father and $5,000.00 from Harry's uncle Batyu as wedding present and we spent most of it on furnishings. The unit was also convenient from the point of view of looking after my mother as my parents lived on the same floor.

I chose a colour scheme of blue; medium blue shag carpet, matching blue flock wallpaper, navy blue dining chair covers but with 'oyster' lounge suite and piano finished bedroom furniture. Harry approved, his mother approved and so did mine. We liked it. It was our home.

On 25th August 1974, we were married. In front of 350 guests Harry signed and dated his wedding speech which we pasted into our album. In it he expressed his *"gratitude and thanks to everybody here who share in our happiness …Love and Respect is in my heart and only my actions in the future will be able to bear witness to these feelings. … My darling wife, Agnes, here in front of all our honoured guests, family and friends I state that I love you and I will do so for the rest of my life."*

Chevron Hotel, Sydney, 25th August 1974

"My love is thine to teach."

William Shakespeare

Chapter Twelve
MY THREE SONS

"Children are like rainbows.
They come in an array of personalities, ..."

A D Brown

Every mother remembers the birth of their children. My three sons were and are similar, and different at the same time. They all arrived on the day they were expected, they were about the same weight and height and behaved in a very similar manner till they went to school. And although they were dressed in similar clothes which they all hated as they told me later in their life, they were different little and grown characters. All three of the boys did all the right things at the right time while they were little. I recorded every movement and motion as did my mother about me in her little black book.

At midday on Sunday 6th July 1975, I phoned the doctor and started to leave for the hospital. After all the preparations for pain I was given a pethidine injection which had no effect whatsoever. Then I was given a gas mask which had no effect whatsoever. Apparently, it was just oxygen. For a few hours pain and more pain followed till Dr Kovacs arrived, as did my firstborn Richard who arrived at 6.35 pm just after sunset with the help of forceps which left no mark on him whatsoever.

BIRTH

CZEIGER (nee Forbat)

Agnes and Harry
are delighted to announce
the birth of their son

RICHARD JAMES

on July 6, 1975

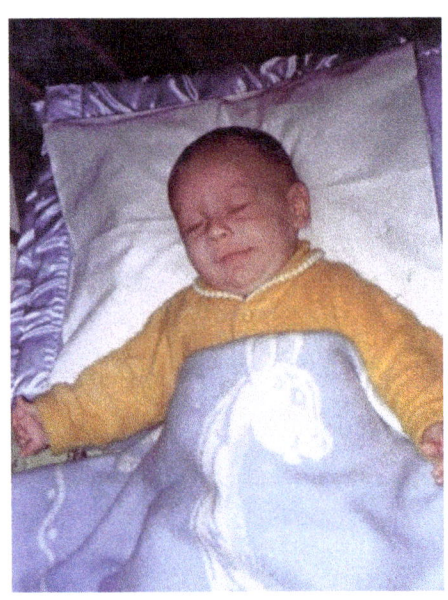

While Dr Kovacs was stitching me, I told him to do a good job because I intended to have two more children. According to Jewish custom, the *Bris* or circumcision is performed on male children on the seventh day after birth, so we went home on the eighth day because I wanted it performed in hospital. And he was a little jaundiced, so it worked out well. And it was done by Dr Weiss, who was a Jewish doctor.

Richard was nice and 53.5 cms long, 3.165 kgs. which was a good average weight. Perhaps because my mother couldn't breast feed me, I was determined to do so. I dreaded the four hourly feeds, and each time anxiously watched the Paddington Town Hall clock which was in clear view from my room. When I told Aunt Irene, she thought it absurd that I was upset and said that I was "not a cow." I relaxed after that, and Richard grew steadily.

At age three months Harry's mother asked if she could look after Richard. Lilly was loving and caring and of course, totally responsible. I was delighted. It served a dual purpose. I could go to work, and Lilly didn't have to work with Uncle. In fact, it became her therapy. I organized carers for my father and four bottles of formula for Richard. No weaning off as was customary. Richard thrived on the bottle.

I set up the little room next to Lilly's kitchen as a well-equipped nursery. It was painted, a new carpet was laid, and curtain was hung. I bought a cot and had a change table made with drawers for nappies and clothes which were mostly Bonds Terri toweling all in ones. Richard had a routine of eating, being changed and playing between his sleeps. When he woke up, and he woke usually with a smile, Lilly tapped her feet, and Uncle came up from his work room under the house to play with him. He was a perfect baby, and his brothers followed suit.

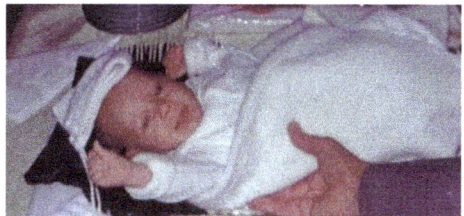

Following another Jewish custom, we had a nice little ceremony to purchase our first-born son for 50 pieces of silver from a Cohen. Whether or not my father realized what was happening, we shall never know but he was the one to hold his first grandchild for the ceremony. When Richard was married, we gave him his 50 pieces of silver.

Two years later, on a June midnight I phoned Dr Kovacs and told him that I thought I was ready to have my baby, and he told me to make my way to the hospital where he would meet me. We took Richard to Lilly making sure that he had his "bimbin" or security blanket with him. He must have inherited the need for a security blanket from me. For years I carried a folded piece of cloth with frayed edges to rub against my face. It was most comforting. How or why I still have it, I do not know.

We arrived at the hospital around 2.00 am, Admission needed to fill in a lot of documents, but I interrupted and told them that I had no time. Of course, they did not like that, but I was wheeled up to the Delivery floor to be prepared. I was not prepared as on examination the baby's head was showing and the nursing Sister gave me a gas mask.

Oh, the relief! No pain. And I was happily chatting away. I must have been very high, for in a haze I heard one of the nursing sisters say, "I think you had enough, dear," and the mask was swiftly snatched away. Then I heard, "turn on your side, dear," and out popped my Bobby around 2.30 am. Perhaps due to an overdose of nitrogen in the mixture, he was a most enjoyable delivery. Dr Kovacs arrived in time to do his stitching work, while I reminded him of the coming of one more baby for him to deliver in the future.

Robert Justin Czeiger was born on 21st June 1977. A lovely round baby, who weighed 3.12 kgs. and was 51 cms long. Harry and I thought that if we had another boy, he should be named Robert with the same middle name initials for our children. So RJC became the boys' initials. Later they only had a couple of arguments about their mail, especially when I opened them.

My second son Bobby was a dream baby, perfect in every way. I decided to bottle feed the second and any subsequent children to avoid any more jealous than was necessary. I even finished reading Colleen McCullough's *Thorn Birds* while bottle feeding my Bobby. He too had his Bris on the eighth day in the hospital.

Roby was five weeks old when I handed him over to Lilly and he continued Richard's routine of eating, being changed and playing between sleeps. And when Lilly tapped her feet, Uncle came up from his work room to play with him. I was delighted. My routine became dropping Roby at his grandmother's house, then dropping Richard at Kindergarten and going to work.

After picking them up, I visited my father in hospital or Nursing Home where Richard peeled and shared a banana which he still remembers. But generally, the routine was going home, looking after the baby, the two years old, and a father with a severe stroke. Harry always spent his time playing with the boys who were fed, bathed and ready for bed by the time he arrived home from work. And especially later he always managed to excite all the boys after which it was hard to settle them.

I decided on a two-year gap between our children, that would give my body time to rest, and they would not be too far apart in age. Because my deliveries were quite quick, I had a vision of delivering my third baby at home, so I booked myself into hospital for a birth induction on the day he was expected. Interestingly in those days having periodic ultrasound tests were performed only when some problem was suspected. Hence, we did not know the sex of any of our babies.

The induction was a matter of an injection and a drip, and over an hour later, assisted by a nurse, my third baby slipped out almost painlessly. Afterwards another drip was hung which resulted in almost unbearable pain. I asked for it to be removed but that required doctor's instructions. My Dr Kovacs was late. Eventually I told the nurse that if she didn't remove the drip then I would. She removed the drip, and the pain stopped immediately.

My third RJC, Ronald Jonathan Czeiger was born on 19th April 1979. He was 52 cms long and weighed 3.400 kgs. Rony behaved in the same manner in most respects as Rich and Rob except one.

BIRTH

HARRY and AGNES CZEIGER (nee Forbat) happily announce the arrival of their third son

RONALD JONATHAN

at the Royal Hospital for Women
on April 19, 1979.
Mother and son are happy and healthy.

Unlike the other two, when I sat him up after feeding, he not only burped, but regularly produced a small overflow until he was about six months old. He was awfully cute, and his brothers showed him off with great pride until he was old enough not to let them bother him.

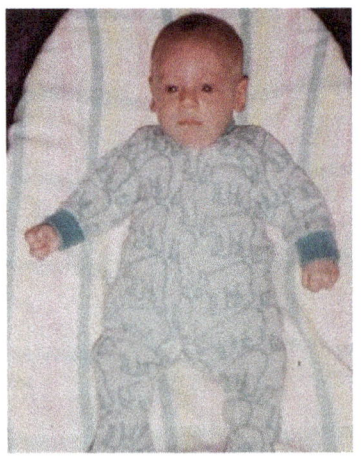

Six months later, the day after I had a tubal ligation I went to Grace Brothers in Bondi Junction with my three sons. I received several strange glances as I pushed Rony in a pram, while Richie and Roby aged four and two respectively held onto the handlebar on either side.

I lost Richard on that Saturday. When I turned around, he was gone. Cold perspiration flowed and a dilemma as to how to find him. I didn't want to leave in case he came back. Then came the announcement of a lost little boy. Unlike me, he was totally calm and smiling when I collected him.

Lilly did not look after Rony. By then Harry converted the factory garage into a *Forbat* shop for her. Next to the factory, Waverley Council opened a free 'Hop in Centre' for mothers to leave their small children for two hours a month while they kept doctors' appointments and such. It was newly painted and clean, with brand new equipment and toys, and was run by a qualified nurse.

While I worked for a few hours, Rony stayed next door and slept in a cot which was reserved just for him. He was a very good baby, and the staff loved him. In time my working hours increased, and he stayed longer. In fact, he stayed every day for a few hours while Richard was at school and Roby at kindergarten, until he went to kindergarten also.

My three sons were perfect babies till they were twelve months old, after which they stood on their feet, spoke in full sentences and they started to develop their character. We encouraged them to learn and to become independent thinking little individuals. They may say that their upbringing was strict. In a way it was with set limits or boundaries within which they were free to function.

I believed and still do that there is a time and a place for everything. There is a place for eating in the kitchen, a time for doing homework before playing and for packing away toys when finished with them before bedtime. And possibly reading time included in bed before sleep.

They had an abundance of toys, Legos, and they were particularly fond of Matchbox cars. Not to stereotype the sexes, I bought them a sturdy dolls house which was made of wood with furniture and small colorful people. No frills of course. But then I was never a frilly person.

I think my three sons' childhood was a pleasant one. Of course, they may remember it all very differently but when they were little, they were lovely. Not necessarily perfect. I did shout a lot for which I must have had darned good and genuine reasons. I did not and do not believe in hitting children, unless they do something dangerous such as running across a road. Then a spanking on the bottom does no harm and may teach them a lesson to avoid "danger."

I think that the boys liked each other and that they got on well, other than the occasional bickering or quarreling, all of which I believe was natural and normal. There were occasions when there was some problem. Once while I was driving, I stopped the car and told Richard to get out. I told him I was going to leave him wherever we were. Eventually he got out of the car, and I drove off.

Actually, I drove around the corner and watched him. A few minutes later I returned, he got back in the car, and we drove home. On another occasion when I told him to get out of the car, he got out without any argument and the smart little man told me that he knew I would not leave him. And he was right. When they misbehaved at home to punish them, I told the boys to go to their room and stay there until they behaved, and/or they apologized. They played in their room happily and had a nice time. But they did settle down. I learnt that it was very difficult to punish bright children.

My sons remember Harry beating them with his leather belt. I must have been absent because I remember only his threatening them. Most of the time the scenes were of playful boys, who may have ended up fighting often when Harry took part in the games. However, I have nothing but lovely memories of my three sons.

What my sons remember is that we always worked. As a working mother, I may have neglected the boys, but I thought we spent sufficient quality time together. I thought we were good parents. We even attended some Parenting group sessions. Harry learned a few things too and to this day he advocates "active listening."

I enrolled them in Hillel kindergarten from my hospital bed as I enrolled them in Sydney Grammar School, the private all boys school attended by my second cousins the Engel and Desiatnik boys. I must admit that I was happy when all three of them went to kindergarten. Not only could I drop them off in one place, but they were very well looked after, happy and learnt a lot. I was never imaginative enough to invent and organize all day activities for them. From the first day of Kindergarden while most children clung to their mothers and cried, Richard ran inside without turning to look back. The other two followed suit.

And I was most happy when all three of my sons were at Grammar. I was in my teens when I attended their Regattas which was the deciding factor for my choice of school if I had boys. Of course, none of them rowed. They took part in rugby, soccer, tennis, and played violin, flute, clarinet, sang in the choir and took part in other activities, but they never rowed. And they looked splendid in their uniforms, especially the winter uniforms.

My first experience at Sydney Grammar School was when the Women's Association had a luncheon, and each lady was to bring a plate. I did too. I took a plate. I showed up with an empty plate. I was not told that I was to contribute some food with the plate. That was not a custom in Hungary or in our social circle in Australia. Another lesson learned.

I was on the Tuck Shop roster for what seemed like forever washing lettuce leaves for the lunch sandwiches. For the sake of the boys of course. I was on the committee in various positions and also President of the Women's Association.

At the auction of one Grammar school fundraising dinner, we bid and won back the art piece we donated, and at another fundraiser we acquired a painting of the Big School which housed the Great Hall. It was in that Hall that I danced my first dance at my first ball and received my dancing prize.

There were many little incidents that the boys must remember from their school days. One was when Richard faked a Scottish accent, and all the teachers assumed that he was adopted until they asked us about his lovely accent. Another was when Richard suddenly came to a complete stop as he ran to a music lesson. He fractured his ankle. He reveled in moving around on his crutches.

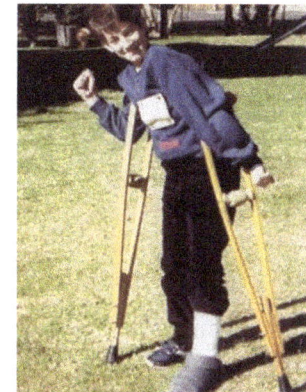

I was furious when Richard was caned by the headmaster. I was about to see the headmaster, but Richard was against it. He said that he deserved the caning. I accepted his verdict that he deserved some punishment and at his insistence did not pursue the matter. But there was no other caning incident.

Roby was kept back after school quite often. I learned that one of his two friends, who were also named Roby, was the cause. Much later my sons told me that they were bullied at school. Why didn't they tell me at the time? To this day I don't know why or how they were bullied or how it affected them.

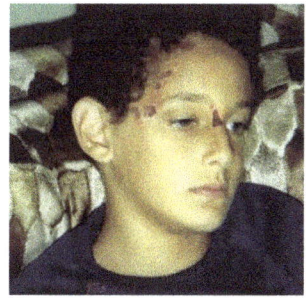

On the first day of school in third grade after we arrived home, Roby had an accident when he rode his BMX in front of our house. He was hit by a BMW, thrown a good many meters and lost consciousness. He sustained no lasting internal injuries, but his fractured leg could not be put into plaster cast because he had a puncture in it. I spent the few nights in hospital with him watching him bear the pain and the pushing and prodding of the staff. It was fortunate that he had a high threshold for pain. He was also home for a while and was a very good boy.

I never thought of myself as a rebel. Yet I took liberties at Grammar. I took each of my sons individually out of school for a day once a term. I lied about the reason for their absence from school. We spent the day doing what they wanted. That was until Mr Harwin, the headmaster called me in to his office to reprimand me. Shortly afterwards I announced to the headmaster that we would take all three boys overseas for a couple of weeks, whether or not I set a precedence. We did visit the Toronto Science Museum, which was fun, interactive and educational. So I did not lie.

I wanted the boys to become doctors. It was a legacy from my Jewish heritage based on my parents' Jewish history. They believed that medicine was a profession suitable for all occasions in all countries under all regimes. No matter how persecuted, doctors could always make a living under all circumstances. It was a matter of survival. Hence, I wanted the boys to be doctors even if they were paid with chickens. At age five, Richard announced that he would not become a doctor. Was it the right decision to send our three sons to such an elite school and one which is primarily focused on academic excellence?

In hindsight I am not sure. I do believe that it was appropriate for Richard and probably for Rony too. Perhaps not necessarily for Roby who struggled at times. I did ask him from time to time whether he would like to change schools and go to one where there was less pressure to excel, but he declined. So did the other two. I know that Roby liked the Regiment and had he joined a branch of the armed forces, he could have done his university studies there too and he could have had a secure future. In hindsight Grammar was an expensive lesson for the boys, but I think it was well worth it.

As the boys were growing up, we had numerous birthday dinners at Lilly's place with numerous birthday cakes. Four out of the five grandchildren had birthdays within a few weeks of each other, so we celebrated them together at the end of June with lots of presents and large birthday cakes. And whatever the shape, her coffee cream cakes were always absolutely delicious. Some would say 'orgasmic.'

But the boys had other birthday parties with other birthday cakes, some of which were made by Erzsi the babysitter. Sydney Grammar had a practice that the whole class was invited on the occasion of a boy's birthday. We also had extended family and friends whose children shared in the celebrations. That meant that each of my three sons had three birthday parties.

There were so many experiences that come to mind when I think of my three sons. They tend to blur into one large mass since decades have passed. When they were little, they ran in three different directions in parks. As they were growing there were play groups, library book readings, Cubs, weekends and holidays with friends and their families. They didn't want to go to camps, but they did go and came home having enjoyed them, or so they told me. And more, much more.

Since music was important in my life, my three sons were exposed to classical music from the time of their conception. Richard wanted to have piano lessons. Too young to learn an instrument? Not according to piano teacher Miss Agnes Waldman. He could start lessons as long as he knew the first eight letters of the alphabet and was able to count to ten.

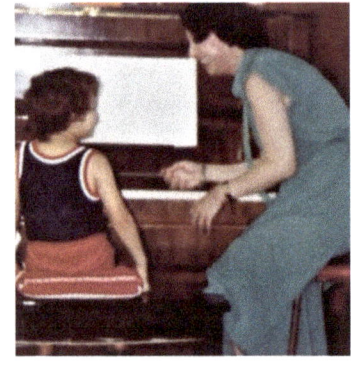

So, the first piece he learnt on the piano was from a music score of **CCDE, CCDE, CCDE**, … drawn in large capital letters and he performed it at his first end of the year concert which we all attended in the heat of summer. Richard was not yet four years old.

He continued with piano till grade seven. He also played the flute and enjoyed playing it in the indoor swimming pool area where the acoustics resounded his performances. The other two boys also had piano lessons. Roby took up the violin, which was not an easy instrument, and three weeks later he sat for a conservatorium examination. His teacher Mrs S, who played in the Sydney Symphony and other classical groups, told him not to worry and to enjoy the experience. I don't know if he actually enjoyed the examination. Does anyone? But he did considerably well, considering he had such a very short time for preparation.

The lead flutist of a Philharmonic orchestra started to play the flute to help his asthma which was totally controlled by the time he became a member of the London Philharmonic Orchestra. I encouraged Rony to take on any wind instrument to help with his asthma. At first he played our cousin's clarinet. He later changed to the saxophone and also played guitar.

For the weekly piano lessons with Miss Waldman, I dropped off the boys one at a time and had to occupy the other two until they had their lessons. We usually went to parks. One week we passed a new glass bus stop with a black *swastika* painted on it. I drove to the first shop that sold paint and bought a spray can of paint. I returned to the bus stop and hurriedly sprayed over the *swastika*. It became a white *swastika*. Obviously, I was not thinking clearly because I was so angry. I stifled my laugh at my stupidity and very quickly sprayed white paint to cover the whole glass. The boys remember the incident to this day.

Over the years I took a lot of photos of my ever so cute three sons. They hated their snapper mother. They either walked away or turned away but more often one or all made silly faces of which I disapproved. I wanted nice images of them. I particularly loved the bath photos. I have some 75 photo albums full of photos, mostly of my three sons. I sometimes wonder what will become of them after I am no longer. Will they last and how will the boys divide them?

When the boys were little we acquired a budgie, several goldfish, a dog, a cat, and a turtle. I believe we started with a couple of goldfish in a small bowl, which eventually grew into a complete oxygenated aquarium for Rony. He also had a turtle which after a time went walkabout and never returned. Then we had a lovely green and yellow budgie, who lived longer than do birds of that kind. Eventually it was scared to death by Brandy the cat. But before her, Richard had a black cat.

We needed a doggie because Lilly shooed away all dogs who dirtied the grass strip outside her house and our three sons became frightened of dogs. To combat their fear, we decided to get a puppy. Harry did the research for a playful guard dog who was child safe.

Enter Sir Rod Ridge, the Rhodesian Ridgeback whose ancestors were lion hunters. A beautiful animal in every respect. His name was Whisky. Since I was never a friend of dogs either, I reluctantly carried the puppy home in my lap. At seven weeks, Whisky was more than half a meter long and quite heavy. Naturally he became my dog. I fed him, I cleaned him, I took him to the vet and so on. After he had all his vaccinations, I took him to Centennial Park on Sunday mornings for obedience training and he was very good and obedient.

At home he did everything perfectly as an obedient doggie would. Once we reached the park, he saw the other dogs, his basic instinct took over and he was off racing after all of them. As a result, he not only failed all the tests, but he pulled out my left shoulder and left it damaged.

All his blue blood prodigy were Blue Ribbon winners at many Easter Shows. We showed him at the Castle Hill Ridgeback Shows where he won a number of first prizes as the Lickiest Puppy and Waggiest Tale Puppy. Richard was ten years old when he showed him. Just a little taller than the fully grown six months old, 47 kilograms heavy Whisky, it took all Richard's strength to hold back the instinctually aroused doggy.

Whisky grew to be a very healthy dog for many years. So much so, that he jumped a six-foot fence, ran down the street and impregnated a Bull dog. The Bull owner was most upset and insisted that we pay the $90.00 for the termination.

Whisky's bark was deep and loud. It was so terrifying that the men who came to read the gas and electric meters refused enter our property unless we held back our dog. But he was a friendly dog too. He greeted guests with his front paws on their shoulder. And because he was strong, they invariably toppled backwards.

He was a very good dog, and the boys loved him. The large Whisky was playful and very gentle with the boys to the point where they rode him like a horse. Initially the large dog ran a mile from our tiny ginger kitten who Roby named Brandy. Eventually Whisky came to mothering Brandy the cat as she slept in the curve of his body every night.

Whisky travelled very well during our weekly trips between Sydney and Bowral. When he became very sick, Roby picked him up and placed him in the car boot for his last journey. I made the decision not to let him suffer any longer, for which Rony has never forgiven me as he was overseas and was unable to say goodbye to our family pet.

When Rony was old enough and independent enough, he bought himself a black and white Border Collie who I sent away to training school to avoid another shoulder problem. Cassie was very beautiful, very well behaved, and a very lovable puppy. I am not sure why she stayed with us a lot, but she was very welcome. And when Harry came home with *"the doggie in the window"* of a Pet Shop, Cassie adopted the small brown eared white furball of a Maltese Shih tzu Terrier we named Brandy who became our 'granddog'.

I don't remember that training Brandy was ever a problem, but we spent most of the time with her outside in the garden. She was adored by all who came in contact with the very cute and cuddly puppy. With time she developed a most beautiful plumage for a tail which later became a stub, but Brandy was still very cute and cuddly.

Cassie was especially welcome by Brandy who was mothered by the then two-year-old Cassie. After she had surgery for the tail removal, Cassie stood guard over her. In fact Brandy came to be like a sheep dog and very much lacking fear while she ran after Cassie around our 15-acre large property. And although it was surrounded by fences, the doggies found a way in and out of the property of neighbours just like the six-foot grey kangaroos did.

We loved our pets, and we did the right thing by them, but they slept in their beds in the garage summer and winter. Winters in the Highlands may have been cold despite the sheep skin lined beds. We may have been seen as very cruel by the pet owners whose dogs slept in their bed with them. However, the doggies happily sat next to me for hours in the study even if we treated them like dogs and not like children.

Brandy developed a severe illness at ten and a half years of age, and the surgery would not have saved her. So rather than put her through treatments that would not have prolonged her life for long, we decided to be kind to her, and eventually she was put to sleep.

Cassie met the same fate two months before. That was a tearful experience when Rony and I held her paw with one hand and each other's hand with the other. The ceramic urns with the two puppies' ashes were placed next to each other in the garden in Bowral at the foot of the water fountain which is visible from our study window.

We no longer needed grand dogs, as we had six very loveable grandchildren. Although none of them have alcoholic names.

And we had a number of ladies looking after the boys. Erzsi (Elizabeth) was a pastry cook at Prince of Wales Hospital. She had an eight-year-old son and to earn extra money she did cleaning. I inherited her from my mother as I was working too.

When Richard was born, she spent most of the time playing with him and eventually she became our permanent babysitter. She loved the boys who were very attached to Erzsi. Their dinner was usually Wiener Schnitzel, and she taught the boys how to 'schnitz.' She was as imaginative with games as with their birthday cakes. She was reliable and responsible.

Our friend Barbara had a law student living with her. However, she needed someone who would clean and cook besides looking after her two boys. Since Harry always wanted a Nanny for our children, I was persuaded to accept the law student to come to live with us and look after our three sons.

Gabriella was a nice young lady, originally from Lismore. She was neat and clean. And she was organised to the point that by the time I came out of my bedroom in the morning, and when I returned at the end of the day, I had nothing to do. That was all great. But what was to happen if and when she left. We came to an agreement that she would supervise the boys to do everything for themselves.

At first, I was reluctant to have this stranger in the house with the boys. A couple of weeks after Gabriella moved in, the doorbell rang on a Sunday. There were four tall, well-built young men in casual clothes at the front door. I thought that this was where the problems would start and that we will have to ask Gabriella to leave. One of them was the son of a friend of Gabriella's parents and they were asked to contact her. In other words, they came to look us over to check on us to see if we were suitable for Gabriella to live with us. Not only that, but they were police officers from Bondi Beach police station. I then relaxed.

Gabriella studied, helped with the boys, and sat with them when we went out. She organised their birthday parties and on the rare occasion when she dated, we met the young man. When she went to a masqued ball, even the boys had to approve of her mask and costume. For a few years till her graduation as a lawyer, we adopted Gabriella and could not have been more fortunate with someone who became part of our family.

In 1985 we fostered a little girl and later a teenage girl. The cute little girl was nearly four years old when she stayed with us for about four months. Jewish Welfare contacted us about fostering because her mother needed to be hospitalized. We discussed whether or not we were in a position to have an extra child living with us. It had to be with the boys' agreement, and we needed to remember that it was temporary.

We signed up for the Foster Parents training program which turned out to be rather a superficial course. Naturally we qualified. One of the exercises was to complete a Scrapbook about our family and lifestyle. The boys took a major role in its production, and it turned out to be a rather fine and memorable document.

Most of the fostering applicants were there for financial benefit. Some people must have been in dire need for the fostering fee. It was $40.00 per week for which I opened a new account for the little girl. We bought a few clothes for her and a pink bicycle. The balance of the money went home with her together with the clothes and the bicycle which her mother refused initially until I convinced her that my three sons would not ride a pink bike. Besides, they had their own bikes.

Rony still remembers that he was moved out of his room as it was the only one with its own bathroom. He was placed into Richard's room and shared the joint bathroom with Roby. Richard enjoyed his freedom in the king-size bed in the upstairs guest room.

At first Ariella cried a lot. That was understandable considering she was separated from her mother. She was moody, had some bad eating and sleeping habits. She mashed up her food with her fingers making an awful mess and slept in a sitting position on the insistence of her mother who said that asthmatics must be in an upright position.

In a very short time, she assimilated into our family routine. She ate neatly and slept lying down, particularly after her family doctor told me what I suspected, that she was not asthmatic. She became our fourth child, and my three boys even doted on her. Because she could not say 'beautiful,' she said 'buful.' The boys still say *buful* sometimes and I do often.

During the Christmas break we planned to drive up the coast to Noosa, but we needed her mother's permission, which came very reluctantly. Ariella decided to test us by asking for repeated pit stops and rejoiced in "false alarm". After a while Harry lost his cool and spanked her on her bottom. After that Ariella became most attached to Harry, and our family of six had a lovely shop-hopping holiday. The separation from Ariella was very hard on all the boys. Her absence was hardest on Harry. She left a void, and in a way, I regretted that we did not try for a girl after Rony was born. But it was far too late.

Sometime later, we were contacted by Jewish Welfare again. Barbara had been fostered before and we had little history about her background other than she was fourteen years old, referred herself because she did not want to move in with her father and wanted to have a break from her mother who had problems.

With Barbara it was easy to lay down the rules. Primarily we expected honesty and the rest would follow. Of course, she had other ideas. She wagged school. She lied about the time she was to come home, about her evening outings at the skating rink and the boyfriends. After the punishment she learnt her lesson, never lied again but we always had some suspicions.

That short stay with our family seemed to have helped Barbara and she planned to return to her mother. A few years later I received a letter from Barbara. In a rather happy tone, she wrote that I should consider her a "success story". She had a job in a legal office, she was renting a flat and she had some nice friends. She expressed her gratitude for our efforts even if she gave us some hard times. Such experiences felt most gratifying.

When the boys reached the mature age of 13 years, they went through their Bar Mitzvah (*possessor of the commandments*) which is the Jewish religious ritual of boys' rite of passage into manhood. Harry came from an observant family and it was most important for his mother and uncle. From my point of view, it was to make sure that they never blamed me in later life for not going through the ceremony.

And they learned about Jewish history in the process. Sadly, Lilly was present only at Richard's *Bar Mitzvah*, but she arranged for each of them to have the same gold necklace.

From Fedor they each received the same gold nuggets as a present on the occasion of their *Bar Mitzvah*. For Ron's *Bar Mitzvah* his G-d mother Marika gave him a lovely locket which he never wore and probably will give to one of his daughters. The doors open to reveal the Ark, where the *Torah* or the Jewish Bible is supposed to be housed. Irrespective of the religious connotation, it is an unusual piece and just very attractive.

Instead of the traditional big reception on the occasion of their Bar Mitzvah, we had the traditional *Kiddush* after the Service and some dinners for family and friends at our home. Instead of feeding hundreds of people with whom they are not very familiar, we offered the boys their choice of parties for them with their friends and a choice of their destination to spend some time alone with their father. They remember them well.

Richard had Samurai fever, so he wanted to visit Japan. Roby chose Daintree Forest as his destination. Rony opted for the Epcot Centre in Florida. Harry enjoyed the special time with each of his sons who still remember their personal experience.

The years between the boys' *Bar Mitzvahs* and their weddings went by quickly. The memories return in fragments and at odd times, as they do. And there are so many of them. Memories, sweet memories may linger, and I recall them as I turn the pages of photo albums.

All three have graduated a number of times with degrees and I was very proud of them as I witnessed their academic processions. Richard has B.A. (Hons), Grad. Dip. Commerce (Marketing), M.I.M. Rob has BAA, Grad Dip Des, M Des. And Ron has BA, Adv Dip Mech Eng, Cert III & IV Auto Mech and others. It is nice that they have all those letters after their name. And all three found employment so that they were never out of work.

The story goes that Richard left home because I told him to hang up his towel. Richard was eighteen at the time and he was angry when I told him to hang up his towel. Without a word, he dressed and left the house. I felt angry, guilty and frightened as I did not know where he went or where to look for him. Eventually he did return and told me that some time ago he rented a terrace house in Newtown with a couple of his friends, and he left me his contact details. When I visited him a short time later, I couldn't believe that he was such a neat housekeeper, and Sundays were his cleaning days. It was all fine, but I missed out on selecting items with him for his first home away from home. I always thought that we would do that together.

Soon Roby and Rony followed by sharing a rented semi-cottage and eventually bought a town house together. But they welcomed my help when they moved into their new homes. Roby and Rony were always closer to each other. However, even today, the three include each other in their lives on important occasions.

There came a time when the serious girlfriend moved into the terrace to stay, and Richard and Alexandra were planning a family secretly. Their first-born daughter Rebekah was ten months old when they married. But it was Rony who was the first to wed after he found his soulmate in Joanna. Consequently, the jointly owned house was sold, and Roby rented a unit where he lived with Monika, who he eventually married. So, the weddings of my three sons were in reverse order to their ages. Go figure. Sadly, Ron was divorced but presently he is in a nice relationship.

Ron 2009

Rob 2010

Rich 2011

After each wedding, besides being happy for my three sons, I had mixed feelings of relief and loss. I felt a kind of relief in relinquishing all responsibilities for my sons and was happy that they found their partner. At the same time, I knew they no longer belonged to me. It is true that they may have left home permanently but the worry for, and about them stayed home permanently. For they remain our children no matter how grown up they may be. That is the plight of us parents. Now that they are parents too, I am sure that they are going through all the worry for and about their own children. So, the cycle continues. I am sure that they will always love their children as unconditionally as I love mine.

Chapter Thirteen
FROM MY CHILDREN

*"A child is never far from your mind, even when they are grown.
However, they eventually give you grandchildren to worry about."*

Looking at my three sons I can honestly say that I am proud of them. I have always loved them and liked them. Even if I did not like some of their actions, for they did not necessarily do what I asked or told them to do or meet my expectations, I did love them.

As small children they were lovely. As teenagers they were confused or rebellious, or even sad. I am sorry. I probably contributed to that, unintentionally of course and the guilt is mine. They are no longer the cute little boys that they were, but they are nice, and as adults they are decent, kind, hardworking and responsible people. They are good husbands, and they are good and loving parents. When I look at them or even just think of them, I am filled with joy, and I just smile. I still love and like my three sons.

And we are six grandchildren richer, all girls except for one boy. And to write about them and their fathers would fill more than one book, for there is just so much. But my sons know about themselves, and they are witnesses to their children growing up together with all the pains and pleasures that accompany growing up. They can record all that themselves.

As my three sons were, our grandchildren too are cute little characters who are growing into nice little adults. Our *Numero Uno*, Richard's Rebekah born in 2011 will always be the closest because she spent the most time with us when we looked after her from an early age while her mother went to work. She is the horse rider. In the same year Roby's son Ethan was born, and he is a keen prize-winning soccer player. In 2013 Richard's Scarlett was born followed by Roby's Belinda the year after. Both girls love to dance and are little performers and posers. Our very sweet and very special Riley was born to Ron in 2016 with ZTTK, a severe disability but with a fortunate happy disposition. She now has a sister Jocelyn who is three years younger, very bright and quite a character.

The multitude of photo images provide us with evidence of their development and the busy lives they lead to which we cannot be direct witnesses as we were to our sons. But we are witnesses to some scenes in their lives often. The grandchildren are not ours, not our responsibility and sometimes it is just nice to give them back. They belong to our children and that in itself is a most strange notion for a parent just as the fact that our three sons are men, and they are nearing fifty years of age. And when we glimpse into their lives, it is with great affection and sheer satisfaction.

So, Scarlett was just sitting by the pool, dangling her legs and talking to the stars, telling them about her day. When she was called in for dinner she said "Bye!!" and waved bye to them. Alex asked her who she's talking to, and she pointed to two stars and said, "Batyu and Mama Lilly." My heart just broke.

Richard – December 2022

On the rare occasion when my three sons organize themselves and get together, then they create something special. And I received this lovely present from them not so long ago.

DEAR MUM

May 9, 2021

Richard   Robert   Ronald

Dear Mum,

It's Mother's Day 2021 – a year that still sounds like it's in the future. Time has been creeping up on me lately and I look in the mirror and realize I'm not 25 anymore… More than that, I'm not just your son. Now I'm a father in my own right with two little ones who look up at me adoringly, imploringly, whingeingly, accusingly, frustratingly, happily and all the other little emotions that come with being a child.

The same emotions I see in them I recognize from myself. Especially with Rebekah. She reminds me so much of myself sometimes and it makes me think of you and how you must have dealt with me as a young boy, and angry teen and later as a (dare I say it) fully-grown man.

So, this Mother's Day, let me take a few minutes to tell you everything you did wrong raising me. You kept me under your wing and tried to protect me from the world when all I wanted to do was stand on my own two feet. I remember so many times when we would lock horns over some trifle, all in order to assert dominance in an attempt for me to take control over my own destiny. But now that I have children of my own, I can see what you were trying to do.

I look at Rebekah and desperately want her to remain as naïvely innocent as she is now for as long as possible. That pure sweetness, once replaced with the cynicism of modern life, can never be recalled. Already she is testing boundaries, realizing the world is bigger than her little family and trying to figure out where she sits in that global dynamic. I want to retain my control over her because I know – absolutely know– that she isn't ready for certain things. Her young mind is still so fragile and unable to grasp the nuances that we as adults take for granted.

She will grow older still and battle me, as I battled you, until eventually I will be forced to let her stand on her own spindly little legs on the slippery, thin ice of life. I laugh when I think back to what you recall as "The Towel Incident" which spelt the end of my time as your 'dépendant'. Obviously, there was a lot going on at the time on top of simply where towels were supposed to live. But now, as a parent, I think I have a bit more understanding of where you came from all those years ago. That and all the other times we battled our wills in my formative years. In the end, I am thankful that you did protect me from the great big world outside so that when I was finally ready to go out there, I did so without the floor falling from under my feet.

Next. You always said 'No!' to everything.

So, what if this stopped me from being a spoilt brat. I was well on the way: what with you and dad having given me almost everything I asked for… I wanted stuff and you wouldn't immediately accede to my juvenile demands! Unforgivable! Still, I suppose this little prince had to be brought back to reality every once in a while.

Also, I think you had a much darker outlook on life than dad. Slightly more cynical and pessimistic. But this as well, can be seen as a positive (especially with dad). While he would dive into opportunities, you would always be more conservative, judging risks more critically than he did. I believe it would be fair to say that if dad had listened to you a little more, some of the family's fortunes might not have been lost on unprofitable ventures. This too I have inherited from you. I am financially conservative and was careful with who I gave my heart to, always waiting to ensure that they were worthy and would treat my vulnerability with respect and care. But, like you need dad to sometimes boldly venture where angels fear to tread, I think I need someone to pull me out of my comfort zone sometimes. Thankfully Alex came along, and she drags me off when I would rather retire to my cave, and she makes me experience the sunshine. Nevertheless, I think my caution and conservativism have held me in good stead. And I think my cynicism and sarcasm are some of my more endearing features.

So, thank you. For all of it.

I tried to think up some other things that I didn't like growing up that you were responsible for but, honestly, I struggled to come up with anything else.

In the end, that's probably the best compliment a child can give their parent: "You didn't screw up my life too badly."

Thanks, mum. You were a great mum.

Love, Richard

With love from Alexandra, Rebekah and Scarlett

Dear Mum

First, Happy Mother's Day!

Another year has flown by, and it hasn't been an easy one, but rest assured there have also been some milestones.

One; you survived a pandemic, the question of sanity…could have gone either way but we're stuck with what's left of it :-P.

Two; you finally made the switch and now live in Bowral while visiting your holiday house in Sydney on weekends.

Three; you have watched your grandchildren, all 6 of them, grow and mostly mature, but definitely delighted.

Four; If Batyu can make it to 100 you most likely will as well so you'll have more time with your kids and grandkids and even possibly great grandkids.

So that brings me back to you in a roundabout way. You must have done something right as you have three healthy children who each have two healthy and happy children each (fingers crossed for Riley).

I have to say that I think I'm a little ahead of my brothers as I managed to throw a boy into the group of girls. Luckily Ethan's other side of the family is the reverse, and they have plenty of boys for Ethan to hang out with and vice versa with Bella.

You are far from perfect but then who is and anyone who thinks they are, aren't worth knowing. What you are, though, is loving, giving and supportive. And that is all anyone needs to be. I like the analogy of you're a cat in lions clothing, those around you may never get too close but those who you have lived with from the beginning can see the protective and loving side.

Enjoy your Mother's Day knowing that even if there were ups and downs and a lot of side-to-sides you have three grown boys who have families of their own and children of their own to raise and love … unconditionally.

Happy Mother's Day :-)

Rob, Monika, Ethan, and Belinda

Dear Mum,

The first rule of writing is "show don't tell". In other words, it is ok to say something like: "he was angry" - as a sentence on its own, it's almost as if the author is pausing to emphasize an emotion. On the other hand, if you were to say something like: "he ground his teeth and slammed his clenched fists on the table" you allow the reader to make inferences, engaging them as part of the story. - Show don't tell.

It's hard to write something cheerful in a time when I am going through something quite difficult. Thinking back now, I feel that my marital separation is probably the hardest thing that I have done, and hopefully the hardest thing I'll have to do. But from darkness comes light. I look at the way you have sustained your family through hard times and come through shining on the other end. I am in awe, and I don't mind admitting that I am a little bit jealous. I always wanted the "nuclear" family and until recently, never had to imagine my life without it. But the fact that you have maintained the Czeiger clan, on its own, is testament to your success in motherhood.

Personally, though, our relationship hasn't been smooth sailing in the least. And while I could point the finger, I do take some responsibility for this. Not to make excuses but I am an introvert, can't help it. So, it has always been difficult for me to express my feelings, and quite to the contrary, I take comfort in escaping and avoiding. Not healthy I know, but can't help it, though I am working on it.

What I have taken from this whole experience is that when everything is swimming, our interactions remain platonic. When, however, the shit hits the fan, you are there with a mop and bucket, gloves already on. It seems that this reaction has a little bit of "worry" to it, but it's clear that the response is mostly a loving reflex. Support is what I needed and, for some reason, felt I had to ask for. But the truth is that it was always there, no matter what.

So, the premise of "show don't tell" is that actions speak louder than words. You always say you "love us unconditionally". And I always wondered why you needed to "tell" me this. Especially when in my hour of need, you clearly "show" it.

As far as Mum's go, I can honestly say you're the best one I've ever had.

Happy Mother's Day from Czeiger Minimus, Riley and Jocelyn

A PICTURE IS WORTH A THOUSAND WORDS!

THE BEGINNING
ADD A FEW YEARS

LEADING BY EXAMPLE
THEN THEY ARE MEN

AND THEN, THE GRANDKIDS

Scarlett and Rebekah - Ethan and Belinda - Riley and Jocelyn

From Harry and the "kids"!

Chapter Fourteen
FAMILY

"Family is not an important thing. It's everything,"

Michael J Fox

There were the Kenedis (originally Klein) on my mother's and the Forbats (originally Freund) on my father's side. Sounds like the Montagues and Capulets. The two families were never warring, although they were never really very close. However, when they were together, they enjoyed themselves. Strangely enough, some members were connected by marriage and to those I was related from both sides of my parents.

Kenedi Erno was a tall attractive serious man. He survived deportation and forced labor camp. One story told is how he was reluctant to volunteer when the Germans called for interpreters although he was fluent in speaking and corresponding in several languages especially German. When translators were called for, Erno would not volunteer so my father forcefully pushed him out of the line which probably saved his life.

It was my mother who introduced Erno to his blonde wife Ibolya. All the Binet women were very attractive blonde women. Iboly was quite vivacious and a beautiful looking woman who was also a relative of my father's brother's wife, Bozsi Fischer. So, I was related to her from both of my parents' families.

It was a marriage that ended in divorce, but they did produce a very good-looking boy, Gabor or Gabi two years younger than I, and who was spoilt by everyone.

After his divorce, Erno became a somber man. For many years he worked as a laborer in a dark dingy airless basement metal workshop. And till the end of his life, he frequently visited his lady psychiatrist, with whom he had an unhealthy transference.

Kenedi Gyula was also tall and attractive, but otherwise quite the opposite to his brother Erno. He had a cheerful nature and was always smiling. He was a practical man, not only able to fix everything but had a pragmatic attitude to complex issues. As the youngest in the family, all doted on him. As a young man and a Zionist who wanted to *aliya* or move to Israel, he grew to be a man of action and seemed fearless.

Gyula married Klari (nee Halasz) and together they had two daughters Anita born in 1946 and Sylvia born ten years later. During WWII he moved around the city freely in his brown leather coat with a *swastika* armband and a machine gun. He procured false identification papers for many including my mother and his wife. He pulled Klari out of the line-up of Jews to be shot into the Danube River. The man had *chutzpah* or guts.

During the 1956 Revolution, there was cause to be frightened with constant street fighting including heavy artillery, tanks and bombings. A knock on our door did cause alarm and we were relieved to find that it was my cool Uncle Gyula, in his brown leather coat with a Hungarian armband and a *guitar* or a Russian Kalashnikov machine gun with its round ammunition case. From where or how he obtained it, we will never know but he moved around the city freely with his *guitar*. He came to check on us.

In the summer of 1973 when I spent time alone in Budapest, Gyula showed me the nightlife ranging from the base bars frequented by lowlife just outside the city, to the elegant restaurants including the one with the famous Gypsy band beneath the Var, or the Palace on Castle Hill on the Buda side of the city. We drank more than we ate and danced to whatever music was playing well into the early hours of morning. Perhaps he wanted to recapture a part of his youth, perhaps he wanted to be close to his sister through her daughter or perhaps he wanted to spend time alone with the little girl who sat on his bicycle bar so long ago. But that whole night was unforgettable.

My aunt Klari was an attractive blonde bespectacled intellectual and an Associate Professor of Languages at the Technological University in Budapest. As a born pedagogue, Klari was an extremely capable organiser. She organised, well, encouraged her husband Gyula to graduate from university as a mechanical engineer and later her two daughters Anita and Sylvia, who are highly intelligent and cultured university graduates. Both became teachers who spoke multiple languages, and later still she also exerted her influence on her grandchildren.

During that 1973 visit, I was walking with her on campus when we met one of her students. She asked him how he spent his vacation, and he answered that he was employed as a 'transactional transport technologist.' Impressive. After he left us, my aunt Klari informed me that he was actually a *trogerer/schlepper*; in other words, he was a labourer. Remember she was a language teacher and with great expectations from students.

Over the years we sent a lot of clothes to Budapest. As an international tourist guide Klari crossed many borders during university holidays. In a backpack, she carried those clothes which she sold on black markets. It helped towards the two years waiting list to purchase their car, the *Trabant* with the motorcycle engine, the Bakelite body with the wide range of colour selection of white or beige or light green, and which we periodically needed to push up a hill until Gyula fixed it.

Later in 1973 my parents brought Gyula and Klari to Australia. No one was to know that both my parents were so incapacitated that it was left up to me to show them Sydney and all the places that were significant in our lives. I drove west to the Blue Mountains, up north and down the south coast, as far as the Kosciuszko National Park. We detoured to places with Indigenous unpronounceable names when we drove cross country just to see some places not on the tourist route.

One day we drove into a one-horse town on the way to the coast of southern NSW. It was already dark, and the only light emanated from a pub. Every town has at least one pub. So, we checked in for the night. Dark and dingy, barely furnished, with a shared bath and toilet down the hall, rusty water, no towels and so on. We had a mighty Australian breakfast, with bacon and eggs floating in a mighty quantity of oil. A true Aussie experience for which I apologised whenever I saw my aunt and uncle but which they took with good humour.

Since Harry grew attached to my family, in 1983 he brought Klari and Gyula to Australia. They had instant rapport with Lilly and Uncle. We travelled some of the same destinations as we did ten years before and some new ones too. With each meeting we spent much time recalling past days we were together with my parents both in Hungary and in Australia.

It was their daughter, my cousin Anita who was sporty and excelled in fencing. She was a prize-winning cello player long before I started learning music. She was blonde straight hair, tall, slim, blue eyes, with fair skin exactly the opposite to me who was dark with curly hair, shorter, solid and had olive skin. She and her mother Klari used to call me *kis fekete* or little black.

I never expected to compete with the girl who resembled a Goddess and was never competitive anyway. Our friendship was cemented with our serviette collections among others from which we exchanged many. All lost with my youth.

Anita's sister Sylvi nicknamed affectionately *tucsok* (cicada) was born just after we left Hungary, and I met her for the first time when she was ten-year-old. She was most attractive, sweet, cheeky, and very likable. With the passing of the years the three of us grew close. And we shared all experiences that life dealt, including marriages, children, the loss of parents, and our cousin Gabi.

Cousins Sylvi, Anita, Gabor and I. 1966

Anita lost her daughter Brigita but still had Adam who bears a striking resemblance to her father, my uncle Gyula. During his roaming lifestyle Adam wrote several books and produced the beautiful Hannah to whom he is totally devoted. When he visited us in Australia, he toured the country while he spent time working on farms picking fruit. Anita's Brigita was always extremely bright, political and as a young woman was a determined achiever. Even when she became gravely ill, she travelled to lecture in many countries. Unfortunately, we had little contact with her children Emma and Aron who are quite exceptional from the reports I received over the years.

Hannah 2017

Adam's visit to Australia was followed by Sylvia's son Kristoff who also had some work experience as an architect in Sydney, although every visiting young relative worked dispatching Forbat garments for a short time. Sylvi's oldest Dora moved with her family to Finland and the children practically grew up there. Recently Sylivi's youngest, Fanni descended on us with her husband and three-year-old son.

Dora, Kristof and Fanni 2022

My cousin Sylvia visited Australia when her three lovely children presented her with a plane ticket for her 50th birthday. She claims that it was one of the most memorable experiences of her life, and she will say it on every occasion of our contact. That was in 2017, and today when we meet or speak, she still recalls those times warmly and with affection as we do.

Dora and family, Kristof and family, Fani and family 2023

My mother felt very close to her cousins Litzi Desiatnik and Irene Engel (nee Kellerman) in Australia who I came to call Aunt and their husbands Uncle. Originally, they were from Wien but fortunately left before 1939. Irene said they arrived with "a lift" which was a large container of household goods including furniture, linen and kitchenware. My mother's aunt *Tante Olga*, or *Die Mutter/Die Mamme*, moved between the home of her daughters until she moved to a Senior home where I last visited her with my parents. She was a lovely lady.

Peter's Bar Mitzvah 1961 – Back row: Ron, Peter, Robert, Uncle Walter, Harry.
Seated: Aunt Irene, Tante Olga, Aunt Litzi and Uncle Ernst

Aunt Litzi married the American Ernst Desiatnik who served in the US armed forces and sailed on the General Harry Taylor which was coincidentally the ship that transported us to Australia. Their son Ronald was born in the USA but obtained his Australian citizenship when he became a barrister or Queens Counsel. He gained a PhD in Law and wrote several textbooks among other contributions to the legal profession aside from teaching. Their second son Robert affectionately called *Bobby* excelled in languages and with particularly fluent French became a translator that included working in the United Nations. They both had families with who we sadly drifted apart.

It was the Engels, Aunt Irene and Uncle Walter, who guaranteed for our migration to Australia while we waited in Wien. They were true to their word. They rented a flat for us and helped my parents obtain work. Irene and Walter worked in their Ladieswear shop *Engels*. In summer they rented a house in Leura and took me along for a few years. I am grateful to Aunt Irene for much, such as giving me the opportunity to learn considerable German, and especially the swimming lessons. However, I am not grateful for her greeting me years later with, "You are fat," even though I was never thin. But she always said what was on her mind. I regret that that was her last conversation with me.

For fun, Peter discovered little acts to torment me. They were either not discovered by his parents or not believed by his parents. One fine day he threw my towel out the window of my room. By the time I discovered where it was, after a heavy downpour my towel was barely able to be lifted from its wet weight. Darling Peter was mischievous to say the least.

Probably the most memorable of his escapades was in Blackheath swimming pool where we had our lessons. Peter suggested a race and I agreed. However, Peter stopped unexpectedly. When I stopped, I could not stand down to touch the bottom of the pool, as we were at a very deep strip along the rail. I have not yet learned to swim and for I don't know how long but long, I was hovering between the bottom and the surface of the pool. I can still see me looking up at the water line of the pool's surface where I very nearly drowned.

Over the years we lost touch with Peter and his daughter Simone. He changed partners a number of times and we were never sure about his occupation. Harry on the other hand, was a different story. He was a first-year medical student when we arrived in Australia, and he affectionately called me '*Die Kleine*'. He became a pharmacist, joined the Australian army, and was responsible for all medical supplies nationwide. After he retired with the rank of Major, he continued the medicine supervision in Nursing Homes.

Leone, Harry E, me and my Harry 1980s

As a young man he married his love, a most wonderful lady from Brisbane. He and Leone have been happy in their loving relationship ever since and they have been enjoying their family of two daughters Bettina and Jodie, and their families. We visited them in Melbourne on various occasions. We are still communicating with them and because we share Harrys, when Leone and I write to each other, we refer to 'your Harry' and 'my Harry.'

Harry wrote his autobiography years ago. Recently Leone completed and published her neat slim volume of a biography, *Melody of Generations*. I thoroughly enjoyed reading it. It seems everyone is writing their life story, so I had better complete mine which has been a work in progress for far too long only to become a patchwork.

Budapest 1956
Back row: Tomy, Erno, Eva, Bela, Miksa
Front Row: Marika, Zsuzsi, Bozsi, Gabi, Nagymama, Kati, Ibolya, Agnes

Then there were the four Freund boys of my father's family, who were quite close to each other. Since money was scarce in their youth and they had one good suit, they often took turns wearing it. All the brothers were very good to their mother. However, the history of their youth is very vague as there was not much spoken about it.

Freund Laci who was the oldest perished in Siberia. A quiet and intelligent man, he was an inventor. Unfortunately, he did not patent his inventions, and though they became successful, he never benefitted from them. With wife Olga he had two daughters, Eva and Marti.

Marti was only about 12 years old and Eva a few years older when their parents were taken away. Apparently, Eva went to the railway station every day and waited for her parents to return. The girls were shifted from uncle to aunt to grandmother. Later Eva married Fritzi Fisch, and they had two sons Gabor or Gabi, and Tamas or Tomy. After the Hungarian revolution, courtesy of sister Marti, Eva, Fritzi and son Gabi were in Toronto, Canada where another son Tomy was born. But Eva insisted on returning to live in Budapest.

It was at a Toronto family celebration that I had a great time with Eva's Tomy and got to know his most hospitable family when we visited Hungary. From my cousin Marika I hear snippets about the life of Gabi and his family, with particular praise for his writing talent. Eva's sons are no longer boys, but grandfathers.

2022

Every time I visited Hungary, and for a long time it was every two years, it was the same routine of visiting all the cousins and aunt. I drove from one relative to another. In fact, that is all I did. And usually with some goodies such as chocolates, cigarettes and Smirnoff. The first and only time I saw the two sisters together was in 1998 at the 'cousins' reunion.'

At age 14 years, Marti emigrated to Toronto and later married Bill Lowy who was also a Holocaust Survivor. They had Debbie and Robert, who had two children each, Jordan and Jeremy, and Cassie and Jonah respectively.

Debbie, Jordan, Jeremy and Peter Sewell   Jonah, Ruth, Robert and Cassie Lowy

As a surprise, Harry and I went to Toronto in 2005 to Marti's 50th wedding anniversary. I presented her with a booklet that recorded most of our past shared experiences. At the celebration I read out only a summary. But I do believe that the document was welcomed.

Because I lived with Marti and her family for a longer period in 1973, we developed a special relationship which remained over the years. We are still in close contact although much of it is at a geographical distance. But memories of my stay with Marti are vivid and ever-present, and I am still attached to my cousin who is a very proud great grandmother.

As a child I had little contact with Erno except on the Sunday mornings when the three brothers were together, and I was the addendum. He married Erzsebet (nee Fischer) or *Bozsi*. They had Tamas or Tomi and Zsuzsi or Suzie. She was a good-looking lady, as was every member of her family. It may be said that that family had only beautiful looking women.

In 1956 Tomi left Hungary illegally while he was conscripted into the army. He happily tells the story of how he knew he crossed the border to Austria, when he saw a sign on which the writing was foreign. From sheer joy he promptly picked up the signpost and returned with it to the escaping group waiting to cross the border. Naturally he did not remember where he got it from. We next saw him in Australia, and later I was a bridesmaid at his wedding.

Sydney 2016

Tomi and I were never really close. He was considerably older just like Eva and moved in different circles. He had a pleasant nature with a constant smile on his face and always seemed happy. His favourite greeting was and is, "*Mi van?*" or "*What's up.*" Together with Magdi, they had a daughter Kathy who married Ron Geiser, and they had a daughter Jacqueline and twin boys Aron and Joshua. It is a shame that we saw them only on rare occasions even though the geographic distance did not prevent it.

Suzie who is seven months younger than me, was blonde and sweet and pretty. Just the opposite to me. When Zsuzsi and I were little, our grandmother looked after us on a couple of New Year's Eves when our parents celebrated together. She did look after Zsuzsi while her mother worked, and hence they had a closer relationship. She never looked after me and rarely came to our home. But the two families did spend some holidays together when we were little, and I know we were always much happier than in some photo images. Still, I think we were cute.

Zsuzsi met, deeply fell in love and married Alex. They had two lovely daughters Tina, and Michelle who married Mark. Zsuzsi is the happy grandmother to her "two boys" James and Thomas. We see each other more in our older age than ever before, never fail to reminisce about the past and always include the famous cousins' reunion.

I do believe that my father was closest to Bela. Perhaps Bela can best be described as a reserved person, but I always felt he liked me. Why, I do not know. He, my father, and I spent many Sunday mornings together. On a visit to Budapest when I saw him last, he gave me a Herend bonbonniere which I gave to his daughter to give to his grandson.

Bela was married to Ilonka (nee Vajda) and they had a daughter, my closest cousin Marika. Ilonka was a highly intelligent woman and liked to socialise. I remember little of her, but my mother thought highly of her. They spent many weekends with my mother's family in Ujpest before the war.

After Bela was liberated from Concentration Camp, he walked all the way home to Budapest as many did. Post war he was in a high Transport Ministerial position, and after they separated, Ilonka spent the rest of her life in the Far East. He married Kati, called the vamp (short for vampire) by my mother who never forgave her for allowing her stepdaughter to leave Hungary with an old night gown that had holes in it.

Marika and I have known each other for all of my life, and we have been close always. She was an attractive girl whose thick black plaits I always admired and to who I looked up. I distinctly remember that we spent holidays together, skipping and walking in the country, and that they were very happy times.

Ilonka, Marika and Bela c1952

My cousin made the courageous move at the age of 20 years to start a new life in Australia. She joined my parents and me in Wien and was with us in Korneuburg *Lager* and on the General Harry Taylor. Late in the afternoon on 25th June 1957 she walked down the gangplank, carrying her packed USA Navy canvas bag on her shoulder, same as the crew of the Navy ship.

The first few years in Australia were hard with no English language and no specific occupations. We saw each other frequently on weekends and whenever there was a family gathering. After a relatively short time, the independent Marika settled into several jobs and rented a flat on the North Shore. Not much later she was a lovely bride when my extremely happy and proud father gave her away to her wonderful husband Paul, in 1964.

Marika focused on her family ever since the two boys were born and she continues to be engaged closely with all matters concerning them and their families. Roby had three girls Liina, Jana, and Pia, and Tomy had Jacob and Asher. It seems to me, that our relationship and indeed our lives, revolved around our families. We celebrated the boys' birthdays and Bar Mitzvahs, their graduations, then their weddings, the births of their children and most of our anniversaries. Also, we took numerous trips together to fill our memories. Tomy and Richard did travel in Europe together, so they have their memories of their shared past journey. And, we have volumes of photographs that attest to all our lovely experiences together.

They say that life is a journey, and just as we journeyed together so did our children though not as often as we would have liked. When our five boys spent some time together, that was in the good old days when they were little. As they grew older, we stopped organising them, and they have met on rare occasions only. They did and do lead busy lives. But we still have the memories and the photos that reflect the times of yesteryears.

It was a rare occasion when some of the second cousins got together as in 1988. And even more so to organise most of the family members to meet in Bowral in 2009 for my Rony's engagement. To think that today, today being 2024, there are sixteen Australian third cousins, and a number overseas, some of whom have never met each other. As our South African friends say, "Shame."

I firmly believe that Marika was largely responsible for steering her sons to achieve and succeed in their profession as barristers. It was a most proud time for my cousin Marika when Rob took Silk, which replaced the title Queens Council. Sadly, Paul passed away shortly after his 80th birthday, before he could witness the event. However, he was surrounded by his family and particularly by all his grandchildren.

The Freund/Forbat cousins also ventured outside our adopted country. The most remembered and talked about trip was when Marika, Zsuzsi, Tina and I spent three and a half wonderful weeks driving around Italy from Rome to Firenze, then onto Venizia and Verona followed by Lake Como. In the process we adopted the Italian attitude of "*tranquillo*" and the adage, "if you can't beat them, join them". Italia had so much to offer and not only the Vino Rosso which never made us even tipsy although all meals were accompanied by her red wine. It was simply wonderful. And we accumulated a lot of memories of that journey. Later we flew to Budapest for the cousins' reunion which was a first. It is clearly etched in all our memories and forever talked about at our meetings.

The cousins' reunion 1998

In 2011 the Seabourn Pride landed us in St Petersburg and the Hermitage. What a great experience to view that which Catherine the Great has amassed for posterity. And we were witness to a most perfect and enjoyable Russian ballet performance at the Marinsky Theatre. We always delight in reminiscing about our cruising holidays and our overseas trips. But there is no place like home and Marika always enjoyed her stay in our Bowral home. We have her bed linen put aside especially for her. For her 80th birthday I presented her with a booklet. I thoroughly enjoyed all the time I spent putting it together with the multitude of photographs which for me are a wonderful reminder of our rich past.

From the time her Rob was born, Marika and I met weekly at lunchtime in her home as she lived close to where I worked. As the cliché from *Casablanca* states, it was "the beginning of a beautiful friendship". We discussed everything, shared intimate and not so intimate details in our conversations. The subjects included the children of course, friends and enemies, and the sad state of the world which continues to place daily unwelcome technological obstacles in our paths. None of that goes down well with my very smart cousin even with her wicked sense of humour.

That ritual of meeting regularly and frequently continued into our twilight years. Even today, we can talk sometimes literarily for hours. And on the phone sometimes into the early hours of the morning. I consider her my closest of relative.

How I met and married Harry in 1974 has been told many times and is well documented. It was four years after his father died and the family was still mourning the loss of a much-revered man. They always referred to him as *szegeny Lajos* or 'poor Lesley.' I never learned much about poor Lesley except that he was a tailor, the townspeople came to him for advice and that he had a good sense of humor. So, I thought of him as a wise funny man. When prompted about information about his father, Harry decided to write about him, and that led to his writing also about his mother Lilly and uncle Gyula.

The family of five members, *szegeny* Lajos, his wife Lilly, his brother Gyula known as Uncle or Batyu, sons Harry born in 1947 and Fedor born two years later, were from Tasnad, in the Transylvanian part of Romania. Tasnad, not to be confused with Tusnad the Spa resort, was not a place of which anyone had heard.

I visited Tasnad, as I wanted to see Harry's birthplace for myself. Well, our Vienna hired Mercedes took up the width of the main street of what I considered a village. Harry showed me a small house with a small gate where a horse drawn carriage would not have fitted, as opposed to the large house in which they were supposed to have lived according to legend. Harry must have taken me to the wrong house. But Tasnad has grown since, we know that.

Since only the youngest and the oldest sons of nine children survived the Holocaust, that is Uncle and the ill Lajos, Uncle always lived with the family. Uncle worked with Lajos and promised him to look after Lilly after his death, just as Lilly promised him that she will take care of Uncle. They both kept their word.

The Czeiger family history was recorded in detail by Harry in "*Recollections*" in 2017 for his 70th Birthday, as far as his memory allowed. Many parts were filled in by Lilly and Uncle who had an incredible short- and long-term memory for detail. From my perspective the Czeigers were excellent in-laws who had a wonderful relationship with my parents. Lilly and Uncle were particularly good to them when they were ill.

Lilly was a lovely lady who loved her family. She seemed to have been supported first by her mother, then her sister, then a cousin and friend in the Concentration camps and then her husband. She was considerably younger than her husband with whom she enjoyed over 25 years of a loving marriage.

In Tasnad, she had one maid to look after Harry and Fedor as babies, one to cook, one to clean and one to iron. She merely fed the boys and played with them. And she read a lot. It was a rude shock for her to have to look after family and do all the housework by herself after arriving in Australia.

As a Grandmother Lilly was wonderful. She loved her grandchildren, handled them very well and she played with them a lot. She looked after Richard and Roby till they were old enough to attend kindergarten. She only babysat once, but her house was always open to my children who considered it their second home. When they were old enough, they took the bus from school to their grandmother and stayed there till I collected them.

Then there were five grandchildren, my three sons and Fedor's Stevie and Natalie, who spent every Friday night at Lilly's place and most weekends together. There were so many birthdays and presents and the cakes that we all remember. Both Lilly and Uncle always had stocks of sweets in the kitchen pantry and hidden in the cupboards in their bedroom, but the boys knew where to find the goodies. Sadly, Lilly missed out on the marriages and lives of the grandchildren, and the great grandchildren.

Uncle worked hard and paid for their house in Murriverie Road, North Bondi within a few years. Later at my instigation, he purchased two units by paying the deposit and the rental income paid off most of the mortgage. After Lilly's death in 1990, rather than wait till he died, Uncle divided his estate between the Harry and Fedor. He was always a generous man.

Harry decided that once his uncle was alone, he was Harry's "responsibility." So, he renovated his inherited Bondi property in such a way that Uncle was at once living with us, he was not alone, and he was independent. That was his wish, and I think he was happy with the arrangement.

Because he was always a family-oriented man, Uncle was always overjoyed to see all the children, and took great pleasure in playing with them, especially when they were little. He was extremely generous to them on their birthdays. He cared very much for the great grandchildren, particularly for Riley who was born with a most rare disability needing very special treatment and equipment. One among the many was some gloves to protect her hand from chewed knuckles. At 97 years of age Uncle took out one of our antique sewing machines and made some gloves for Riley to her mother's specifications. He was always there for them and is missed.

When I first met Fedor, he was a nice-looking young man, attached to his family and a hard worker. Fedor was the brother-in-law for whom one should wish, and he deserves credit for many of his actions. On one occasion a carer poured tea down the back of my father's black and white Grundig television, and it died instantly. Since it was his only distraction and occupation, we needed it replaced quickly. I phoned Fedor who was always very much into electronic gadgets and within an hour he brought a colored TV to my father.

On another occasion Harry was overseas on one of his business trips and I was home alone with my three sons. One of the boys became sick with a very high temperature and he needed medicine. I phoned Fedor and he came straight away to pick up the doctor's prescription from the pharmacy.

And then there was the pièce de resistance. The story of *Forbat* has been told as was her one time of crisis. What was omitted was Fedor's rescue mission. Briefly, in December 1989, the then Westpac bank manager froze the business accounts when the company needed to borrow further finance to pay interest repayments. Consequently, the business came to a halt. But only for a day.

Fedor asked how much was needed to continue to function and immediately wrote out a cheque for $150,000.00 without any question or condition. At that time, that was a large sum. Well, it still is. The cheque was never used, but it certainly gave me a feeling of security. As it was not needed, I have written "cancelled" across the cheque with capital letters, but I have retained it to this day as evidence of Fedor's act of unquestioning and unforgettable generosity.

Fedor took Liz on their first date to our first wedding anniversary celebration at Hunter's Lodge. I do believe that Fedor wanted to get married, and that he was quite impressive with his blue convertible Cadillac. They were married six months later, and it was a lovely wedding. They had Stevie and two years later Natalie. She married Warren, a wonderful man, and they had three lovely boys Ryan, Cooper and Chase who all had their *Bar Mitzvahs* already.

It seems to me, that our relationship and indeed our lives, revolved around our family celebrations. We celebrated the children's birthdays and *Bar/t Mitzvahs*, then their weddings and the births of their children, and many trips together. What *Mitzvahs*. Both our photo collections exude thousands of images of the birthday dinners, presents and especially the times with Lilly's chocolate chestnut birthday cakes, whose recipe was lost to the world along with that of her soup both of which we loved and called orgasmic.

Our five children spent a lot of time together other than the Friday nights and birthdays. To name but a few, they swam together in our swimming pools when they were little. They had picnics together. They all walked into the Roscoe Street Synagogue on High Holy Days and made Lilly proud. They all went to the same Hillel kindergarten, and they shared a piano teacher. They also enjoyed Fedor's Lake Macquarie holiday home with all the water activities.

We celebrated many of our birthdays and anniversaries together. Liz always put a lot of thought and skill into her presents. Knowing how I treasure photographs, for our 30th anniversary, she went to much trouble selecting and arranging the photos in the windows of the wooden box with little photo albums inside it. It has been happily sitting on our coffee table in Bowral.

Natalie's Central Synagogue wedding was beautiful, and it was followed only a few years later by Rony's colourful wedding. That was special in that Fedor acted as *Shadchan* or matchmaker when he introduced to him the bike riding Jo. They were soulmates, though years later they separated. Other weddings followed and without consciously noticing, the family grew in numbers with the arrival of the grandchildren who are growing fast.

2004

2009

Fedor and family 2022

My attachment to family extends to Harry's extended family as his to mine. The Czeiger family tree branches are dense in Israel and reach out to North America. I had the pleasure of meeting all the relatives Harry met on his 1973 tour. It was then that we were both in the same suburb in Toronto, when he was visiting his cousin and I was visiting mine, before he and I knew each other.

Over the years we spent considerable time with Harry's second cousins particularly the Toronto Kleins and the San Diego Geroes. I have exchanged many letters and photographs over the decades with the two lovely ladies Dora Klein and Zsuzsi Geroe.

Much like three brothers Harry and Fedor grew up in Tasnad with Robi Klein who emigrated to South America and later moved with wife Dora to Canada. They settled in Toronto and after a short time his mother Ilonka, who was Uncle's cousin, and Dora's whole family joined them. Robi visited us in 2002, and Dora was present at our Roby's wedding in 2010 in Australia.

Zsuzsi was from Oradea Romania and her husband John Geroe from Hungary, before they settled in San Diego. She did extensive research into her family history which she published. She also translated her aunt's poems. Both Zsuzsi and Dora speak a number of languages, are teachers and enjoyed the long letters attached to all my photographs I sent to them as the children were growing up. Dora still insists she misses my letters. I treasure our very special relationships, even though I became rather slack in my communiques.

Klein Clan 2024

Of course, Harry keeps in touch regularly with all the relatives including mine. We spent many enjoyable days with them all.

The 'reluctant Centenarian' Uncle Julius with great grandchildren at his 100th Birthday 2021

Geroe 2018

I was brought up in the family way. That is to say, family has always been important to me. Naturally, feeling close to my family members, I have always been honest with them. Through the years that has led to a number of unintentional offenses for which I have apologised. If truth be known, I have great difficulty with nontruths. But what is true is that I have always felt an inexorable attachment to all my family and continue to do so.

"There is nothing either good or bad, but thinking makes it so."

William Shakespeare

Chapter Fifteen

FRIENDS - PART 1

"The friends thou hast ...
grapple them to thy soul with hoops of steel ..."

William Shakespeare

The line between good acquaintances and friends is blurred. Since we have a lot of both, we don't need to categorise them. We merely value them and appreciate our relationships with them. We can even bundle our relatively newly acquired in-laws in there somewhere as we had some very lovely experiences with all of them in Australia and in England. In the past, some of our business acquaintances became our friends. Hence, there are all too many to mention.

We have kept all our friends. Life does interfere in the frequency of our meetings. However, even if we have drifted apart in the years that passed, whenever we came together it was as if time stood still, and we continued where we left off. Our relationships remained the same, enduring. As Marika L said, "I somehow feel that you are family…a deep connection."

The Gals were my parents' best friends. Their friendship lasted for over forty years till my parents' death, after which my relationship with the family continued. The Gals were more than friends. They were considered part of our extended family.

My father and Andi met in their twenties when both were apprentices in menswear shops. My father often spoke of how much he learnt at *Hertzeg es Fodor* and later at Andi's family haberdashery business.

They were friends before they were together in Forced Labor Camps about which they spoke often, but we as children remember only fragments. Only three survived with Andi out of the original 1000 inmates.

Gal Andi (top left) and Freund Misi,
my father (top right) c 1943

The thin little woman Szabo Kati *neni*, and her jolly tall rotund husband hid the Gals, my mother and many others. There were periods when their one room flat in what was a predominantly Jewish area that was known as *Chicago* contained up to nineteen Jews. While in Hungary, I often visited Szabo Kati *neni* with my mother. They should have been inscribed in the book of Righteous among the Nations.

Gal Kati was a lady. She was a quietly spoken, gentle and religious woman, who blessed me every time she saw me, which was quite often. I received a pendant from her when I was very young and being very young, I chewed on it much of the time. Since I wore it every day till my twenties, the enamel rubbed off the Raphael cherub on one side and the writing on the other. But I can still make out the words: *Isten vedjen*, or G-d protect you.

On one occasion, Kati asked me to go for a dress fitting. She told me that the elegant three-piece checked outfit from the exclusive children's dressmaker *Kellen Marta* in Budapest, was to be a surprise for "a girl who was just my size." That was the present for my fifth birthday, from this most generous lady. I wore that skirt with its matching top for many years.

Kati's Check Skirt 1953

All my birthday presents from Kati were extravagant and beautiful. Later in Australia, every year on my birthday a box attractively wrapped in cellophane and tied with a colorful ribbon waited for me when I arrived home. In it there was always some small valuable gift together with a carefully selected lovely card, written with her beautiful even pearl hand and heartfelt words.

The Gals' oldest son, the bright and attractive Tamas, succumbed to fumes from a heater at age three. A terrible punishment for parents with which they had to live all their lives. According to what I remember being told, the two sets of parents assumed that he was to be my future husband.

Tamas

Johny was born two years after me. For the first few years he did not speak. One day when the Gals came to visit and from the courtyard, they called to us on the first floor as was their custom. There was little Johnny about three years old, in his white shoes and white knee-high socks, and he shouted the two syllables, "Ag-gi." My name. That was the beginning of his perfectly fluent language which was good enough to hold the doctorial position of university lecturer to date.

Two years after Johnny, Steven was born. He was always a sweet smiling boy. The brothers were always close and very well behaved. When they came to our home, the two young men always looked at their mother for permission to have a second slice of cake. But Kati usually nodded her agreement with a smile.

Then came the 1956 Revolution when there was a mass exodus by Jews, and my parents and I left illegally. That was traumatic for both Kati and my mother. For many weeks and months there was correspondence between my parents in Australia and the Gals in Hungary about the pros and cons of emigration, until they arrived in Australia legally.

Although the friendship between our parents continued, Johnny and I were more like cousins, and moved in different social circles. But we always came together to celebrate special occasions, and our spouses were welcomed into our extended family. Johnny found Judy who was and is very much like his mother Kati; quiet, considerate, and caring. In 1973 I was absent from their wedding as I was overseas husband hunting. But over fifty years later, the marriage is as good as it was at the beginning.

The Gals 90th birthday celebration

And then along came the intelligent and talented blonde David. He was a cute little boy, adored by his parents and grandparents, and like all children, grew up too quickly. He married lovely Mel who we may not know very well, except that they are happy together and with their Jacob who brings no end of joy to Johnny and Judy.

Coincidentally, the relationship with the extended Gal family continued to the third generation in an indirect way. Johnny's cousin Mary and husband Robert's son Alex is one of the *trio of friends* of my son Roby at Sydney Grammar School.

The Family 1994
***

My very first friend was Kertai Juli in Budapest. She was my best friend for three years. Strangely enough I did not stay in touch with her after we left Budapest, yet I continued my relationship with my cousin Anita through correspondence. And I did have some very good acquaintances along the way.

It was in first year High School that I met a new friend who was coincidentally also an Agnes and coincidentally also a newly arrived Hungarian migrant. She had curly hair also, slightly protruding front teeth, was intelligent and rather artistic. We composed a poem together about puppies. It was not a very good or memorable one, despite the fact that she was very creative, even kind of Bohemian.

Agnes relished speaking Hungarian as most newcomers did revert to speaking their mother's tongue, and many emigrants still do. She must have been well indoctrinated in the communist system not to speak about Jews or other religions in public because she had replacement words for them; Jews were '*radios*,' and non-Jews were '*gramophonos*,' so a stranger would not understand to what she was referring. The distinction made little difference in our school, where nearly 50% of the girls were Jewish and with European backgrounds. I did not experience anti-Semitism at all, though once or twice I was called a "bloody foreigner." That left no mark on me.

In second and third year my best friend was another Hungarian girl called Ninocska or Nina. I called her by the endearing name of Ratty because I liked that endearing character Rat in *Wind in the Willows*. She was a very mature girl for her age, very bright and had a much better command of English than I. She seemed worldly and compared to her I must have been a rather naïve young girl.

She too worked after school and on weekends in her father's shop in which she started full time after she obtained the School Certificate at the end of third year. So, we had a lot in common. In hindsight I am very grateful when at 14 years of age she allowed me to invite myself to her family party which was my very first adult social outing. And the gentleman Benedek made it memorable.

In senior high school, the Romanian Rosemary or Rory and I gravitated towards each other. We were both newcomers to Australia. Early in our relationship I failed to keep an appointment we made to meet at Bondi Baths. There was a family *Bar Mitzvah*. When it was too late to meet her, and I was unable to contact her, I felt a tremendous amount of guilt.

I apologised profusely but that did not pacify her or her family, until her parents met my parents and me. Then our friendship was cemented, especially when in school we sat together in the last row in the corner seat in the classroom where we could not be seen smoking.

We were friends long after school even though she moved to the other side of the Harbour Bridge. Sometime later, Rory married Milton, and I was one of her bridesmaids. They are still together having had two children and their retired lifestyle consisted of spending considerable time travelling. She and I still meet and each time we continue where we left off previously. Rory has not changed.

Perhaps the reason why I had close friendships with one girl per year was that DHGHS was rather cliquey, and the girls did not accept us into their circle due to our lack of good English language or our accent, and also due to our low socio-economic status. It may have been because they all had serious boyfriends who they eventually married and we posed a threat, although we were already in relationships too. Naturally, at our reunions all was denied by the other girls.

***

At university Elizabeth was my best friend, of Polish origin, she arrived in Australia in the early 1960s. Since she was educated in an all-girls Boarding School with rather limited experiences, she was rather naïve as far as boys were concerned. Not that I was so experienced since my life was rather a sheltered one too. I had to explain most of the punch lines of jokes to her.

At one of the Hillel Graduate meetings, while not thinking about matchmaking, I introduced my friend Elizabeth to a Max. They seemed a most unlikely pair, she a gregarious extravert and he a calm introvert. But they became attached and married. I was a bridesmaid at their wedding and met many of their family and good friends. And she didn't even have to change her initials.

When Harry and I were invited to one of their dinner parties, all the men were solicitors bar one who just then was appointed as the youngest Magistrate in NSW. In those days dinner started around eight o'clock. It was all very pleasant but around ten o'clock Harry was ready to leave. He stood up, I shook my head, he turned and sat down at the piano and began to play. The party continued and lasted very pleasantly well into the late night. We shared special occasions, and most recently and most happily we celebrated Max's 80th birthday with their family and friends. Elizabeth and Max or Maxwell as she always called him, continued to be our friends even after he became our solicitor, despite the fact that I did not like mixing business with friendship.

***

Similarly, we have remained friends with Barbara and Ray ever since Barbara opened her Anywhere Travel agency. And we still travel with her. I recall first meeting Barbara at her engagement party which I attended with my then fiancé. I thought her fiancé Ray was very happy and very much in love with Barbara and still is. How nice for Barb. She and I went to the same school though I did not remember her. Harry on the other hand has known her since he had some business contact with her father.

I next met Barbara when we were ladies in waiting at our Obstetrician Dr Kovacs. She was three months ahead in her first pregnancy and two years later we were ladies in waiting again when she was three months ahead in her second pregnancy. And we met again later through our boys at Hillel kindergarten and then at Sydney Grammar School.

Barbara and Ray are a most hospitable couple. As with our friends we spent many occasions together including all the celebrations for birthdays, anniversaries and such. As Barbara was and is a great organiser, once she organised a picnic lunch for a group of friends and their children. And to occupy the sporting boys, cricket was on the menu. So, when Daniel batted, the ball mistook Harry's shin for the wicket, caused a clot and weeks of incapacity.

When Barbara organised a Caribbean cruise for the four of us, it was a *tour de force* cruise to be remembered. The islands were most incredible as was the ship's treatment with champagne and canapes served at the water's edge when in port. And there was that unforgettable flight affair when we were piloted by Ray. And our friendship still continues.

***

Our friends Lynda and David introduced us to another of their friends originally from South Africa. It was about the time when John and Marilyn moved into their home with their two daughters Misty and Mandy, and Mother Millie a few houses down the street from us in North Bondi. Their attractive and most useful presents are sprinkled throughout our homes.

When I am thinking of them, I reflect on times spent with them, and whether or not I have returned their generosity. Early in our relationship we celebrated an anniversary, and they surprised us with two large aqua bath sheets which were such good quality that I still use them after more than thirty years. So, on most mornings, I quietly thank Marilyn and hope that it will continue to last as our friendship.

John is a rather large man well over six feet in height while Marilyn is a small petit woman. Although they look rather an odd couple, they are not odd but rather lovely people. John studied law but only practised for one year. He then went into jewellery retail, which with a partner expanded from 2 to 52 retail stores. Left retail and took over a diamond-cutting operation. At the same time, he became involved in engineering.

Over the past 38 years he has built gas-fired power stations in WA, maintained and updated other power stations, and built 4 of the world's desalination plants together with many other water and effluent treatment plants. John holds a PhD in hydromechanical engineering. He said he learned more from bush mechanics who had to make the plant work with a minimum of spares than he learned from university. A privilege to have him call me his friend.

Besides being an animal friend, Marilyn has green fingers and is particularly artistic. She paints beautifully and is rather crafty as illustrated by the glossy decoupage finished wooden box she gave me. I also have little gift reminders from her generous Mum Millie.

For the last few years John and Marilyn have enjoyed living on the water in the Central Coast. It is a few hours from us and when we do visit, we are always treated to a delicious lunch usually involving seafood. It is a pleasure to see them even if we would like to see our friends more often than we do now. As Marilyn says, "shame."

***

Ernie Friedlander OAM was one of our business associates who became a friend and more. Early our relationship was much like adopted brother and sister as we were both only children. Also, because Ernie looked to my father as a father figure and my father treated him like a son. For my 21st birthday, Ernie gave me a lovely brooch with three small aqua stones, which I treasured as it was my first and only one for a long time.

Ernie started working as a salesperson in my parents' business. In a short time, he proved himself to be an honest, hardworking, and responsible person. In a relatively short time, my father offered him a one third share of the Forbat company.

The personal relationship between the two families was a close one. The Friedlanders were invited to all family functions and vice versa. We celebrated Ernie's engagement to Leah and their wedding, and the arrival of each of their three bright and truly attractive children. Ernie and my parents also shared subscriptions to the Opera House and membership in *B'nai B'rith Lodge* where Ernie is still making a difference. Hence the accolades.

Leah, Ernie, my parents and I, 1963

That relationship with my parents continued till 1975, when both my parents became ill. When Ernie and Leah, and Harry and I became equal partners based on the terms set down by my father for the partnership, our personal and social relationship became even closer. Ernie and family were present at most of my children's birthdays when they were little and some when they were more grown. They were present at Bar Mitzvahs and weddings and many other family functions. After all, Ernie is my son Roby's G-d father.

Ernie and Leah introduced us to Berida Manor in Bowral in the Southern Highlands. We spent extended weekends there with them a few times in the year. It was our only true holiday. And oh joy, without children. And oh joy, later we built our house there in Bowral. Ernie and Leah are still present in our lives.

***

Ms Ita Buttrose AC, OBE, journalist, editor, publisher, author, television and radio personality, ABC Network chairperson of late, and more was also a business associate who became a friend. It started in 1992 when Harry contacted Ms Buttrose about manufacturing her fashion label. And so, *Ita's Collection* was created and promoted in her magazine *Ita* as well as in other magazines. Her clothes were good quality, easy care and wear, and relatively inexpensive. In short, a successful collection, which she herself promoted even in New Zealand. But when the magazine *ITA* closed, so did her collection. It seemed that the two were associated with each other in people's minds. Shame.

However, our relationship continued. Ita opened our Fashion Stop fashion outlet and involved us in a number of fundraising functions. We were at family events such as Kate's wedding. Ita was at our 25th wedding anniversary and over the years we enjoyed many meals together. We were present when Ita moved to the Southern Highlands where she edited the magazine *Highlife* for a couple of years and featured Ron on the page of a man, his Ute and his dog.

We were included in her writings. In her 2002 publication of *A Passionate Life* Ita writes about Harry's proposal for her collection. For her 2005 co-authored publication of *Motherguilt*, Richard and I were interviewed. Afterwards, guilt was much discussed, but I would have to reread the transcript to be able to comment on whether or not I claim any guilt. We had a very pleasant association and special friendship with the lady.

***

Margaret Carter was someone we met through our contact with Woollahra Council. She was the Alderperson who swayed the alderpersons to reject our neighbour's objection to the proposed white paint on the outside of our building. A highly intelligent, well-read person, who loved the arts.

Maggie, as she was known to her friends, began her career as a QANTAS Stewardess. Do not snicker. In those days the ladies had to have special qualifications. The first requirement was a Bachelor of Arts degree and the second was a certificate from the June Dally-Watkins etiquette and deportment school.

She spent considerable time at ABC, working with overseas guest artists who she met and accompanied in Australia. She name dropped over the many years we knew her and the colourful experiences they all had together. Danny Kaye who she escorted in Sydney comes to mind because I was at an incredible studio taping of one of his 1966 shows in Los Angeles.

We decided to join Maggie on a couple of her travels. One was the Adelaide Festival followed by a two-day Indian Pacific journey to Perth with one brief stopover at Coolgardie, a kind of one-horse town but with a lively red-light district. I found the whole trip delightful and the dry repetitious Australian landscape most interesting. It was just like one of our paintings of that region. Arid. But Margaret River with its vineyards was a true contrast and we enjoyed all that it offered including the private concert by Anna the Russian pianist at the Leeuwin Estate.

Our next trip with Maggie was to Europe. It was a musical one, a tour lead by Christopher Lawrence musician, broadcaster at ABC national, later at BBC, with a wealth of knowledge and a most companionable gent. We were also accompanied by then governor of NSW Dr Marie Bashir, who is not only a violinist and a psychiatrist with numerous accolades but a most pleasant personality. And all on the tour were so totally overwhelmed by the experience of visiting *Auschwitz* that there was silence on the bus for hours. Much later, only one person spoke, and all Marie Bashir could say was, "Oh, the children. Oh, the children."

The highlight of the musical adventure was the last stop in Prague. It was New Year's Eve 2004, and the program was Mozart's Don Giovanni which was first performed on stage in Prague. With the help of some intermittent snacks our performance was stretched out till midnight, at which time there were fireworks on the roof of the Opera House and the orchestra returned to play Big Band style music for the audience to dance on stage. It was a unique experience and another memorable one with our friend Maggie.

***

The Southern Highlands had a certain attraction for Sydney people. Ita moved to Bowral and Maggie moved to Bundanoon for a time, but eventually they both moved back to Sydney. Another person who seemed to have followed us to the Highlands was Harold, who is an intelligent and articulate man with an exciting and colourful background in journalism and broadcasting. He has been writing corporate histories and his biography of late.

We first met Harold in Sydney through Agnes whose two daughters were at the same Hillel kindergarten as our boys. Once we were at her Nicki's wedding. Many times, our Roby transported her Karen to Oatley campus of the university that they both had attended. And we had many pleasant dinners with Harold and Agnes.

Harold's Bellevue Hill home was exchanged for a Burradoo property that Harold and new partner Sam took great pleasure in renovating. Harry showed interest in the building works and over the years had some minor business dealing with Harold that ended swiftly. Shortly after Sam left Australia, Harold returned to Sydney, only to move later to Cairns to marry his Sigy. But we still have frequent contact with him.

***

When we moved to the Southern Highlands, it happened frequently that Harry went to town and phoned to say he is coming home shortly with some friends. Once when I opened the front door, recognized, and greeted our friend Dr Paul, and saw our Maltese Shih Tzu dog called Brandy being cuddled by a lady. Harry announced that, "This is Brandy." I replied, "I know Paul and the dog, but what is the lady's name?" Well, it was Brenda but because they knew each other from their youth, the lady was nicknamed Brandy by Harry and his brother. I still call her Brenda.

Paul has many interests. He is well informed of world events, likes classical music, and plays piano and guitar. He is a very active sports person, who plays golf and tennis regularly and frequently. He also skis and recently ventured on a motorcycle expedition in outback Mongolia. And he loves to engage in debates. Although it was during Paul's marriage to Brenda that our friendship developed, we knew him from the time when our youngest son was best friends with his son in kindergarten and then in Primary School. Rony spent a lot of time at their home after school and I was told by the babysitter that she liked having him as a calming influence.

Harry has been playing golf regularly with a group who happen to be doctors, and I seem to have had some association with some of them. Hence it is not six degrees of separation. It is less. One is Adam who I knew when I worked at King George V. Another is Sam, a South African man whose wife Eva is in my book club. Eva is a very bright artistic lady, very widely read and a great asset to our book discussions.

Sam is simply a lovely man who was most concerned about my health when I had medical problems and was very helpful with extra information mostly to put Harry's mind at ease. But he is a genuinely caring person. I don't know if he is the oldest in the group that Harry refers to as "the boys." And it is always nice to catch up with the "boys" and their better halves when busy schedules permit.

***

It was Susan who introduced us to the Southern Highland Jewish Community, where we met some new friends. Susan was a temporary Bowral resident while she was selling winter woollen coats to the locals. Since her business became successful, she closed her Sydney *Hers and Mine* shop, sold her Sydney home and established herself in Bowral permanently.

Many people move from city to the country. Some like Carol and Eli who have travelled far in Australia and even further overseas, have returned to the Highlands more than once. Our more recent friends Brigitte and Charley who also regularly travel between their Sydney and Bowral homes have become our cruising as well as Rummy Cubes playing friends.

One couple stands out from when we first joined SHJC. And Dr Peter Spitzer was an outstanding person. He was a General Practitioner in Bowral and just returned from his overseas trip as a Churchill Fellow. He was the only medically qualified Clown Doctor in Australia who started the Clown Doctors with his wife Judy. All other clown doctors were professional performers trained by Dr Spitzer. The history of the clown doctors is documented in the Humour Foundation which is the current organisation for clown doctors.

Peter was quite a character when he appeared everywhere as Dr Fruitloops with his red nose, flat green golf hat, smiley stick, and of course with his rubber chicken. He was always ready to entertain and to create a happy atmosphere wherever he went.

Judy and Peter welcomed us into the community and into their family. Whether it was burning off garden refuse at his home, or dancing at New Year's Eve at our place, or driving north to Port Douglas, it was always lovely to spend time with them. And Peter never let an opportunity pass without humour such as the unexpected shower of colour at our Ron's wedding. He was a lovely warm human being and one who deserves to be called a *mensch*. Peter was a good friend who is sadly missed especially by Harry even today after many years.

The amount of space each of our friends and close acquaintances occupy in these pages is not commensurate with the extent of our friendship. There are many more, too many to mention and too good just to list. And our feelings are present for all our friends whenever they may appear.

To me fair friend you can never be old.

Shakespeare

Chapter Sixteen

FRIENDS - PART 2

> *"A friend is one who knows you and loves you just the same."*
>
> Elbert Hubbard

Phillipa and Trish were colleagues of mine at Royal Prince Alfred Hospital in Camperdown in Sydney. However long our working association was, it is as friends that we have remained. I have often written to Phillipa, especially during Covid and following years.

And it was around then that the warm and sweet smell of toasted bread wafted into my pleasant memories of my stay in Goulburn. My placement was after Phillipa, who was a hard act to follow. We often talked about how different our backgrounds were, she a true blue Australian and I a Hungarian born ex-refugee. So once again I am reminded of our past as I wrote to her of our friendship of over 50 years.

My Dear Phillipa,   *29 September 2021*

We met in 1970 at Royal Prince Alfred Hospital where we shared an office. Within a few months we had a nice working relationship that grew into a nice friendship. I was not quite 24 years old and later, much later I found out that you were a few years older than me. Perhaps mentally and emotionally yes, but physically you never appeared so. On the contrary, especially now that you have reached the milestone of four-score years, and you are very much a most admirable sprightly lady.

When my turn came for the period of about three- or four-months placement in Goulburn Base Hospital, I followed in your footsteps as best I could. I delivered Meals-on-Wheels, I attended the AA meetings for the first time in my life and cleaned the house of the blind lady with diabetes and other ailments. But you set a very high standard, and everyone missed your genuine empathy and committed presence.

A few years later I got married, stopped working as a Social Worker due to certain family commitments and you continued to leave your indelible mark on countless people's lives. When you retired from Social Work, you continued to do good work. You volunteered, helped and left more of your footprints. You still do. When we closed our factory and I retired, I continued to do some administrative work. That is the main difference between us. You made a difference whereas I left no mark whatsoever. ...

You proved your capacity for caring and support when my fiancé of one night broke up with me over the phone. I was sitting facing the window with my back to you and I just sat there in silence. I was lost for words. But you were there, and you just sat behind me, feeling with me silently. So, if I didn't thank you then, I thank you now.

When you came to visit during my term, we had a picnic with chicken and wine in some tall grass somewhere near Ulludulla on the coast, where the sea gulls threatened. Then we spent a weekend further south, where I drove you to morning Mass at six in the morning and evening Mass at six in the evening. And except for those early mornings, that was fine, as our religious difference was not only never an issue, but it also never came up to affect our relationship. Nothing ever did.

You know that Trish and I had a history together outside the RPAH Social Work department. It included the children when they were little. Trish's daughter Tashi and my son Richard were born around the same time, and they even lay together once when they were about four months old.

Trish and I differed considerably in our outlook. One instance was that for many months she carried the baby Tashi in a Wrap on her front, even while doing such housework as vacuuming. She was a firm believer in that her newborn should continue to feel her mother's heartbeat. I, on the other hand, was a firm believer in lying my sons squarely on their backs in their cot and leaving them alone to sleep to grow. Our religious histories also came into some discussions in our relationship.

Over the years we had family outings and many pleasant dinners with Trish and Gary, including the ones in their home. Unlike me, Trish liked to cook dinner herself, and she did so while we were waiting. And waiting. She always started after we arrived and sometimes, we started our meals quite late. But that was because we always talked a lot. Or I did.

We also celebrated together. Ingrid's wedding was very special indeed. Traditionally Sicilian in every aspect with horse drawn carriage and Sicilian Renaissance costume. The ceremony was in a charming small Chapel followed by a colorful and musical reception in an orange orchard. When Harry narrates the event, he invariably embellishes it with some characters with guns much like in the film "The Godfather." I saw none as we drove around the whole island, although the first dark night was rather eerie.

But to return to another history. One day at RPAH you said that you would love to go overseas but could not afford it. You said that you could never save enough money. I offered to help. So, I took your salary, dealt out enough of your money for you to live on and banked the rest.

Sounds harsh and domineering. However, by early 1973, I accumulated a sufficient sum for you to purchase your return ticket and have some spare. You organized accommodation with some friends in Kensington, London and then we spent that short but most memorable time on the Island of Kerkyra (Corfu.) A mere 12 days but it felt and still feels as if it was much longer, probably because we filled every day with some exciting outing. And I shall never return to the island, so that my memories may remain intact and unaltered by all the changes caused by time.

Just yesterday I accidentally caught the last episode of Lawrence Durrell's "The Durrells." How wonderful it must have been to have lived on that island in that time when it still maintained that certain nativity, the tail end of which we experienced when we were there. It was just fantastic, and so is the memory which is the most vivid in my mind and a favorite of my overseas trips.

Remember the Pensione with four rooms where we stayed and where the owners who lived on top of the mountain served those delicious fresh Continental breakfasts on the veranda of our villa? Remember the glorious transparent aqua color of the Aegean Sea? Remember the very small Fiat in which we drove around the island? Remember the Church at Paleokastrisa, a name that took me ages to learn to pronounce?

It was on Kerkyra that I hitch-hiked once and only once in my life. And it was on Kerkyra that I danced on a table once and only once in my life. You know, I can't quite remember that. Then there was the Sunday cricket match in the center of the island. Your brother took part in it. These are all fond memories and will continue to treasure them.

The poor black and white images I took with my Minox spy camera are the only photos I have of my first overseas trip with my parents and of our time in Corfu. But they do recall the events and therefore they are very precious.

The year after our Greek Island journey, I got married, stopped working as a Social Work, had three children and got lost in their lives and in our business. Harry and I marked special occasions such as birthdays, anniversaries, and weddings, and you and Trish were there to celebrate them with us. We met regularly if not frequently, many times with our friend Trish and although our preoccupations were and are different, we managed to share each other's experiences, you more than I because you are such a good listener, and I talk too much.

For a good many years now, we shared living in the mountains, you in the Blue Mountains and I in the Southern Highlands. It is a wonderful lifestyle, and I am glad that we have this experience. It also lent itself to restrictions such as Pandemics very nicely thank you. Covid, and now the new strains that have 'done us in', have done us literally indoors. We settled into a way of enjoying the activities for which we had little time in the past, such as reading, listening to music, watching movies at random and you have the additional talent for painting. All sheer pleasures for content persons.

I end by saying that it was nice and easy talking to you, even if it was not the same as talking with you. But either way, I always feel free to be honest without having the need to reform the words that speak the truth. Thank you, my dear friend. Take care, stay well and safe, love a

To our Friend Lynda on the occasion of one of her birthdays, I compiled a booklet that was something like the composite of our shared lives from when we first met. Some things have changed but distant as our relationship may be due to the distance from Sydney and Bowral where we are, to Sanctuary Cove where she is, our friendship still continues.

Corbett Garden, Bowral 2017

My dear Lynda!

Our relationship has been a lengthy one, and perhaps the occasion of this special birthday is appropriate for me to document some of the times we had shared. Friends are hard to find and even harder to keep. But through thick and thin, we had remained friends for well over 40 years. Most of our experiences centred on our families, the children, celebrations of birthdays, anniversaries, and other significant events, as well as houses and homes.

You, Harry and I met in August 1974 at my wedding of which my parents dreamt for their only daughter. As all the staff were invited you were there also as our salesman's, Peter Gero's wife. You gave us a lovely porcelain duck which is perched in my China cabinet, still ready to take flight. Over the years, you gave us a number of ducks, which were amongst other very generous gifts you bestowed upon us, such as the cane lounge suite for the Rumpus room in our last house. In our photo album, you are happily dancing at the wedding.

Lynda (rt corner) August 1974   Duck

In the late 1970s we spent numerous days on weekends by your pool side in March Street, or at ours in Vaucluse. You were always ready to invite and entertain our friends in your home, whether or not they reciprocated.

Tuesday evenings at Czeigers at Vaucluse Road 1978

We had a weekly routine. Every Tuesday night we played cards, initially Canasta and later Bridge when you and Peter came to our place. We were social players, hence they were always very friendly games; they were, as Leah would say, "a bid and a giggle." And the games went on for decades and at times some friends like Yvonne joined us. We still have a weekly routine, but now it is for dinner and usually at 21 Espresso restaurant.

During that period there were the birthday parties for our boys and your girls who were always there together with Ernie's, amidst our family and friends.

Harry was occupied with running our *Forbat Styles* business and building our house, when he embarked on another venture. It was a children's range manufactured with his uncle Julius, under the label '*Uncles*'. They were most attractive clothes, and your Dannie and Richard looked lovely in them. Although they were both shy at the beginning, they had real fun at the photo shoot in 1979.

After you married David Sharrat, there were our birthday celebrations, yours, David's, Harry's and mine. I think we took more photos at mine, and I feel very honoured to have immortalised our friendship. My 40th birthday was a surprise event organised very secretly by Harry and Liz. We had a back room at the Coachman restaurant in Surry Hills all to ourselves. It was a very happy occasion, and all went very well, until the main course. Only one meal never arrived. It was David's. And none of us have forgotten it. I am sorry. That was followed by Harry's 40th birthday at Hunters' Lodge with another duck from you.

For Harry's 60th birthday, you presented him with a painting. You knew we did everything in threes because of our three sons. So, your painting of a large brown bear with her three cubs, using a brush with a single hair took over six months. It was and is appreciated as a unique piece of your art.

As the years go by, some memory tends to go too. I cannot remember the occasion or the place. However, we were together with you and our mutual friends Marilyn and John, and Barbara and Ray, for another lovely dinner with plenty of good food and wine. It must have been enjoyable because of all the smiles. Over the years, there were many such evenings. And I cannot remember an unenjoyable evening with any of our friends.

One of my birthdays was celebrated at Catalina on the water in Rose Bay. If the wonderful venue were not enough, I was very surprised by a Hummel figurine planted on a lovely chocolate cake. You can see my surprise. For another one of my birthdays, there was a leisurely lunch held at Pier 1. The venue was no longer the Fun Fair of old, but we had the view of colourful sails on Sydney Harbour in 2000.

As the decades pass in our lives, we mark the milestones with more celebration of food and wine. My 60th birthday was celebrated with our immediate family and you of course, at one of the most up-market restaurants, the Aria which faces the Opera House and the Harbour Bridge. I have never sent back wine but on that occasion, I did when I noticed that the expensive  brew ordered was off and felt fine about it. The following year was our friend Harold's 70th birthday held at his home in Burradoo. We had fun led by our friend Dr Fruitloops, the one and only original Clown Doctor.

Then there was the big celebration when your David turned 80 years of age. Pink Salt in Double Bay was dressed in flowers, and ribbons and bows of pink, only missing the buttons. Wonderful atmosphere, plenty of drink and good food. Not to speak of the great speeches by you and the family. The beauty of it all was the presence of all the children and their children. What more can a young man of four score years want? It was a lovely party.

Pink Salt, Double Bay May 2010

There were anniversaries too. Our 10th wedding anniversary was held at the Hunters Lodge which was one of the very few places where one could dine, wine and also dance. And we also danced on our 25th anniversary at Bondi Beach at Danny's which unfortunately is no longer. Our 30th anniversary was celebrated in the Hunter Valley. We had dinner on Friday night, toured the vineyards to taste different wines, some cheese and chocolate on Saturday by bus, and later danced the night away with décor by Dr Fruitloops himself.

Of course, you are famous for your homes. You and David have been 'doing up houses' since you have been together. A way of life and a way of earning a living to be sure. You have bought, renovated, decorated and sold well over 20 stunning homes in the Eastern Suburbs of Sydney with the exception of Clontarf and the weekenders, and there was one in England, which is another story.

Vaucluse 1988, Burradoo and Dorking, England 1989

Over their history, the styles of the houses have changed from your English influence towards more modern designs, although some of the furnishings have lasted from way back, with the Lynda signature on all décor. The gardens themselves were always blooming and blossoming in their green glory as everything you touch thrives. All I can say is that the lady has style as well as talent.

For special occasions, you were always ready to open your home to your friends and you were always a most gracious hostess. Just before her wedding, together with her family and friends, Mandy enjoyed the shower tea you arranged in your home in The Crescent.

The Crescent 1993

It was a tradition for many years, that Boxing Day was held at your home. Every year, there was a standing invitation and when you were not available, even Richard missed your view, the lavish food and wine that was always abundant. Your pools were enjoyed by my children, dogs and adults in every one of your homes, and they were all most memorable occasions.

Crescent 1996/1997

One of your first homes is especially memorable. Not only because it housed your antique billiard table, which was once owned by Queen Victoria but also because of your generosity. You offered and opened your home for Richard's 13th birthday Bar Mitzvah celebration when we were living in a small rented house.

Your Wentworth Road, Vaucluse home was a beautiful place with a grand winding staircase, large wall tapestries and floral upholstered lounge suite, with a crystal chandelier over the dining table laden for a feast, glassed in sunroom overlooking a magical garden and the Harbour. It was a superb setting, nothing of which was forgotten by those who were there.

Wentworth Road, Vaucluse 1988

You were in England when we had Roby's Bar Mitzvah at Murriverie Road, Bondi in 1991, but you were back in Australia by the time we finished building our house in Bondi just in time for Rony's Bar Mitzvah. Once again, we had a small reception at home, and our immediate family and close friends including you stayed for an impromptu dinner.

You have always been a water person. Your homes were on the water, you had swimming pools in your homes, and you had a number of boats. So, it was natural that Dannie's engagement was on the Harbour. Another memorable event.

Then there were a number of outings we shared. We went south to the Southern Highlands at tulip festival time to Corbett Garden. Eventually you had a lovely French provincial style house there for a few years, until it was too hard to have a Sydney home and travel between it and a weekender. Then we travelled to north to warmer climate to Noosa together with the Whittens. I am not only totally un-photogenic but was gaining weight. But why you, with your size and shape hid behind a rock, I shall never understand. Anyway, Noosa has always been one of your favourite places and I think it is fair to say we enjoyed it too.

Noosa, Gold Coast

Before you bought the house in Burradoo, you had a good taste of being in the Southern Highlands. The Sutton Forest family property was large enough for some Llamas to graze freely in 1991. When you invited us to spend weekends with you, my three sons had no end of fun with you and your ATV. However, there were other past times to occupy us all. Somehow everyone was busy working on house plans, or building a maquette, or a model car or painting some part of the model or just playing board games. But altogether they added up to great weekends and wonderful times spent together.

In the early 1990s, our great organiser friend Barbara organised a group of us to attend a couple of out-door concerts. The jazz concert starring James Morrison was held at Vaucluse House and despite the hard ground, the picnic which overflowed with wine was a great success. The music and the balmy night proved to be a memorable and even romantic. It was wonderful.

Everyone celebrates New Year's Eve. The very first time the Harbour Bridge was lit up with the fiery 'waterfall', we were in awe of the spectacle that was centre stage of our home in Vaucluse. Once when my relatives from overseas were visiting, we did venture out into the city, amidst the throng of millions to experience the reality of it all but took refuge in the Ballroom of the Regent Hotel at Circular Quay for most of the night. Although the décor was a sparkling blue, we were not. However, of late it is so much more comfortable to watch the fireworks on the big screen in the comfort of one's home.

New Year 1995 and 1999

And just for a change, after the eve of the millennium, we have been dancing in our Bowral home for a number of years. Whatever occasion we celebrated, we all had fun. I must confess, I was not looking forward particularly to Melbourne Cup days. As you know I am not one for dressing up and the hat was always a problem because I only ever owned a white pill box for my wedding which I converted to blue for Mandi's. But hey, I went shopping and bought a cute small black number. But you looked lovely in your acquisition for the occasion, as you did most every year when you attended the Cup of the year.

Bowral 2001, Bondi 2009 and Cosmopolitan, Double Bay 2002

There came a time in your life when you decided to move to England. So, you sold your possessions including your house on Wentworth Road and left for the far-off shores of the country of your birth. A major change indeed, especially when you were not sure if it was the right move because of the girls. And so began a two-year correspondence between us for the duration of your stay in England.

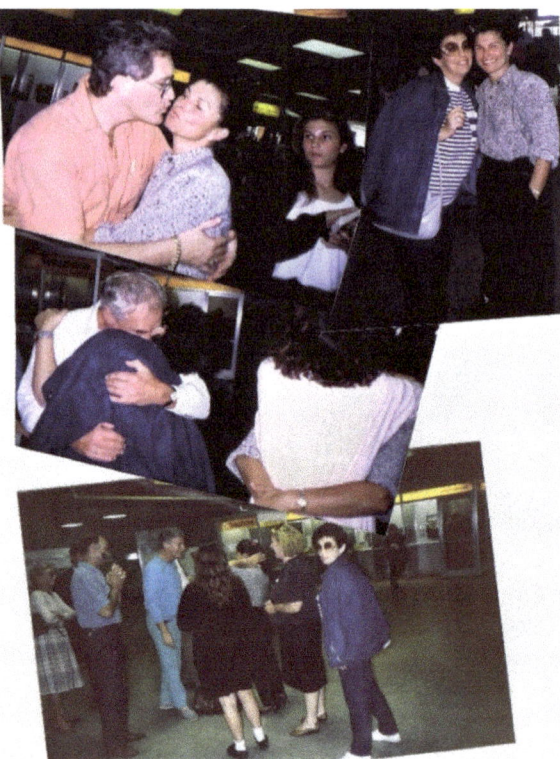

Kinsgford Smith Airport, Mascot 1988

Your first Aerogramme arrived a few weeks after you left. Written on 10th December 1988, it contained in great detail, the state of affairs in which you found yourself after landing in England. You wrote about the uncomfortable weather, the hotel accommodations, the high cost of rentals and food, the house at Hampstead Heath, and especially the mood in which you found yourself. On the one hand, you embarked on an adventure with some trepidation and on the other hand you were quite anxious and impatient to establish a home and permanent lifestyle.

But you were justified when feeling miserable, missing the girls, family and friends and being quite unsettled. Subsequent letters early in 1989 contained much the same. *"It is so hard to think."* By March you exchanged contracts on Petersfield Farm, Dorking, Surry. And your mood changed, as you came into your element of doing up the Manor house.

No ordinary house the one you bought. It was, as you wrote,

"... a 16th century farmhouse. It has 6 acres and is approx. 25 miles from London. ... 1 hour by car but only 30 minutes by train. ... It's not a large home ... has 4 bedrooms, 2 bathrooms with an annex with two beds + 1 bathroom. Needs a bit of work ... it has 1 very large lake + 1 smaller one. Full of fish, ducks + geese! It also has 2 barns +1 small, 2 stables + a small summer house. ... It has so much character, beams galore – only 6'6" ceilings and lovely lead light windows. We were told Winston Churchill stayed once and helped build a wall in the garden (he did brick laying) It's an important house in the area and full of history."

David sent a note with some photos of your house. *"We can't wait to move in. It's a bit old, but the minimum siding will give it a lift!"* He also wrote that you had April snow. And you were having a nice time.

You began to settle down in your new surroundings, with a new car, Peter's wedding announcement, packing for the May move into your new home and a trip was planned to Sydney in July. That decision must have given you some comfort regarding the girls. We had a good laugh at your antics with the tractor and David, even though it was not funny but dangerous.

By the middle of the year, you threw yourself into doing up the house but this time it was different. You learnt that it had 14th century beams and 400 years old trees and more history. You renovated keeping it within its 'heritage' and did a most beautiful job, while always caring about the garden and the animals that ate from your hand. Yes, you must have missed your friends in Sydney, and we missed you too.

So, we decided to visit and even stayed at your Manor house for a few nights at your most welcoming invitation. What a pleasure that was!! Oh, yes indeed, we had a great time, and it was a most memorable one for all the Czeigers including Lilly.

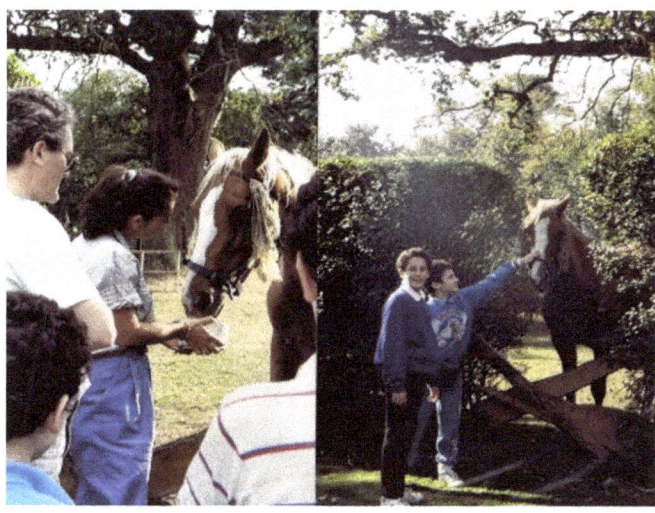

Kinsgford Smith Airport, Mascot 1988

When we arrived in September, although not quite finished with all of the renovations, you welcomed us with all the comforts of home in your little bit of English paradise. What can one say about your typical English furnishings, your English country garden with its lakes and of course all the animals. Ah, Marigold!! What a beauty of a horse you were, and even if you stepped on Lynda's toe, Rony had the most wonderful ride. We also shared a couple of day trips to quaint parts of old England, and we went together to Madam Tussauds' Waxworks where not only my three sons had fun but so did we. It is obvious that you and I have different tastes in some things, such as you liked Benny, but it just adds colour to our relationship.

Surry and London 1989

While living in Dorking and tending your farm, you and David managed to travel around England and Europe. Among the many countries, you took trips to Spain, Portugal, Ireland, Italy, Israel, Egypt and part of America. You always entertained family members and had the girls, and your mother stayed with you many times. When you finally decided, you sadly sold your Manor house and returned to Sydney in November 1990.

Touch of Class on Sydney Harbour 1987

Although you were born just outside the water sign of Cancer, you have always been a water person. Your homes were on the waterfront, they all had swimming pools and for many years you owned a boat. We have such wonderful memories of sailing with you. From leaving the dock to tying up at the end of a day on Sydney Harbour, every outing was a pleasure trip. We had meals on board, we had drinks on board, and we fished on board. My second experience of fishing was with you. In fact, you taught me and my sons how to hook the bait, how to throw the line, how to unhook the fish, and although the boys were reluctant at first, they too always released them, and we all always had a great time.

Czeigers and Whittens, Darling Harbour 1988

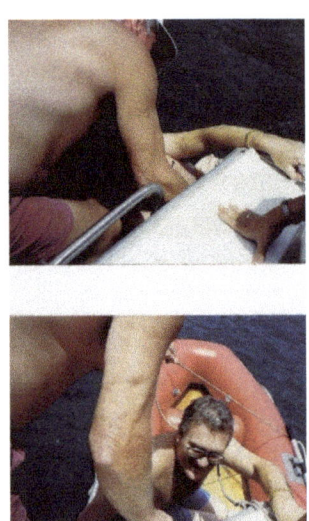  

Night Rider at Pittwater 1991

Amongst your yachts, there was the 40 feet revamped Navy boat by the name of 'Touch of Class', and she was just that; classy. There was the Riviera 35 named 'Night Rider' and the 28 feet Bertram. Berthed at various spots, at your buoy in Vaucluse, in Rushcutters Bay and at the Newport Marina, we either stepped onto the deck or rowed out in a dingy. There was a slight hitch when Harry rowed away from the boat. We watched helplessly while the dingy was taking water and prayed that it would not sink before it reached the boat. Harry was not a good swimmer. But he didn't drown. On other occasions, you always welcomed our friends, as well as a select group of our business associates, who all shared wonderful times on the water with you.

Night Rider at Rushcutters Bay 1992

But the most memorable was that one long weekend the four of us spent on the *Touch of Class* on the Hawkesbury River. We still talk about it. To take the classy lady from the Harbour to the river, we had to sail out through the heads into the Pacific Ocean. As the story goes, all except Harry was seasick. That is not necessarily true as I was not sick, but then I couldn't drive a boat anyway. And certainly not in three storey high waves. So, Harry took the wheel and to keep parallel with the shoreline, he steered us towards the white waters. What did Harry know about white waters or even driving a boat? Only in the last few minutes did David steer us clear of the reef of coastal rocks, on which we would have capsized with certainty. After that little incident, David drove us without a problem.

Once on the river, we had calm waters. We fished, we ate, and we drank as we sailed on the river surrounded by the Australian bush, reminiscent of Kate Granville's *Secret River.* In the evening, we docked and had a seafood dinner on land. We slept on the boat at night and woke to the sound of birds and a blanket of mystic mist that covered the waters. What magic moments I remember, as we watched the sun rise above the hills with Champagne in hand. You and I fished while David and Harry cooked a delicious breakfast for us. Then we baited our lines again and waited for the slippery little suckers to bite. And they did, and we threw them back again, all except enough little fish to cook for lunch. And you and I discovered that we could work together most efficiently in a tiny galley kitchen, as we anticipated each other's moves. And all I can say is, "Oh, what memorable times we had together. And they were good times!"

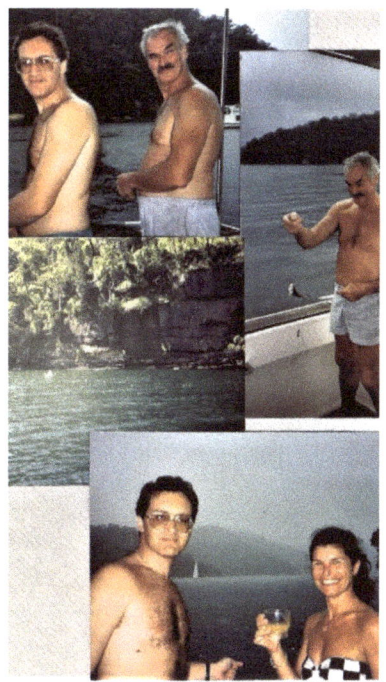  

Touch of Class Hawkesbury River 1987

Cruising is a passion of yours. Seaborn is the Liner that you prefer, and you introduced us to her ships. You do as many voyages with them as you can. I believe that they add up to many hundreds of days. You have travelled the world over and covered the five continents. Whenever someone mentioned a destination, you would surely say that you have been there too and perhaps more than once.

Because your feelings about cruising must have been contagious, we booked to join you on one of your trips. Since it was our business trip, we met in Los Angeles, together we drove to San Diego to meet with Harry's cousin and then we drove north, staying overnight at the Madonna Inn on the way to San Francisco. There, we boarded Cunard's *Royal Viking Sun* and sailed south to Acapulco among the other exotic cities. We met some nice people along the way and had a ball. We had several balls actually, as we spent New Year's Eve on board and another one with clowns. David obviously had a lot of fun too. And while the two of you went on a flight to some Aztec Pyramids, we were to bus to Mexico City, which you have seen already. Instead, we visited a colourful Third World little town because of a short three-day revolution. Still, it was memorable.

Los Angeles to San Francisco 1997

Formal Evening on the Royal Viking Sun 1997

The Royal Viking Sun and San Francisco 1997

When you are not cruising the seven seas, you busy yourself with your house and garden. And you busy yourself with our house and garden. Never was there a time when you could not improve our Bowral landscape that Harry designed with minimal research and much consultation with experts over the years. Each time you visit you walk around in our garden and weed as you move along the flower beds. And each time we clear some plots and replant with whatever you suggest.

Bowral 2010

Bowral 2016

For example, we now have a couple of small fields of lavenders that are thriving. The thirty or so roses that blossomed for at least ten years and which Harry killed, have been replanted a third time by David who stripped to the waist to do the work. Sadly, the roses bloomed only for a couple of years because of the bunnies. But later you recommended that the bed be replanted with irises. Now Van Gogh would be proud of our strip of your rich dark purple irises that set off your lighter lavenders. And the garden looks better for it all.

I mentioned previously your talent for design as well as your hospitality and generosity. You have opened all your homes to our family and friends from near and wide. One such was a New Year's Eve when your Wharf Road pool was filled with them from Sydney, Bowral and Toronto. Yet another occasion that is still talked about.

That pool was adorned with sea sculptures that cascaded onto your private Kuttie Beach, where your dogs pranced amongst the unwanted public. And yes, I must mention that you always had a couple of dogs, and yes, there was Winnie who alone sat on a dining chair at your table. You cared lovingly for all of your dogs, and they all loved the Maltesers you fed them for dessert every day.

In hindsight, we probably spent more time with Lynda and David than with any of our other friends. The last few years were hard on Lynda while she cared for David alone. During that time, we did cruise with them not long before sadly he passed away a few weeks before his 93rd birthday in 2023. But Lynda braved to cruise on her own when a year later we sailed the Mediterranean Sea together. And after a brief rough spell, that voyage truly cemented our friendship.

True friendship resists time, distance and silence.

Isabel Allende

Chapter Seventeen

HOMES

"Home is where our story begins, and every departure is a new chapter."

Annie Danielson

For nearly four score years, I have lived in many houses between Budapest and Bowral. Some of the buildings were rented and some owned, but all were our homes for a time and each one of them held some outstanding memories.

Till I was ten years old we lived in the same home in Budapest. It was a u-shaped building with a cobble stone central courtyard which extended into the garden in Csaki Utca 37 in Budapest XIII which was renamed Hegedus-Gyula Utca after the 1956 Revolution. Our home was one of the five apartments on the first floor of the six-storey block, which I roamed freely. Our flat consisted of two rooms, bathroom, toilet, kitchen, and a maid's room which was rented out for many years.

When we illegally slipped out of the country in the middle of the night in December 1956, we moved from one temporary home to another, first in the Hotel Wallenstein and a Boarding house in Vienna, then in a Lager in Korneuburg and briefly in Salzburg before sailing on the General Harry Taylor to Sydney. After Kings Cross, our homes were in Bondi till we moved to Rose Bay, Vaucluse, and back to Bondi. However, after a while, we also had a home in Bowral which we still have and treasure.

We arrived in our Australian home in June 1957 when we were deposited in a flat in 99 Victoria Street, Kings Cross. We came to discover that a Potts Point address was more prestigious. Today the Boarding house contains offices, art studios and such. We were still to discover that The Cross did not have the patina of some of the Eastern Suburbs. In the years to come, my father would boast about our palatial home. He started by saying that we had a large home with many rooms such as our pink and green room and numerous other rooms, all of which were occupied by the neighbours.

Actually, our home was subterranean. We lived in a basement flat, in two small underground rooms with uncomfortable old beds, two defunct fireplaces, and no windows except an air shaft or air vent that opened to the ground floor garden above us. Just outside our garden door there was a cockroach infested kitchenette.

The broken toilet was housed in a shack on the other side of the garden and to get to it, I regularly had to push the rusty reel mower to cut the lawn. The bathroom was three floors above us and for hot water we needed to have a consistent collection of pennies to feed the hungry little hot water tank. But my mother was happy that the three of us were together and alone in a clean flat with clean beds and a small fridge full of food.

Perhaps it was fortunate that we were reported to the police for working with one motorized sewing machine in that basement flat even if it was jealousy on the part of the Polish man who was the other subterranean dweller. Between early 1958 and 1971 we rented flats in Bondi. First, we rented the newly painted clean top floor from Mr. Bayer who owned the hardware store in his corner building which also housed the surgery of the General Practitioner Dr Havas, on the middle level.

My mother wrote to her brother that;

"the new accommodations at 356 Oxford Street, Bondi Junction, previously an old factory, was actually two rooms, which had to have new plumbing, electrical wiring, floor covering, and a kitchen established in a small balcony with new fittings and a fridge. We bought three boxes which served as bases for three very good mattresses. The luxury was that everything was brand new and our own. The most important element is that we managed to leave that slum; we can live under relatively normal circumstances, sleep in good beds and we have decent living quarters."

With Mr. Bayer's kind assistance my father managed to construct a so-called wardrobe with a back, sides, and top from Masonite. To cover the few clothes it held, my mother sewed a curtain for the front, and from matching fabric she made bedspreads for the three box beds. In that carpeted room the beds doubled as the dispatch area for the manufactured garments which were packed each night before we went to sleep.

Linoleum covered the floor of the larger factory room, the hallway which housed the dining table. Just outside the door was our 'tea-kitchen,' a small corner space at the top of the stairs and it housed our very first very own refrigerator. Later we added an extra small piece of furniture, my combined radio and gramophone or record player. This then was our home and factory at the same time. Perhaps it was a meagre home, but it had all new necessities and the three of us settled into a new lifestyle.

When the factory started to grow, we had to move. 9A Bennett Street, Bondi was close to Bondi Junction, off one side of Bondi Road. My mother had a penchant for new buildings. We were the first tenants to move into a two-bedroom flat on the third floor of a brand-new building. It may have faced the garden, though there was an ocean view but only if one leaned out far enough from the lounge room window.

Our great investments were purchasing solid Parker furniture, which not only lasted for many years, but today it became fashionable as Art Deco style. I still have two armchairs that have been recovered a few times.

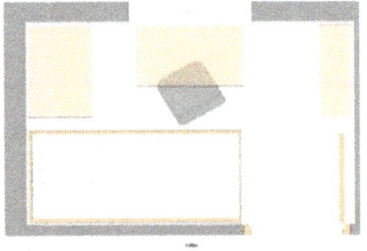
My room was so tiny that I could barely turn around in it literally. Measuring roughly three meters by two meters it fitted my bed, a small cupboard, a small bookshelf, and a desk under the window. Once my mother came into my room to get to my cupboard. Because I was studying, I had to stand up and push my chair under my desk so she could pass. But it was my very own room, and I loved it.

Much later, I bought my father's car from my salary. It was stolen and we reported it to the Police, who promised to take some action. However, the following day, to our great surprise my Valiant was parked around the corner and it was totally undamaged. Only the fuel gage was empty.

A few years later, we moved into Mrs Breiner's house at 29 Penkivil Street, Bondi, the street on the other side of Bondi Road. It was another brand-new three-story building and again we were the first to move in. Our moves were usually when I was studying for end of year examinations. We now had a somewhat larger two-bedroom flat rented on the top floor with a street frontage and the same Ocean View as before but directly from our living room.

My room was larger with a built-in wardrobe, an art deco design burnt orange 'day and night', today called sofa bed. It looked like a very stylish lounge settee during the day, but every evening it had to be opened and made into a bed. That is the room where I ended my relationship with my first boyfriend on that fateful February day in 1967.

Once my parents' business was well established, my father looked for an investment. He believed that brick and mortar was an answer for financial security. He purchased a piece of land in Rose Bay and built a block of nine units.

I was happy to be involved with him through the whole project. One change we made to the plans was an extension to the first-floor front unit with the intention of purchasing it for our family. And so, in 1970 we moved into Unit #1, 14 – 16 Chaleyer Street, Rose Bay once again at examination time. I had a spacious room with a walk-in wardrobe and an en-suite of my own situated on the opposite side of the lounge room to my parents' rooms for some privacy.

We considered our home was one of sheer luxury, symbolized by our modern crystal chandeliers. It was spacious with three comfortable bedrooms, one of which was used as a study by my father who always brought work home. We had an eat-in kitchen. The bathroom was large enough to fit a washing machine and dryer. My parents commissioned custom-made built-in furniture made by European master craftsmen, Mr Redi and the upholsterer Mr Mitrovitch. Much of it travelled with me to new homes and was even used by one of my sons for many years. I still have all the armchairs.

Ironically this home was within walking distance of my old school. But by then, I was at university and working. While I was away on a weekend with my mother, my father traded my car into a classy brand-new metallic rust brown two door Valiant Regal with beige hard top. That was the second car for which I paid from my salary.

At some stage I purchased the back unit. Unit #3 had three-bedrooms with a different floor plan and was rented out. A few years later when a front unit on the second floor came up for sale, I convinced Harry's uncle to buy it. He did and I think he appreciated it.

Life seemed to cruise along peacefully for a time. I worked and studied. I enjoyed my busy social life which included the opera and concerts series. However, that building was a most useful vehicle. It was the first of my association with the process of building development which was to be followed by a few later.

After our wedding in 1974 we moved into my Unit #3 which became a blue sight to behold with a sea of blue shag carpet and matching blue flock wallpaper. The kitchen was orange, and the main bedroom had Italian maroon piano finish with white intarsia. We were happy except for my mother's illness. Shortly after she died, my father became an invalid, and he too needed help. In 1975 Harry and I moved into my parents' Unit #1 to look after him. By then we had our first-born son Richard for whom we enclosed the balcony with glass and it became his nursery.

My Harry, the 'builder architect' never ceased to look for opportunities. He saw the advertisement for a house with sizable land in a nice area for $148,000.00. When he looked at the two-street frontage property, he stood on top of the garage and was awe inspired by the view. He bargained it down and phoned me with the new figures. I can still see myself standing next to the phone listening to him and then hear myself saying, "Buy." Within a day we paid the 10% deposit of $13,000.00, signed and exchanged contracts. We then organized the required $100,000.00 loan and signed the necessary mortgage with a high interest rate of some 17.5% to become the proud or otherwise owners of 5 Vaucluse Road, Vaucluse.

I am a Scorpio and not a trusting one. How or why, I agreed to enter into what for me was an unheard-of commitment, I cannot remember. But I must have done some calculations about repayment of such an exorbitant debt, as I was extremely definite about agreeing to the purchase of the unseen property. Harry must have been a brave man, and I supported him all the way, probably because I was caught up in his enthusiasm.

The Vaucluse property was a locked up deceased estate in which Harry saw great potential. First it needed to be aired before it was possible to stay in the house for any length of time. It must have been built for an entertaining lifestyle, because more than half the house was one large lounge room. It also had one large bedroom, three very small bedrooms, a bathroom that had five different sizes and colors of tiles and a white ant-ridden kitchen. In short, the place was unlivable.

Because we planned to live in it only for a short time, it was a challenge to spend on it as little as possible. We steamed off two or more layers of peeling wallpaper and painted the walls off white in the lounge room. We stripped the kitchen totally and installed the cheapest practical Knebel kitchen for $1,200.00. I was still in my orange phase. We stripped the old floral carpet and replaced it with a cheap but durable green nylon one. Instead of taking up the bathroom tiles, we covered most of the wall and all the floor with off-white bathroom carpet. All the carpets were cheap fall offs from Jack Ezra' *Carpeteria*. Our blue painted and carpet outfitted bathroom became a kind of feature of the house. Certainly, it was a lasting topic of conversation.

The whole house redressing was completed relatively quickly and in 1976 we moved into our new old home, which was clean and if truth be told, looked quite good. We added a few little touches such as a couple of glassed in shelves that were for the beginning of our China collection and connected our stereo player. Had it not been for Fedor's new $50.00 circuit breaker, Harry's stereo installation could have killed him. However, the electricity instantly switched off and Harry landed on his back with only a slight headache and a damaged ring.

Our second son Roby was born into our temporary Vaucluse home. His small lemon painted room had his cot and the specially made waist high change table with three deep drawers. Hence, I never had a backache as I never had to bend down. That piece of furniture was most welcomed by all who inherited it. I also had one made for our grandchildren.

The large loungeroom enjoyed many events. We had all the boys' birthday parties where the attendees increased in numbers each year and where the children could play freely on the washable green nylon carpet. We played cards regularly with our friends. We had a very pleasant space in our Sunroom where we sat and watched the many different performances on our simply splendid Sydney Harbour while we sipped drinks and ate Bon Vivants.

While we were happily settled supposedly briefly, big plans were afoot for the fulfillment of the potential of the big building block. Harry's design of a three-level house was excellent and required little contribution from me. But I always added just that little. It was a most enjoyable experience to be able to work towards the realization of our dream, even if we needed to sell Unit #1 in Chaleyer Street to afford the cost of the building. Cyril Smith the architect, lodged our plans and within a short six weeks we read in the Wentworth Courier that Woollahra Council had approved The Development Application. It was a most unusual occurrence that the official letter of approval arrived in the mail well after the publication.

It appeared that we were meant to return to the blue unit too before we sold it. Our third son Rony was born into that temporary home, and the other two boys settled nicely into their shared room. No one paid any attention to all the blue for two and a half years.

At night Harry and I spent many hours placing and moving little shapes of paper cut to exact measurements that represented furniture, positioning lights and power points, and all that was necessary to finish our house. Those nocturnal activities were an absolute delight.

Harry was a very efficient builder and finished the construction within thirteen months. During that time, we worked in the factory and managed to supervise all the construction stages daily.

In 1980 our new home address became 2B Gilliver Avenue, Vaucluse. Interestingly and coincidentally, we moved into our very own new *Forbat* factory in Mountain Street, Ultimo at the same time. Because Vaucluse Road was a very busy one, we sealed it off and turned the house around as it were. The entrance was from the back street, and the living area was on the top level to capture the magnificent view and accommodate my father who had problems with walking and stairs. Sadly, he died before completion of the building.

Our mansion, as someone called it, was quite large and complex for such a young family. It was most unusual for a young family to have a huge structure for a first home. The entry was adorned by a glass dome from which a chandelier hung. Or is it hanged. Either way, it never leaked when it rained. The top floor had a study, a guest bathroom and a guest room which was occupied later by our helpful student Gabriella. There was a family room attached to the kitchen which opened into the dining area which was part of the lounge room separated by my glass China cabinets, and there was a music alcove.

Entry into the living area revealed a picture postcard view of Sydney Harbour. The Harbour Bridge was situated in center stage, with the Opera House and the City on the left, the North Shore on the right. Port Jackson from Fort Dennison to Shark Island was situated in the front. A glorious view at any time especially on New Year's Eves when we had many family members and friends who marveled at the fireworks especially the waterfall lights.

The same Harbour view was available from the middle floor where our main bedroom was situated with its doorless bathroom. Our very large oval bath that fitted the three boys and their two cousins comfortably on many occasions lacked the same views.

Each of the boys had their own very spacious rooms. Rich and Rob shared an adjoining bathroom and Ron had his own. The boys had a large play area that could accommodate a whole class of boys for birthday parties even without the huge balcony. Also, many birthday parties were held in the rumpus room on the ground floor that led into the top garden that led into a lower garden which contained the fenced off swimming pool. Our double block land was so large that looking down from the balconies, it appeared that our pool belonged to the neighbour's house.

I was never very sociable with any of our neighbours, and with good reason. Not to be trusted. *Beware of strangers bearing gifts*, may have originated from "Beware of Greeks bearing gifts," from the Trojan Horse mythology, but she was neither a Greek nor a truly welcoming neighbour. Merely a stranger with a pot plant who later decided to sue us.

Our house design had one flaw which was that for technicians to read the electric and gas meters, they had to enter our house. We needed to build a staircase down the side of the building for access for them. Previously Mrs Neighbour objected to our family room window looking into her bedroom, so we altered our plans by raising the height of the window. We could not see out, but the window let in sufficient light into the family room. No problem.

Then Mrs Neighbour objected to the stairs we needed for meter inspections on the grounds that it would become a "public thoroughfare" that faced her loungeroom. Since the space between the fence and the house was well within building regulations, we thought she had no case. Mrs. Neighbour sent her QC husband with two of his QC friends to the Land and Environment Court. Harry took Cyril Smith the architect and a Waverly Alderman who had building experience. In a very short time, without even calling the architect as witness, the decision handed down by the Court was in our favor and Mr Neighbour paid all costs. We built the stairs down the side of the house, and it was used rarely and mostly by meter readers.

I do believe that we lived a very full and happy life in that grand mansion of a home for many years. It was an ideal construction for a variety of events. We even hosted a semi-legal fundraising function with protective police cars cruising our street for the duration of the event. We hired roulette wheels, poker machines and professional croupiers. Poker cards were played for relatively big money, and it all benefited the kindergarten.

We never had a housewarming, but we had a House Cooling where we raised a nice sum also. Over the years I collected small objects which I either did not use or planned to give as presents when we were invited somewhere. I wrapped them all and the neat little packages together with some red wine donated by our *Ragtrader* Magazine editor friend Fraser were all sold by him as auctioneer. The Prince of Wales children's cancer research received a donation of hundreds of dollars and copies of the certificate were sent to all who contributed. It was a pleasant and stylish affair. The piano alcove housed the string quartette from the Sydney Conservatorium of Music, and they complemented a silver service dinner for 50 of our family and friends, many of whom remember that evening to this day.

The day after that most successful night of House Cooling celebration, we had a most successful end of year Concert for the boys together with all of Miss Waldman's students, which included their first and second cousins. It seems that the fact of the house cooling allowed for more permissive behaviour and in the following days, our guests took liberties. One of them was that they felt very much at ease. Some even lay down and went to sleep in the lounge room after lunch, as did our friends Harry and Ray.

January 1986 marked the end of our time in our 2B Gilliver Avenue, Vaucluse home which we had to sell. Harry will always remind me that we did not have to sell it and that I "panicked" him into the sale. We actually had a substantial loan of $780,000.00 that blew out to the tune of 2.5 million dollars. I had great difficulty accepting such an extremely high debt and refused to live with it. So, it may be said that I was responsible for the sale of an unbelievable house and home. And to add insult to injury, had we waited for another six months to sell, we could have sold it for a very much higher price, as did our friends.

But we did pay back much of our outstanding debt and had enough left to purchase another property. I suppose that the successive homes we planned, designed and built may have seemed like an anti-climax, but each had some story and a special meaning of course.

We looked at a lovely little white picket-fenced family cottage in Village High Road, Vaucluse. It was a charming home carefully tended by the wife who, after we were to buy it, asked me to look after her beautiful garden. I didn't have the heart to tell her that we considered her doll's house and garden for a demolishing job with Harry's vision of development potential.

We agreed that we would not spend more than half a million dollars. So, Harry first entered the bidding process as the auction slowed down to the half-million-dollar mark. The bidding stopped at $548,000.00 after which Harry tried to impress on me that in a couple of years the extra $50,000.00 was not going to matter in the great scheme of things. And Harry was right.

It was on a rainy night when we were driving home, Harry at the wheel. We were on our way to celebrate when our car was hit from behind and we were pushed into the car in front in Rushcutters Bay. The metallic burnt orange Merces was a write off. So, on my 40th birthday in 1986 we were on the verge of owning another new home and a new car to boot.

Early in 1987 we were packed to move to the rented 57 Portland Street, Dover Heights opposite a park. It was comfortable living with a glorious Harbour view. The owner was planning to develop it for his son eventually. We made it homely with our paintings and the kitchen furniture which later came to be resprayed to fit the décor colors of our new home. It also motivated Harry to continue his painting, most of which he gave away.

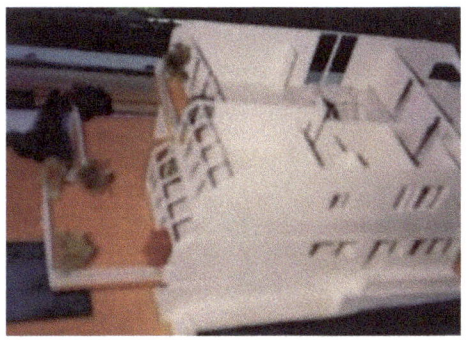

While there, he was quite productive, even creating a couple of bronze resin reliefs. He also constructed a maquette of the three stories house as required by the Council to accompany building Development Applications. One neighbour object to the proposed building's white colour that would reflect the sunlight too much. Harry lobbied the Council Alderpersons, and the objection was overruled with the help of one of the Alderpersons Maggie who became a longtime friend, and eventually so did the objecting neighbours.

The building began in March of 1987. Once again Harry and I worked in the factory and supervised. One day the construction hit a snag. That is, it hit a sewage pipe that went across the property similar to Gilliver Avenue. My challenge-loving Harry resolved the problem by encasing the pipe in concrete and then building the pool on top of it.

As I watched our full-time laborer work at the same snail pace every day, I was convinced that the building would never be finished. I soon learned that he needed to move at such a slow even pace so as not to burn out. And the building did finish in the good time of eleven months. Another one of Harry's efficient building efforts. In February of 1989, we moved into 18 Village High Road, Vaucluse which was referred to as our black and white home. Coincidentally, at the same time we moved into another of our new *Forbat* factories in 23-25 May Street, St. Peters.

The original design for Village High Road was proposed by an Award-winning architect Viv Fraser with an unusual but practical design for the long sloping site. There was a division of the house connected by an indoor swimming pool with a bridge above it. It was an exciting and very modern style.

However, we decided to go ahead with Harry's plan drawn up by architect Fred Heilpren. It had three bedrooms for the boys facing the street on the top floor. The main bedroom with its ensuite looked out to the whole of Sydney Harbour's Port Jackson with view of the Harbour Bridge, as did a common area for the boys with space for an antique Baby Grand Piano coated black to match the black Beethoven's relief on the wall above it. Oh, but they were grand.

On the street level, Harry's passion for a sunken lounge room faced the same Port Jackson Harbour view. And there was a wood log fireplace in the corner. It was a few steps up to the dining area adorned by an Italian crystal chandelier tall enough to fit the space of the atrium. The kitchen looked past the family room which opened onto a verandah overlooking the Harbour. And a flight of stairs led down to an indoor swimming pool which later came to be photographed for a magazine.

Although this house was designed with our family's requirements in mind, it was also designed with the intention that it be sold as soon as practicable. And sell we did. It was easier to leave my prized chandelier which required scaffolding for the problematic disassembling, and so it was sold as extra to the house together with the black wall to wall built-in unit.

Once more in 1990 we were in a position to need another one of our rented new homes. Number 3 Lyon Street, Dover Heights was a house with a doorless double garage just a block away from Fedor and his family. Sadly, Lilly passed away and Rob's Bar Mitzvah was a rather damped-down affair. But we did have a small luncheon in the small house. We also had some animal adventures with our dog Sir Rod Ridge who impregnated a neighbouring dog, Ron's fish, and his turtle that went walk about permanently.

That year Harry was the project manager for the construction of the building of Fedor's home on Fischer Avenue, Vaucluse. That house with its colonial columns was just around the corner from where we once lived in Gilliver Avenue.

After Lilly's passing Uncle decided to gift his family inheritance to the two boys while he was alive. His assets were assessed and divided equally between Harry and Fedor. Thus, his two units were willed to and received by Fedor and his house with the land was willed to and received by Harry.

Uncle did not want to live in his home alone. He did not want to live in a unit. He did not want to live with us. And he did not want to move from that area. Harry, who felt that his uncle was his "responsibility," resolved the problem by designing a house in a way that Uncle had a spacious comfortable one-bedroom unit within it with its own entrance.

In order to maximize the area usage, Harry cleverly designed a 'renovation' retaining the existing outer walls, rather than building a new structure and losing from the area. The plans for Murriverie Road were passed by the council, we moved Uncle into a rented flat for the duration of the construction and organized a garage sale and so the house was emptied.

However, when construction began, some problems surfaced. Besides some sewage pipe obstruction, first the next-door neighbour's garage collapsed and then the street collapsed into the garden. After shoring up all the sliding walls of sand with solid concrete bricks, all went well and smoothly. The building was completed in another relatively short period.

In September 1991, after thirteen months of construction, we moved into another three-level house at 130 Murriverie Rd., North Bondi. That also was the first new building in the street and set a precedence for other developments.

A complete three-bedroom unit was planned for the top floor, with an Ocean view to Bondi Beach. The street level housed Uncle's complete one bedroom unit on one side of the stairs and our bedroom, walk in wardrobe and en-suite on the other side of the stairs, big enough for what is called a 'bed sitter.' In fact, the house had the potential to be divided into three separate flats if desired.

The bottom floor housed the rumpus room, a glassed-in heated swimming pool and a double garage that fitted three cars. The boys grew up there till they decided to leave the familial home.

I found an aqua tile I liked and decided to work on the décor around it and because it was a difficult color to match, white became dominant in the scheme of things. The double door refrigerator and the Baby Grand Piano had to be lifted with a crane over the balcony through the lounge doors. My built in China cabinet behind the fridge faced the living area. Some referred to it as a shop window. But I did take pleasure in rearranging some of my pieces and still do so.

In 2010 we decided to renew the look of our home. New carpet and a coat of paint. Also, I conceded to white marble stairs and partial marble flooring including in the kitchen where we replaced the bench top and splash-back with glass. Oh, the change was amazing. Well, we liked the face lift. The house had a new appearance.

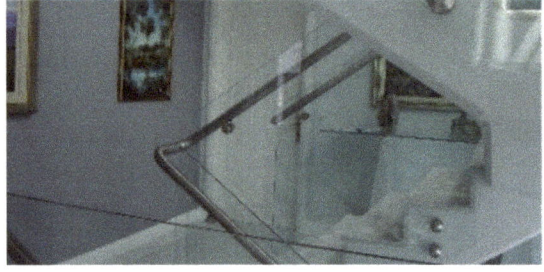

And speaking of lifts, we seriously considered installing an elevator, as carrying packages up two flights of stairs was becoming increasingly difficult. I came to realize that I have never walked up the two flights of stairs to the top floor empty handed. I was against investing more money as I was planning to leave that house as soon as possible. Yet we stayed for over thirty years while Uncle was alive.

In late 2021 we sold Bondi and planned to move to a smaller home. The clearing of a house and home of thirty years of accumulations was a mammoth task. We were to rid ourselves of everything except the barest minimum. And it was an amazing sight to see the triple car garage filled to the ceiling with what I can only call "stuff." Together with thousands of boxed books for *102.5 Fine Music*, over six trucks removed stuff. All that resulted in a feeling of complete relief. A kind of light weightlessness.

In 2017 a group of compatriots who arrived in Australia on the General Harry Taylor gathered to celebrate their 60th anniversary. One of the ladies, Judy Gelb, showed me her residence and then the rest of the building. I was most impressed by the whole complex. There and then I decided that that is where I would like to live at this time in my life. I told Harry "I was going to Moran." His first visit dissuaded him totally. His reason was, "Too many old people." That is the mantra of the elderly. But soon Harry relented.

It came to pass that an independent living residence quite suitable for us was going to become available. We placed a holding deposit on the two one-bedroom units combined and then exchanged contracts. Harry selected the peacock blue setee and the rest followed from there. I was convinced that it was emerald green but just after my Cataract surgery I was proven wrong. It was indeed a lovely peacock blue that changes colour in different lighting.

This was not a good investment. It was expensive for the size of the unit. It had a high monthly fee that was higher than any strata would be in the area for an equivalent size unit. It could be sold only to Moran and at a price about 35% less than the purchase price. All that added up to a bad investment. Some of our good friends warned us, not that we were unaware of the fact. However, it is an acquisition for our lifestyle and now.

Moran was most accommodating and allowed us to make three alterations after the contract exchange. Before settlement we built a wall of bookshelves in the study, replaced the kitchen benchtop with aqua coloured glass and changed the shelves and doors of the cupboard in the lounge room to clear glass.

It was a relief to move into our very new home with just the essentials, brand new furniture, two resprayed pieces and only the old familiar China pieces to be placed in the new glass cabinet. We are happy in this, probably the last of our new homes. Now when we move to Bowral weekly, it is most convenient to just lock the door of our unit and leave all the worries to the management.

 In 2022 April we moved into Mark Moran, Unit 202-203, 2 Laguna Street, Vaucluse. In the past I did all the packing but this time I was unable to do anything. Yet the move was seamless due to the work of Andrea who came from Tasmania a few times to help. Sometimes she took instructions from me, sometimes she just did what she thought I would do. She moved as I would have done, she filled and emptied boxes. She packed and unpacked sometimes with Harry, and I just sat. Without Andrea, I could not have made the move, and I am forever grateful.

Since the early 1980s we have been regular visitors to Bowral in the Southern Highlands. When we decided to look for a property, I laid down specific criteria that it had to be about three minutes from town, three minutes from the hospital and three minutes from the ambulance and fire station. It was in 1997 that we purchased a third of the quarry of 15 acres. Harry bought a container that was supposed to have been an Olympic demonstration unit. It had everything that we needed to spend weekends on the vacant lot. AV Jennings built the house in record time. Construction was completed within six months as per the contract.

 In August of 2001, just a couple of months before we closed *Forbat Style*s, we moved into our primary residence, Lot #2, Orchard Road, Bowral. Years later after Lot #1 was subdivided, ours was renumbered to 17 Orchard Road though I still call it Lot 2.

Most properties have a name so, for something original and imaginative, we decided to call it "*The Quarry.*" For over twenty years we have been travelling to Bowral every week and every time we leave the quarry, we wish to return to the tranquility of that area which was and still is part of our many homes.

"It's a funny thing coming home. Nothing changes. Everything looks the same, feels the same, even smells the same. You realized what's changed is you."

F. Scott Fitzgerald

Chapter Eighteen
MUSIC

"Without music, life would be a mistake."

Friedrich Nietzsche

I have always loved music. If education begins in the womb, I must have been exposed to music from conception and was surrounded by it all my life. Although around seven years of age I was small for adult theatre, my mother took me to my first opera. It was Verdi's *Rigoletto* at the Budapest Opera House. I retained the image of the dark hunchbacked figure that swept across the length of the dimly lit stage. The Court Jester who wove his red lined black cape in harmony with that distinctive baritone voice echoing an aria of resounding pain at the loss of his daughter, still haunts me. I was suspended in disbelief, at once frightened and fascinated. I still see myself as a little girl leaning forward to be closer to the magic and the music.

For me that performance of Rigoletto has not been matched yet. It was the beginning of my true love for opera and the continuation of my love for classical music. So, when decades later a car was driven across the stage in the Sydney Opera House and still later when the lead actor stripped to his shorts which he then proceeded to remove under his dressing gown, somehow all seemed rather inappropriate and stripped of any magic.

My father shared his love of music with me. He had a natural feel for music, a good voice and an aptitude for the violin which he taught himself to play. Whenever in later years he picked up my violin, he demonstrated that he knew how to handle the instrument. He played with good technique, mostly by ear and with great feeling. It seemed to me that he had considerable potential. Ah, what potential has been unfulfilled and what opportunities have been lost, all due to life's circumstances. His particularly, and perhaps mine too. Shame.

I must have been nine-year-old, when by luck of the draw of my parents' Hungarian Government Bonds paid off and allowed us to purchase the latest model of gramophone together with some of my father's favourite records. And so, he and I continued our sessions of conducting some of the worlds' greatest Symphony orchestras with some of the greatest conductors such as Zsolti and Toscanini. Much later, I spent time studying the techniques of the great conductors including Leonard Bernstein's all of whose classes were most instructive in every respect of musicality.

It is no mean feat to conduct an orchestra, particularly an invisible one, but from an early age on Sunday mornings I stood in front of our radio and did just that with my father. I learned about the positions of the instruments in the orchestra, why there were different formations for some compositions, and even when to turn the pages of our imaginary music score. Beethoven's 5th Symphony had special significance as it did for many Jews, but my father was very familiar with it and all the other composers to whom he introduced me.

Often, we sang with the great opera singers of the day. My father accompanied Mario Cavaradossi in *Tosca* to his own interpretation of lyrics which sounded something like: *Cher Pessachino, Moderasso Forte. Ich Ge Soforte*, and when I hear it in my head, I cannot help but smile at his combination of languages. I sang with Simandi Jozsef, one of Hungary's great tenors, who sang well into his very senior years and whose *Bank Bank* by Erkel Ference I still remember performed in the Budapest Opera House.

My repertoire was varied as I learnt Operettas of Franz Lehar, Imre Kalman and others, as well as some popular *schlagers* of the Hungarian diva Honti Hanna such as: *"Hetre ma varoom a Nemzetinel,"* and *"Legyen a Horvath kertben Budan,"* which I sang as a child and still do as an adult which must date me. No doubt my parents danced to her chanson in their youth. There were a few 78 vinyl records including a selection of arias sung by the great tenor Beniamino Gigli who became our favourite. Once I saw him perform from a wheelchair, but his voice retained the same fine lyrical quality.

Then there was Mario Lanza who emulated Gigli and had a beautiful "lirico spinto" voice. I loved his opera arias as well as his Neapolitan songs, all made him popular by his films. For years I sang with him and all the songs he recorded. I have always retained a high standard and sang only with the most splendid of talents, first with Gigli then Pavarotti, Dame Sutherland, and Callas among other greats.

In mid-2000 I believed that I discovered the multi-voiced tenor, Jonas Kaufman with his unique timbre. I predicted he was a new sound with great potential for opera, little knowing that he had already made his debut in a number of international Opera Houses and had a vast repertoire recorded. When I heard him in 2015 in the *Munchen Konigsplatz* singing *Celeste Aida*, I was most impressed with that exceptional quality of his voice especially the head notes. I was somewhat concerned about his voice and then he cancelled a number of programmed appearances. However, he came back with a vengeance.

But to return to my youth when I was about seven years old, I was old enough to start my formal musical education. However, we missed the entrance auditions. Every year there was a quota for the enrolments and once the selection of forty-eight students out of hundreds of applicants was complete, the doors were closed literally. My father begged the judges to hear me. Eventually they relented, opened the doors and listened to me.

It was quite a long test session with the required hand signs, humming, repeating tunes and scales, clapping, tapping rhythms, completing tunes given the first three piano notes, and other methods. It also included singing a variety of songs. I chose one I sang at school on Mother's Day.

Nincs senki olyan szep, Nincs senki olyan jo,
Nincs senki olyan mint az en Anyam.

[There is no one as nice, there is no one as good,
There is no one like my mother.]

I passed my audition and became the constant 'extra' student. Before I could take up any musical instrument, I had to do two years of theory of music by the Kodaly Method. I loved it and excelled in it. Kodaly's teaching was a social, cultural and musical experience. It is based on learning by singing, the human voice being the most fundamental of instruments; on hand signs or *Solfege*, that is the correct hand sign associated with a corresponding note; on rhythmic proficiency alongside of tonal Solfege; on group collaboration from clapping to choral singing, to instrumental accompaniment; and on the cultural connection or an affinity to folk songs that Kodaly Zoltan had as did Bartok Bela, with the aim to create a "kind of visceral connection to music." All those elements were included in the audition.

The Kodaly method and Solfege was not yet commonly used in schools in post war Australia till much later. So, when my children first came in contact with do, re, me, fa, so, la, ti, do in *Mary Poppins* and *Close Encounters of the Third Kind*, it was all very familiar to me, and I was able to demonstrate the hand signs to them. That is how they learnt the signs attached to each note of a scale. In the common octave scale of eight notes, the first and last are the same. If one listens very carefully, one can actually hear that there is no difference between those first and eighth note in the octave. I learnt that much later when I was studying the numerical relationships of celestial spheres and harmonics of instruments.

My parents and I discussed my playing an instrument. I inherited my mother's petite hands which were clever. In fact, mine were smaller than hers and never expected to reach the span of the octave. In hindsight it is obvious that there are small child virtuosi who manage the piano's octave beautifully. So, the next choice was the violin where the hand can be shifted into varying positions for the fingers to reach all notes.

Since I was about to start the violin when we left Hungary one of our investments in the second year after our arrival in Australia, was a second-hand quarter violin and lessons. As I was growing my mother sewed new shoulder cushions for my instruments. Each of my violins was replaced by a larger one and each was shinier with a much rounder sound than the previous one. I broke several strings over the years especially the metal E, whereas the cat gut D and G were more enduring. To this day I can place four of my fingers in the correct basic position on the fingerboard and sometimes still do so on tables as if on the A string on the violin. But I have forgotten much, and I am not sure I could read music.

My lessons were with the gentle Mr. Thorpe, an Australian gentleman who was a Second Violinist with the Sydney Symphony orchestra. Every week I practiced for five to ten minutes, before I caught the bus to Bondi Road for my lesson. Naturally he could tell just how long I practiced. Either he had infinite patience with me, or I did have some talent. Perhaps a bit of both. Yet I managed to keep up with the requirements and at the end of each year I sat for the Sydney Music Conservatorium examinations.

Drink To Me Only With Thine Eyes was my very first piece of music for the Preliminary Grade examination in 1960. After a while I could play with mine and thine eyes shut. I still remember the fingering of the first few notes.

I received a mark of 90% with a comment that I made a "successful start" and that I had "a natural aptitude for the instrument." It was signed by none other than Sir Bernard Heinze one of the renowned Australia's conductors.

Those very encouraging high marks allowed me to skip First Grade. The following year I sat for the Second-Grade examination and wonder of wonders, I gained Honours again. That despite the fact that during the year little time was spent with the violin and much time was spent with the school musical.

I was busy even outside school hours with rehearsals for my principal role as *Pish Tush*, a Noble Lord in the Gilbert and Sullivan production of *The Mikado*. Since I knew it all, subsequently I sang throughout all performances much to the chagrin of the audience around me. What was disappointing with most of the Opera House Gilbert & Sullivan productions including overseas ones, was that there were contemporary political quips inserted into the dialogue. Call me old fashioned, but I did not find it humorous. It seemed to interfere with the ambience of the production.

The Dover Heights Girls' High School's G & S productions had to be authentic and correct to the letter, as it was written in the original libretto with precise directions. We learnt a lot about stage movements as every small step had to be exact and without faltering. And all the lyrics had to be pronounced 'succinctly' as instructed by both music and production directors.

Oh, how I enjoyed it all. The first year the extra drills were a nice experience with Miss Graham, the English Mistress to correct my American rhotic 'r' particularly in the word "really. The word "really" appeared many times in my role and my "really" was really contrary to that of the very British pronunciation of the word "really." What was more painful was the practice of flicking open and closed the large heavy wooden ended fan with the one hand. For me it was more difficult than for the other principals with my nonsporting and rather small hand.

The following year I was involved in another G & S school production. In an all-girls school, the voices tended to be high, and I could easily sing Alto. I could sing the solo parts of the female roles also because my soprano voice improved with my age, but there was a shortage of low voices. Therefore, once again I was given a male role. But this time it was the principal role of Captain Corcoran in *HMS Pinafore*. My then best friend Rosemary was my Boatswain who I ordered about.

Once again, I enjoyed everything about the whole experience, the solo and chorus numbers, the words, the music, the stage positions and movements, the costumes, the makeup, and all that was involved in a musical production that was directed very professionally. I learned just how much work was involved in a theatrical production and I took great pleasure in the accolades we received after each performance. I must also add that having seen a number of G & S professional productions including *The Mikado* and *HMS Pinafore* in Australia and in England, our amateur all girl production could match any one of them in every respect.

They were very high standard productions indeed and at the end of each the cast was rewarded with usual accolades and huge bouquets of flowers just as adult professionals. During all of the performances of both *The Mikado* and *HMS Pinafore*, when I looked out into the auditorium, I could not avoid seeing my father. Seated in the centre of the sixth row from the front, arms folded with a huge smile on his face that was very characteristic of him, his eyes were on me constantly.

During those years I studied very little and practised the violin even less. By then I was fifteen and also wanted long fingernails, though I never did have any long fingernails till my mid-seventies. My parents and I came to a joint decision not to continue either with the pressure of making me practice or the cost of the lessons. Thus ended my career as a violinist before it would have begun.

Since I loved to sing and always sang, I suggested to my parents that I would like to have singing lessons. My mother was probably right when she said that I would not practice singing very much either. But ever since I can remember, I have been exercising my vocal cords when I was alone, especially when driving alone and in the shower as any bathroom has good acoustics. When I accompanied some great singers, I sometimes could not hear them or distinguish between our individual voices. Strangely we morphed into one.

The voice is a natural instrument and a very sensitive one. I remember Pavarotti spoke about his voice in the third person when he said, "The voice must rest," as if it were something separate and not a part of him, much like some musical instrument one carries around in a case. I suppose in a way that is what it is. Once only I thought of singing as a profession. However, my career would have been fraught with the risk of chronic tonsilitis from which I suffered in my youth. Besides, who knows if I would have been good enough to be good.

In 1958 in Sydney, we acquired our very first piece of furniture. The combination of radio and gramophone system was modern and made from light wood. The 45 single of Liszt's *Liebestraum* was my very first record, followed by a few 78s and then the large 33 LPs or long-playing records. I thoroughly enjoyed playing them most of the day particularly when I was studying for exams.

Because we only had a few records I played them so frequently that the grooves wore out. And because I just turned over the records repeatedly, I never knew the difference between the two one act operas of Leoncavallo's *Pagliacci* and Mascagni's *Cavalleria Rusticana*, or between Tchaikovsky's *Capriccio Italien* and Rimsky Korsakov's *Capriccio Espanol*, or between Dvorak's *New World Symphony* and Smetana's *Moldva*. The beginning of *Capriccio Italien* accompanied Tibalt's funeral procession in a most moving Russian film production of *Romeo and Juliet*.

Probably in the second year after arriving in Australia, my parents purchased tickets to the opera productions in the Elizabethan Theatre in Newtown. Seated in the very top row of the very top level, the performers were so far away that we could see them only with opera glasses and even then, not very well. But the voices reached up to us and they were heavenly. We heard Joan Sutherland well before she went overseas, together with the not so tall rotund Donald Smith who was a marvellous tenor. It was a shame that he retired so early in his career only to sing in his country Pub. Later J C Williamson and other companies brought some very fine singers to Australia, and I saw and heard many.

Once in High School, I attended the Music Conservatorium's recitals and had weekly tickets to the concerts in the Town Hall. I rarely missed a six o'clock performance on Tuesdays and I always had to run up the stairs just before the doors were closed. Unfortunately, my seat was on the first floor opposite the pianist, so I could never see the hands of the pianist. From the time when the Sydney Opera House opened in 1973, although our seats were at the end of the fourth row close to the doors, I was to run up the concrete steps under the white Sails to concerts, ballets and opera performances at eight o'clock just before the doors were closed.

One of the critical Blogs of Lady Maleficent. (2018)

Having just turned another year and received the usual wishes for a happy birthday, one gift from one cousin was a concert ticket. And what a treat that was.

Ashkenazy conducted Zukerman playing Bruch's violin concerto #1 and the Sydney Symphony Orchestra played Mahler's 5th Symphony in the same program. The beauty of it all was overwhelming, – enter Lady M, this time with a 'but' – despite the fact that I was not happy with the solo instrument. Zukerman's violin seemed to lack a clarity of ringing, of crispness, and his playing lacked a fire which I expected. However, he and the orchestra were in perfect harmony, and the SSO gave a most outstanding performance, of which Mahler should have been proud.

The thought that persisted throughout this pleasurable experience was about the value of such art. Not just that of the contribution of the Jewish artists involved, Zukerman, Mahler and Ashkenazy. Not just about the fanatics' dictum of annihilation of that people which is another and a huge topic. It was that the culture of classical music is absent from the current generation. A generalisation for sure, but much of the preference of contemporary music can be called preference for noise.

If you have one of those old-fashioned devices called radio, move the knob one notch away from 92.9 FM or 102.5 FM, and there is ear-piercing noise, which they call music. Oh, it is moving alright. Moves one out of the space where from where it is blaring. Not to speak of the damage to the ear drums later in life. But, oh, the absence of what music is! To live life without the presence of the beauty, the joy and the magic of what is music, is sheer unadulterated loss of beauty.

"Music is the language of G-d."

Max Bruch

I am quite aware of what is called modern music whether Hip Hop or some other version of contemporary music. Although in my youth I danced to Rock and Roll and such, in my later years I could never bear to listen to the latest style of "noise" amplified by the sub-woofers. It jarred my hearing sensibilities and all other sensibilities too. That may sound pretentious, but I am not. What I inherited was a feel for "music," which is contained in classical music. It is what has accompanied me all my life.

Music was always playing in the background when I studied in high school. It was present in the background when I was rote learning names, dates and places for modern history and the capital cities of countries for geography in school. Quiet light classical music played when I was writing essays and assignments at university, though I became more daring later and had movies playing. Musical ones, of course.

For one milestone birthday, I could request my present and my three sons presented me with some films about composers. Richard did organise it supposedly with his brothers. Or so I would like to remember. Now while I work, I have a spare computer on which to watch any one of my music gifts. I can choose from a few and I have watched and listened repeatedly to them. And each time I am so moved that words fail me. Oh, the pure pleasure of the music.

A Song to Remember (1945) about Frederik Chopin, the sensitive romantic and the raging revolutionary is beautifully portrayed by Cornel Wilde (and piano played beautifully by Jose Iturbi.) But the scene that stayed with me most was when Liszt plays a Chopin piece for the first time. He recognises Chopin. "Ah, the composer," says he with delight and the two shake hands while they continue to play the composition with four hands.

Song of Love (1947) is about the Schumann's. Based on the true story of Clara and her loyalty to her husband the great composer Robert while she retained the friendship of Brahms and Liszt, and eventually promoted Robert's work. What a wonderful scene when after Liszt played (by Henry Daniel) her 'wedding present' from her husband in Liszt's spectacular embellished and elaborate style, she plays it simply, with "love, unadorned."

Song Without End (1960) about the passionate Franz Liszt was superbly portrayed by Dirk Bogarde about the troubled temperamental and talented pianist composer. "Torn between his music, the church and his loves," his music (played by Jorge Bolet,) triumphed as demonstrated by his numerous performances, all of which began with the ritual removing of his gloves.

The Magic Bow (1946) about Paganini may be an insipid love story, but the fire of the man and his music (played by Yehudi Menuhin,) was interpreted brilliantly by a somewhat dark Stewart Granger. And the rather old black and white film, does not only not detract from the music, but it may also add to it.

All most memorable. And then there is the unforgettable gem *Callas Forever* (2002, Dir: Franco Zeffirelli (story and screenplay, 112 mins.) A great performance by Fanny Ardant as Maria Callas, Jeremy Irons as producer Larry Kelly, Joan Plowright as journalist friend Sarah, with Jay Rodan as Michael and Gabriel Garko as Jose.

It is a wonderful film that illustrates Maria Callas' unique voice, her artistry and her passion, and one which offers something more and more remarkable from each new viewing and listening. It is Zeffirelli's "loving tribute to his long-time friend" the Diva that was the great Callas. Perhaps it is worthwhile to look at this creation in more detail. It is one that I can watch and re-experience its passion and music.

The recluse Callas is visited by Sarah in her home to try to get her out of her self-imposed imprisonment. On her piano there are photos of Onassis, of conductors and various roles of operatic performances; all very reminiscent of the photo displays of roles of Norma Desmond in *Sunset Boulevard*. Callas considers Onassis beautiful. Sarah asks if she was wearing her glasses to which Callas replies, "I saw the beauty. She didn't."

We watch part of her final what she calls her "shameful" performance in Japan, which acts as "a reminder for her never to set foot on a stage again," When Larry visits Callas in her home, we watch Callas at night giving voice to the lyrics of her recording of *Madam Butterfly*. As she relives her performance and reaches the final high note, she is overcome with emotion and collapses in a heap on the floor, sobbing uncontrollably for her lost voice, lost musical career, and her lost life.

Larry returns next morning to tell her that he wants "to see Maria Callas again." She appears in a Chanel outfit with a navy organza coat floating over a navy spotted white dress with matching accessories. Street onlookers gasped in awe and admiration at the stunning vision of the Callas that she was. Larry demonstrates to Callas the proposed script for *Callas Forever* to film her and match the soundtrack of previous recordings of her famous roles. He says that "technically it's perfectly possible" to "marry the sound with the picture." Although she objects that "it's *dishonest*" because it is not her singing," she comes to see that it is her voice, and it has to be her. But when she says she is confused, Sarah tells her that "It can make [her] live *forever*."

But she does *Tosca*. The image of Ardant as Callas wakens to herself singing Tosca is so close to the performance of that role on stage in the film of the real Maria Callas that it is uncanny. The setting of the candelabra on the piano, the red drapes, the dress, the lighting on her face are all so very much matched to that of the original. It is almost the real Callas.

Callas chooses *Carmen* because she never sung her on stage, and it has been "haunting" her. She finds it hard to record because it is not sufficient to move the mouth. Even at rehearsal it requires "everything, the vocal cords, the muscles in the neck, the diaphragm; everything is singing." Hence the actor for the role of Don Jose must be a singer as well as have the right look. The experience of filming is full of passion through music, dance, and the voice. It exudes all: the fire, the sex, and danger that is *Carmen*. Yet at the end of the filming Callas forbids its release because, "*It is a fraud*." While the production maybe magnificent, it is false as it is an illusion because she no longer has "the voice."

And "there was such a voice" as when she sang *La Mamma Morta* from Giordano's *Andrea Chenier* in a wonderful red lit scene in another film titled *Philadelphia* as the Tom Hanks character describes the voice of passion, of love, of heartache, and of the "divine." And her voice was divine.

In between the filming we are introduced to a painter's impression of Maria Callas through Larry's new friend Michael. He is hearing impaired; was deaf and post-surgery the first sound he heard was a sound that was a "beauty not of this earth"; it was Callas singing. We then see a classic portraiture of Maria Callas on the cover of a book with her hands framing her face. And all the while playing in the background, there is Costa Diva from Bellini's Norma.

Michael's studio is like Act I of *La Boheme*. Callas is enchanted by the young man's paintings, especially the one with the red waves that seem to move. Red is her favorite color. Michael says, "It's you. It's what I feel when I hear you, because I feel colors, vibrations… they're waves of sound moving into the air." Michael shows another painting. It's his favorite, blue waves surrounding a white circle. It's *Norma*, the "splendor of the moon with incredible music" of Costa Diva and "a feeling of peace and serenity." As Callas motions for him to be silent while she listens and admires the painting she says, "Sometimes I have visions inside my head. You've read my heart." And *Callas Forever* eventually ends with Callas in Paris walking away while her signature song *Costa Diva* plays in the background. A most powerful moving creation by consummate artists who produced a vivid what may have been the last part of the life of the great Maria Callas. Simply magnificent.

A most beautiful sentiment expressed by Mstislav Rostropovich:

"The artist must forget the audience, forget the critics, forget the technique, forget everything but love for the music. Then, the music speaks through the performance, and the performer and the listener will walk together with the soul of the composer, and with God."

"Music begins where the possibilities of language end."

Jean Sibelius

"If music be the food of love, play on."

William Shakespeare

Chapter Nineteen

OLD AGE

> *"There is nothing particularly interesting about being old."*
>
> Katherine Hepburn

The year was 2021. The month does not matter as it was the second year of the global pandemic of Covid-19 which morphed into other forms such as Delta and Omicron. It was a time when lockdowns and quarantines were necessary, while the virus grew exponentially. It was a tough time when the enforced social isolation may have had negative effects such as development of mental illness, though at my age it may not matter much. It was also a time when large gatherings were banned, yet Black Lives Matter demonstrations were organised around the world. Irresponsible I think or perhaps just untimely.

Reluctantly many have settled into the obligatory lifestyle of staying at home. I settled down to a routine that was comfortable and similar to previous years. There were a lot more communications by means of the internet. True, we lacked the outings to the Opera House, and the frequent meeting with family and friends, but somehow, we managed to keep contacts and occupied ourselves without much disturbance. My friend Phillipa and I agreed that in a way it was a welcome variation to our life.

Many had exchanged a multitude of humorous material about the pandemic which was sprinkled with the stuff that old folks are made of. And that is because *Old Lives Matter*. An interview with Bette Davis comes to mind in which she said, *"Old age ain't no place for sissies."* Well, that is a truism if ever there was one. Katherine Hepburn was very adamant in her interview when she referred to aging that, *"It is a shame that an agile mind is trapped in a rotting body."* Yet she continued to swim in her lake every day throughout the year even in icy waters. She was a tough lady to the end.

Because in these last few years many normal activities were suspended, we were particularly prone to spend time on reflection. And on regrets. One is that I discarded all my photographs of all my boyfriends on the eve of my wedding. Mistake. Another is that I did not become a doctor. Big mistake. In my next life I should listen to my parents who wanted me to become a doctor. They assured me that doctors can carve out a living under any political regime, even without knowledge of foreign languages and even if payment is with poultry. Perhaps in my next lifetime.

If I remember the first few psychology lectures correctly, humans develop peaks in the mid-twenties. Past the ages of about twenty-seven, millions of brain cells die that do not regenerate and the system starts to deteriorate. It may not be common knowledge and that is just as well. Yet each generation lives longer, and while poets are preoccupied with their mortality, we now have to be preoccupied with the quality of our longer lives. And plan for it.

It seems so unfair that just when one's relatively long life of hard work and little play is at an end, and time would become available for pleasures not afforded previously, that one has to be preoccupied with ailments that become the primary focus of one's life. Many elderly battles with aches and pains. The suffering causes anger and frustration, even depression. Perhaps loneliness is one of the most difficult to bear as the years pass. Those are among the curses of the aged.

There is a perception that we who are mature or senior or elderly or simply old, are incompetent. Many may prefer us to be invisible. But on the contrary, we aged tend to rant and rave, complain, and make ourselves what others consider nagging nuisances. Movies have been made such as "Grumpy Old Men." And ageing parents have provided endless material for comedians. We certainly can identify with it all, and even laugh. But more likely in hindsight.

We do face difficulties. Seniors battle with new systems of technology that place unexpected obstacles in the way of accomplishing the simplest of tasks. They fight the new 'protocols,' they converse with machines until their patience runs out and stage battles with the so-called 'tech support' person in foreign places. For Australians, it is Mumbai or the Philippines.

In our age in this day and age, not only technical support is necessary, but physical support. And because we are not invisible, when we appear with our grey hair and a walker or walking stick, some may keep their distance from us. On the other hand, we may unexpectedly elicit the care and generosity in some others who offer some assistance when needed. That does not seem to be a sad state of affairs at all.

However, aging is not pleasant, and it is not a pleasant task to look at the problems of aging. Yet when I look at my peers, they are all very busy filling their days with activities, not only with essentials ones such as visits to doctors, tests, procedures and replenishing their medicine supplies. Everyone needs a purpose, to look forward to something or just to get out of the house. Many simply may be in a state of denial, refuse to accept aging and try to escape the inevitable.

It may sound morbid, and one should not indulge in the morbid. However, cemetery plots have become more topical in our later ages because of their increasing need for use. Also because of the increasing costs of plots. Some time ago I have purchased two cemetery plots in the New Lawn section. They are not far from our parents who are buried under elegant granite, whereas our headstones are uniformly plain needing only names and dates engraved. Our sons will have little burial organisations and expenses when we die. Of course, many people will not die. They will merely pass away.

I don't mind speaking about it. Not because I am looking forward to it, although some may think I do. That has been a point of contention for a long time among my family and friends. When I was approaching my mid-fifties, I made a casual statement that "I am ready to go." I must stress that I did not say that "I wish to go". I said that I was ready to go. I had a good life, my children were well on their way to independence, and I was not needed. I was ready, except for clearing out my cupboards, of which I have done considerable while moving to a smaller home. And now I am left with more time to plan.

However, I do have some concerns about my China cabinet. It contains mostly handcrafted porcelain pieces that my mother started to collect. Harry and I added many small handmade coffee cups and saucers from our overseas trips. Each piece has a little story attached to it and although lacking any great financial value, they all hold considerable sentimental value. True, it has meaning only to us.

I fear my China pieces will be discarded after I am gone. That would be a shame. For me this problem surfaces daily when I look at my many little treasures. Those lovely fine objects, some of which I have enjoyed most of my life, have followed me to every one of our new homes. I am very much attached to them. I find great pleasure in looking at them and remembering their history.

To return to the subject of the inevitable, I have always accepted death as the end part of life, and its finality. I have always been afraid of pain and don't want to suffer. I expect no one does. And no one wants to depend on some other to perform the most basic menial tasks to care for oneself. So, I have given instructions to my oldest son to act appropriately according to my wishes when the time arrives. And how reassuring is that euthanasia, or *Voluntary Assisted Dying* (VAD,) has become legal in 2023 in all Australian states.

I would love to be present at my funeral, to see who shows up, to watch the proceedings, and more than that, to hear some of the comments about me. Of course that is impossible. But I would like to make sure that the service is carried out to my specifications. And those are simple. Just the *Mourner's Kaddish* (mourner's prayer), no speeches and just a little music. I would like "*Valse Triste*" by Sibelius to be played. All that is short enough to remember if not to celebrate my very ordinary life. Let those present think of me however they please, and silently.

I am always asked for my medical history and that of my family, but I only know that of my parents. My mother died as a result of lymphosarcoma, and my father suffered a cardiac arrest and a stroke of which he later died. So based on my parents' medical history, I should have a heart attack on my way to chemotherapy. Not a happy prospect to which to look forward.

But prepared I have been for a while with a packed bag for the hospital. Unfortunately, my hospital bag has been used often in the last few years. For much of 2022 and 2023, I was suffering from pain I knew not before. Oh, the horror! I was bedridden most days for weeks at a time, and every small movement hurt. I learned the meaning of 'invalidated.'

There were doctors' visits, tests and medication of which most were for pain relief. Some had little effect, and some had adverse side effects. The hallucinations were new to me, but I met some fascinating if not frightening characters, with whom I had some very interesting conversations. Since they were illusory, we stopped those medicines and stayed with one whose common side effect the hospital constipation police checked several times a day.

But I digressed. It is easy to do. There is nothing funny about forgetting, forgetting names, dates, places, and events at times, or even on occasions dropping things, being unable to open things, and falling behind our quick stepping children and grandchildren. However, being totally unaware of placing car keys in the freezer may be a distinct cause for concern.

I mentioned anger and frustration at aging in aging. To misplace reading glasses may be frustrating, but it is a natural memory loss with the passing of years, and it is frequently shared with friends. On those occasions of forgetting, it is perfectly acceptable to say, "I can't remember the word, but it will come to me, and I'll let you know later." When I say that I invariably I add, "I will not call in the middle of the night," despite the sleepless nights that may be a very common malaise.

Ironically, I used to fall asleep in Yoga classes when I learnt about relaxation. That was in my young past. Not so in my old present. Perhaps I am not sufficiently tired and should exercise. Both professionals and layman highly recommend some form of exercise regime for a healthy cardiovascular system especially in old age. And I agree. I admire those I see on the street running for their lives. But that is all I do. I admire them.

I believe exercise is healthy, but I don't believe in starting any exercise regime for me in my late seventies when I never exercised in my life before. Yet I agree whole heartedly with Maxine when she said, "I really think that tossing and turning at night should be considered as exercise." Well, I certainly do a lot of that. I am writing now in the early hours of the morning.

There is method in all my madness. I was very determined to move into Mark Moran Vaucluse. Initially Harry objected on the ground that there were "too many old people." Eventually he relented, and I am most pleased that early in 2022 we settled into our most comfortable new home. The unit is light and amply spacious for the two of us with our new furniture. It is the ideal place for independent living for us seniors who in future may need to be wheeled across the corridor to the nursing care section, and then to be wheeled across the road to the cemetery. But because our plots are in Rookwood, we may need to be wheeled just a little further.

For me old age has come at a really bad time. Not that there is a good time, but mine came suddenly and with a vengeance. It is still punishing. There is the adage, "You are only as old as you feel." Well, I may not feel old, but my body does.

When someone asks how I am, I usually reply that I am fine. And I am. Of course, there is something wrong with every part of my body, but I am fine and well. Well, relatively well. And since my body is a temple, ancient and crumbling, it may take another volume to enumerate all that has gone wrong with it, particularly painfully after seventy-five years. But I will not go there.

But to return to a time for reflection. In the past few years, whether or not due to Covid, I spent more time looking at my reflection in the bathroom mirror. In the process I talked to the image that I could not ignore. The other me. I discovered a kind of familiar stranger, a person other than the me who I remembered, but of a much older age.

Venus de Milo, Louvre, Paris, 204cms

Then I looked at some of my photos from my youth especially the ones in the slinky ball gowns that my mother made for me. I thought I looked rather lovely in those photos. I approved of my appearance indeed. I decided that it was true that when I was young, I was shapely, and I had a shape that may have resembled the shape of a Goddess. Something akin to that of the statue of Venus de Milo, even though she lacked arms. I, on the other hand, have prosthetic shoulder joints.

I have learned that the scientific fact of time and gravity enacted upon the anatomy, is not an experiment in physics. The fact of the matter is that with age, everything about the body matter changes. And drops. However, even though I am old, I claim that I can still resemble a Goddess.

However, the sad truth is that my shape closely resembles the shape of the statue of Venus of Willendorf. Not a pleasant sight. And not quite the meaning of plus ca change, *plus c'est la meme chose*, which I used in a lot of my assignments. But it is of comfort to know that even in old age, I can still resemble a Goddess. Even if it is such.

Venus of Willendorf, Nturahistorisches Museum, Vienna, 11cms

To be sure that I am remembered as more attractive in appearance than Willendorf, I have a selection of photographs that I may distribute particularly to my descendants. Whether or not in silence they remember me, I do care about the mental pictures they may retain of me, if any.

So, I offer a few of what I consider as somewhat flattering visual images of me, though they are not necessarily recent.

They say that there are exciting and challenging times ahead as our life spans are lengthened. One wonders about the truth of that and if it is all worthwhile. After my more recent surgeries, my sons keep dwelling on and laughing at their 'bionic woman' mother, while some others may think that I have a fetish for total reverse hip, shoulder and knee joint replacements. I must admit I find it strange that parts of me will outlast me. In the meantime, while my short-term memory is interrupted periodically, my long-term memory, my reflections and recollections became attractions of my past. And that was the main purpose of this journey which may have been difficult, but all the musings filled me completely with sheer unadulterated pleasure.

Old age is like a plane flying through a storm.
Once you are aboard there is nothing you can do about it.

Golda Meir

CONCLUSION

This is an abridged version of what I intended and what I have written. Perhaps influenced by some friends who are writers or have written, I have reduced what I had already written which is safe in a file storage. Also, it is not possible to condense seventy-eight years of life experiences into one book. And I did have more than one in mind before I started writing.

I have included some information about my family background. I practically grew up without grandparents, but the ones I adopted were very significant in my life. When I think of them which is often, it is with great affection. I also think of my parents quite often, and not only on anniversary dates. They were good people, and good and loving parents. They are still so very much with me, that at times one of their sayings or an incident about them just pops into my mind unexpectedly.

When I think of my childhood in Budapest, it is with pleasure as I was surrounded by love and affection. I do not think that our migration was an adventure in the strict sense of the word but more like just another journey or event in my life. I believe that I settled seamlessly into our new life in our new country. It was certainly without any distress. And by the time my education was complete, I was actually thinking in English.

Much like the *wandering Jew*, we moved many times. But each place, each house felt like a home. Probably because I always lived with my loving family.

I have not included the writings of our travels. There were many business trips on which I missed out while looking after our children. When they were old enough, we tried to combine the overseas business trips with a few days of family visits. They were not always successful. The first three or four times we were in Paris we were unable to spend even a few hours in the Louvre.

When we were able, we travelled with our family and friends. With Maggie we were on an unforgettable European musical tour. Then we toured in Australia with her. With our friends Barbara and Ray, we toured the Victorian wine district and cruised the Caribbean, among other voyages.

We can look back with pleasure on the shared cruises with our friends Lynda and David who first introduced us to the Seaborne cruises. And we cruised with them a few times. We were on Seaborne cruise with Fedor and Liz along the east coast of Australia as well as in the Mediterranean Sea. There were others, and all were most enjoyable and memorable.

For our 50th anniversary we decided to return to the Mediterranean; the cruise itinerary was from Monaco to Monaco, including ports in Spain, and on islands South of Italy and South of France. It was one of the deserved presents for Harry who was simply marvellous when he looked after me for nearly two years. He stepped into an uncharacteristic reversal of roles as he did everything without exception, never complained and was ever so kind. So, before I embark on my next project titled *"My Life With Harry,"* I would like to pay homage to the man who contributed to my very privileged life which involves our Bowral home.

Harry had and has much pride in his property and tended his land most diligently. In the first year he planted over a thousand saplings assisted by our youngest son Ron and his faithful Border Collie Cassie. Despite the fact that only a smaller number actually grew into trees, his philosophy remains as unshakeable as his efforts to grow more trees. "Since Australia has been good to us and since we now own a piece of her good earth, we should put something back into the land." And I felt much the same.

For a long time now, he has been putting his back into toiling and working his land. And regularly, he has been putting out his back too. Ever since August of 2001 we have been enjoying the different pace of the country and tried to make it the more dominant in our life. Now we tend to spend most of the week in Bowral. Our sons Rich and Rob and their families frequent our country home more than Ron, especially when we are not there.

A lot of our attention focuses on nature and her needs. Often, I wake to the whistle of birds I cannot name and to fog through which I cannot see. Not unusual in the Southern Highlands at any time of the year. If it rains for days, we are glad. We have never been so conscious of water for our newly planted trees or plants, and for food for the cows and calves, even though they are across the fence and belong to the neighbours.

We spend a lot of time admiring our flowers and watching the grass grow; sometimes literally.

Our country home together with the accompanying new and diverse life is only one of Harry's achievements. It is therefore only fitting to fill part of my narrative with his feats and deeds and activities, from all of which I have greatly benefitted. The purchase of this most unusual property in 1996 was perceived by family and friends not merely as foolish, but an outright stupid move. Who in their right mind would buy part of a blue stone quarry? Only Harry could be so whimsical. But as usual, he had the vision of yet another 'potential.' I complied as I did with many of his ideas that seemed to be good at the time and later, we came to regret not buying the whole of *The Quarry* as we later named our lovely country home.

It's quite a change from the first few months after we moved into the house when Harry started the landscaping with grass. On an October day, I watched him spread bags of grass seeds. For hours he walked around wheeling wide arcs with his arm. He covered most of the area around the house as the sun popped out for a few minutes between showers. When he finished, within ten minutes a windstorm blew up and together we watched all the topsoil fly by the window, seeds and all. The grass never grew, till Harry ordered some long strips of turf to be rolled out with the help of our friend David, and regularly the gardener rejuvenates the soil with special chemicals. And if it is patchy, it is due partly to the drought in odd years. It is no laughing matter that two decades later, Harry is still working on the landscaping. But it is very close to what for us looks and feels like our little haven.

To help him tame his barren quarry without physically damaging himself, Harry acquired a number of machines. I call them toys, but all the farmers have them. From outside come strange noises followed by the breathless Harry rushing into the house sweating and swearing, as each of the machines take turns to break down just to frustrate him.

The first mechanical toy was a second-hand notorious ATV (or All Terrain Vehicle) which usually stopped after a very short time. Numerous parts were replaced. The brand-new lawnmower also gave him trouble initially – until he realised it was simply out of fuel. On slopes it would not start, and our land is mostly sloped. On one occasion, the desperate Harry phoned for a mechanic. After prolonged shouting, our motorcycle mechanic son Ron must have exhausted his capacity for distance diagnoses and treatment as well as his patience. Then the call ended with him telling his father, "Try the CHOKE ON button?" It worked.

Periodically, I could hear the crushing crunch of rocks breaking the slasher blade. It was out of commission for many months at a time until the broken blades were replaced. Then Ron was called again to fix the machine only to injure his back.

The whipper-snipper consumed reels and reels of plastic as it regularly tore during the cutting of the long wild grass and eventually Harry's elbow was injured. The elbow complaint may have originated on one of his golf course outings, when he hit the ground instead of the ball too many times. It is but a small addition to his chronic bone problem with which we have lived just the same all our lives.

The rural activity to which Harry took with a relish was the rock movements. Chunks of blue stones revealed themselves either through contact with machines or by just lying around. They needed to be picked up and loaded, then transported and stockpiled in one spot somewhere. Eventually they needed to be picked up, loaded, transported, and piled somewhere again. Then they were set as dry or wet walls. We already had quite a few but Harry said we need more. One can move a lot of rocks and build a lot of rock walls on fifteen acres. Almost as much as Harry's endless movements. The space underneath the rock wall was ideal for vegetable and fruit garden. And Harry's uncle, Batyu or Uncle as everyone called him, was always very keen to help plant whatever Harry thought we should grow.

One morning I awoke to the sound of the rattle of the trailer. Harry was outside riding his mechanical horse and collecting more rocks. I later found out that it was for some wall down the hillside. When I said that we have enough rock walls, he replied that he is beautifying the place for me. Harry's actions speak louder than his words and I have to listen to his efforts. He wanted to surprise me with a flower garden. I thought it was a lovely thought. However, unfortunately that spot is not visible from the house.

Not wishing to pursue the point when he came inside and ignoring his chronic complaints about aches and pains, I noticed that Harry lost some weight, but he seemed in good physical shape. We have the perfect homeostasis of body and mind. As I gain weight, so he remains slim. Harry invariable stands in front of the mirror admiringly and I hear him say, "Look at that fabulous physique." As time passes and his physique alters, so does Harry's perception. He still stands in front of the mirror. However, now I hear him say, "Who is that old man in the mirror?" or "Look how I am aging."

On an on-and-off rainy Monday in November, I was in our study reading and watching Harry in the garden. He was levelling the top step of a set of stairs that led to the bottom of the rock wall. I was comfortably sitting in my very own spacious, firm cushioned armchair and recalled the history of the number of times it acquired a new look.

I became very attached to that solid piece of furniture after some thirty years. Both Harry's and my backgrounds are such that it conditioned us to value all our possessions. Of course, Harry was unaware of the fact that I spent countless hours sitting or semi-reclining in that particular armchair, talking to him for months before we were married. So, it had greater sentimental value.

The armchair became an issue in the Bowral décor. Harry said that the armchair was too old. True, it belonged to my parents, and it was already recovered a number of times to fit into the colour scheme of our previous homes. But there was nothing wrong with it and 'they don't make them like they used to'. After a few weeks of repeated discussions, we arranged for my large bulky armchair to be recovered with a matching 'puff' or ottoman. My talking armchair became my reading one.

2002

In the meantime, Harry bought himself an attractive leather recliner which was a lightweight masculine piece of leather 'functional art', supposedly shaped to meet the human form. I watched him constantly shifting in it and changing positions until he just did not use it at all. When reading, he insisted on sitting in my armchair, and forced me to have to search for a comfortable seat.

It soon became obvious that I had to organise a 'his' armchair that was just as comfortable as mine. Fortunately, Uncle bought himself one of those mechanised armchairs that had a back that reclined and a footrest that could be raised, and it did some other tricks.

And so, another spacious, firm cushioned armchair with a puff identical to mine, became available to be recovered. True, it took nearly half a year for it to happen, but when 'his' armchair arrived, I felt just as comfortable in it as I used to be in mine. Harry has never relinquished my armchair and now both are covered in plush navy velvet to fit the new colour scheme of the furnishings that the sun faded, and time wore down. And I am still attached to them as to some of my other possessions.

2022

One of the plans was to plant vegetables at the bottom of the rock wall. And we did plant tomatoes, shallots, cabbages, carrots, strawberries and more. They all grew beautifully, especially the strawberries, until chunks were eaten from them. Perhaps it was the cabbages that invited the herds of bunnies, who were there in colonies already and feasted on all our crops. So, the vegies and fruit did not last.

We have been totally unsuccessful with our lemon trees. We planted them in different suitable warm areas sheltered from the cold harsh winds, but still they didn't grow. We were told that they respond very well to human urine. Many a gent emptied his bladder on our lemon trees, but to no avail. The resultant fruit was a shrivelled up small soft greenish yellow ball that dropped before its time. Once and only once did we have a few small yellow lemons. Still nothing like the large evenly yellow juicy lemons grown by Uncle on his balcony in Bondi. Every now and then we try with a new plant, and we tend it with great hope.

Soon after we started the landscaping, we started planting roses. One or two in the bed of some thirty roses had to be replaced but each year they grew, blossomed, and bloomed. After every cut back at the end of winter in August or early September as our native Bowral friend Judy advised, Harry was convinced that I chopped them too much. But they came good and grew, blossomed, and bloomed again. I cut each little branch carefully above the little budding shoots. I took great pride in the trimming and great pleasure in the blooming of my roses. For years they thrived with their different colours and varied perfumes, all thirty bushes of them in my bed of roses. I took great pleasure in looking after my roses and great pride in watching them.

Until one day, all thirty rose bushes died all at once. Again, Harry said I cut them back too much and killed them. I disagreed because they were fine after my last cut. Our friend Judy said that roses were hardy, and they could not be killed by cutting them back. On the contrary she said, the further they are cut back, the more they thrive. She also said that only poison can kill them, and that very likely, that is what happened when weed killer was used around them. It only takes a little breeze to blow the poison onto the roses. That is the only way ALL could have died at the same time. And they were very beautiful when alive and they adorned our desk in the little vase.

Afterwards we attempted to plant roses again two or three times, but they never grew. Our friend Lynda suggested lavender which is another hardy plant and one that needs little attention. For a while we had a number of small lavender fields that grew small lilac carpets, including the longer strip of what once was the rose bed. Now it is a display of blue irises, marking the beginning of spring.

It was in the spring of 2008 that the four rows of vines were planted. Uncle came to Bowral to help with the planting and the tying. They were tended with care, then trimmed and tended with care some more, while Uncle came many times to work on the vines. It all looked very attractive, and we were proud of our tiny vineyard.

2004

And the grapes that grew were healthy for a couple of seasons. Harry wanted to bottle the wine, so he bought a press. For a while we did have some nice green and red table fruits. He obtained some juice from the grapes, but it was never going to be wine. Unfortunately, no matter how well the vines were tended and netted, the birds got to the grapes. And so, our vineyard was very short lived as were the fruits on the trees.

2005

One morning I awoke to the sound of magpies or currawongs. I opened the door to clean fresh air, dew covered leaves and grass glistening in the warm sunshine. To the east behind the trees, the town and the valley were hidden in a dense mist. Oh, what a joyful sight. Until I saw Harry.

When he came closer to the house to spray the roses against whatever bug spotted their leaves brown after his vegetable patch against snails, I saw a large green tank strapped to his back, a hat and bare legs minus his trousers. Never having had any inhibitions, if I reminded him to put some clothes on, it was only to shield him from the harmful sun rays. But it took a while for him to come inside. When he did, he brought some roses with him when we still had roses. Once he even found a single strand of three tiny snow drops.

Later he settled at his computer at our partner's desk which he designed and had made for us. I was situated in the kitchen as I am often and looked towards the study. I stood there and couldn't help seeing the sharp chin go up and down while Harry worked. Some part of his body always needs to move. It's as if the incessant motion drove the work. As with every one of his ventures he undertakes, he is intense. In this instance it was his novel writing. Suddenly the rhythmic movement stopped. Then Harry stopped in frustration and said, "Oh, … I don't understand my book." And once again the writing of the book was postponed.

For many years Harry's desire was to paint and sculpt. So, behind our house he built a lovely spacious studio which would have been ideal even for master classes. He told his artist friends that he will organise workshops with them. He told me that he needed inspiration and that I should pose for him. But because there is a huge incongruency between the notion of me as an inspiration and me as a model, it was a long time till Harry put brush to canvas. And I am not sure what or who he used as his Muse.

Months later, Harry was engrossed in watching the computer screen again. He often took to writing notes, long letters out of some correctional need and even odes to his sons on their birthdays and Bar Mitzvahs. He told me this time it was an "Ode to Father", which was an extension of "Why do I remember so little about my Father?" And that was little. The attempts must have been prompted by my questions about the man who died four years before Harry and I met, and who for me was always an enigma.

Every week Harry spent much of the days outside on his land. When his mobile phone rang, I looked for him and I called him. Out of sight, I shouted to him, but he did not hear. I yelled, I screamed as I walked around the house, but he still did not hear. I started to sing. I changed volume, frequency, and key to no avail. Harry's quarry echoed with every sound, and we agreed that the acoustics would be quite suitable for a production of an 'Opera in the Park', or to be more accurate 'Opera in the Quarry'. Yet he did not hear me, either because of the noise of one of his machines or his selective hearing or just his hearing. So, I gave up and returned to my activities, be they domestic, accounting, or academic. Either way they were pleasurable.

Once Harry suddenly reappeared with our dog Brandy. The little white mop ran circles around him. She trotted close to his legs then ahead and then back, dancing ovals and ellipses as the fancy took her. As I watched the two of them and glanced at Harry's little paradise of colourful cerise bush roses in full bloom, I thought pleasant thoughts of my three absent sons, and I imagined, that is how bliss must feel.

For over twenty years we travelled between the town and the country. The frequency of changing residences sometimes caused sensations somewhat akin to a form of schizophrenic disorientation. These occurred mostly when one failed to register whether the town or country fridge contained the fresh foods that were required. But the bathroom positions were at times simply hazardous. When getting out of bed in the middle of the pitch-black night, it does make a difference whether one turns to the left or goes straight ahead. And the bruise marks are a testament to memory and age.

✲✲✲

We no longer have to check on the grape planter and caretaker Batyu. Uncle Julius passed away at the ripe old age of 100 years. The 'reluctant centenarian' did enjoy his family celebration. We no longer have Brandy to carry between town and country. Now the main reason for our travel to town is to visit the children, the grandchildren, and our friends. And all I can say is country Bowral always feels wonderful, and it is where I feel at peace with the world.

Harry continues to spend much time in the garden weeding, blowing away leaves and whatever his body allows, but mainly riding his lawn mower cutting grass which we still watch as it grows differently within each season. While he works to beautify our lovely country property, I continue to watch and criticize. In a way not much has changed in all that time we have been in the Highlands; except we have no need for a grand dog since we have our lovely grandchildren.

For over two decades, our 'retarded' (retired) life in Bowral has been most pleasant and at times even productive. For most of those years, I have been keeping our accounts and those of Ron's Flywheels business, reading for my two book clubs and socializing with some of our friends in the Southern Highlands as well as spending time with our family and friends in Sydney and Canberra. All the children and grandchildren are involved with their busy lives and that is as it should be, but we see them regularly, especially Harry who is totally besotted with all six of the grandchildren.

The completion of this production took a long time since life interfered in the process. What I wrote is a compilation of a strange mélange of material. I wrote at intermittent intervals and included past writings. Hence it is irregular and in places even repetitious.

In the process, I learned to appreciate how hard it is to write, that it requires solitude and incredible discipline. That it can be an all-absorbing past time which excludes the people one loves and normal activities. Much of the time I lost myself in reflections which I not only found interesting but enjoyed thoroughly.

As I look out our study window, I see a blanket of dense white mist. It seems eerily like the end of the world. Nothingness. *Tis something*. What was a bluestone quarry has been transformed into a living breathing garden that changes with the seasons, even daily, with the weather of course. And it will do so long after we have departed. But for now, I sit and watch as the mist lifts and the scene clears from the ghostly to the familiar variety of greens with splashes of bright colors and blue skies in our peaceful little paradise.

When I stopped to think about my past, I found I lived an ordinary life, a rather unimportant one and perhaps even insignificant one. There were times when I wondered why I persevered with the writing. But then I remembered that the intention was for my children and perhaps even grandchildren to learn a little about my past and about me. Perhaps it will be of some interest to them, and if not now then later when they have reached that age of attraction.

In the meantime, Harry and I will continue to travel between town and country, between Moran in Vaucluse and the Quarry in Bowral. We have the best of the two worlds. I am ever so grateful to be able to live and enjoy such a privileged life.

Bowral 2024

*I rewrote the ending to "Farewell to Arms,"
the last page of it, thirty-nine times before I was satisfied.*

Ernest Hemingway

MY FAMILY

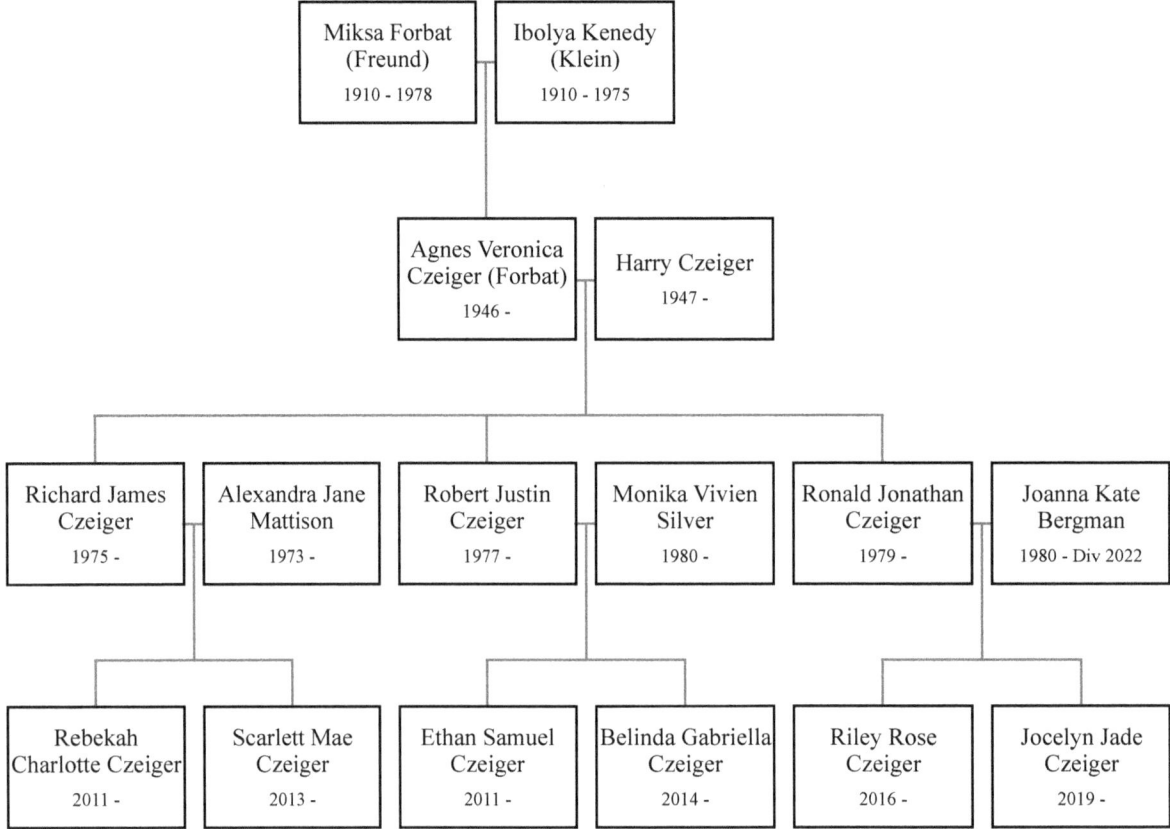

MY MOTHER'S FAMILY

NOTE:
The names in this family tree start with surnames.
They were born and currently reside in Hungry.

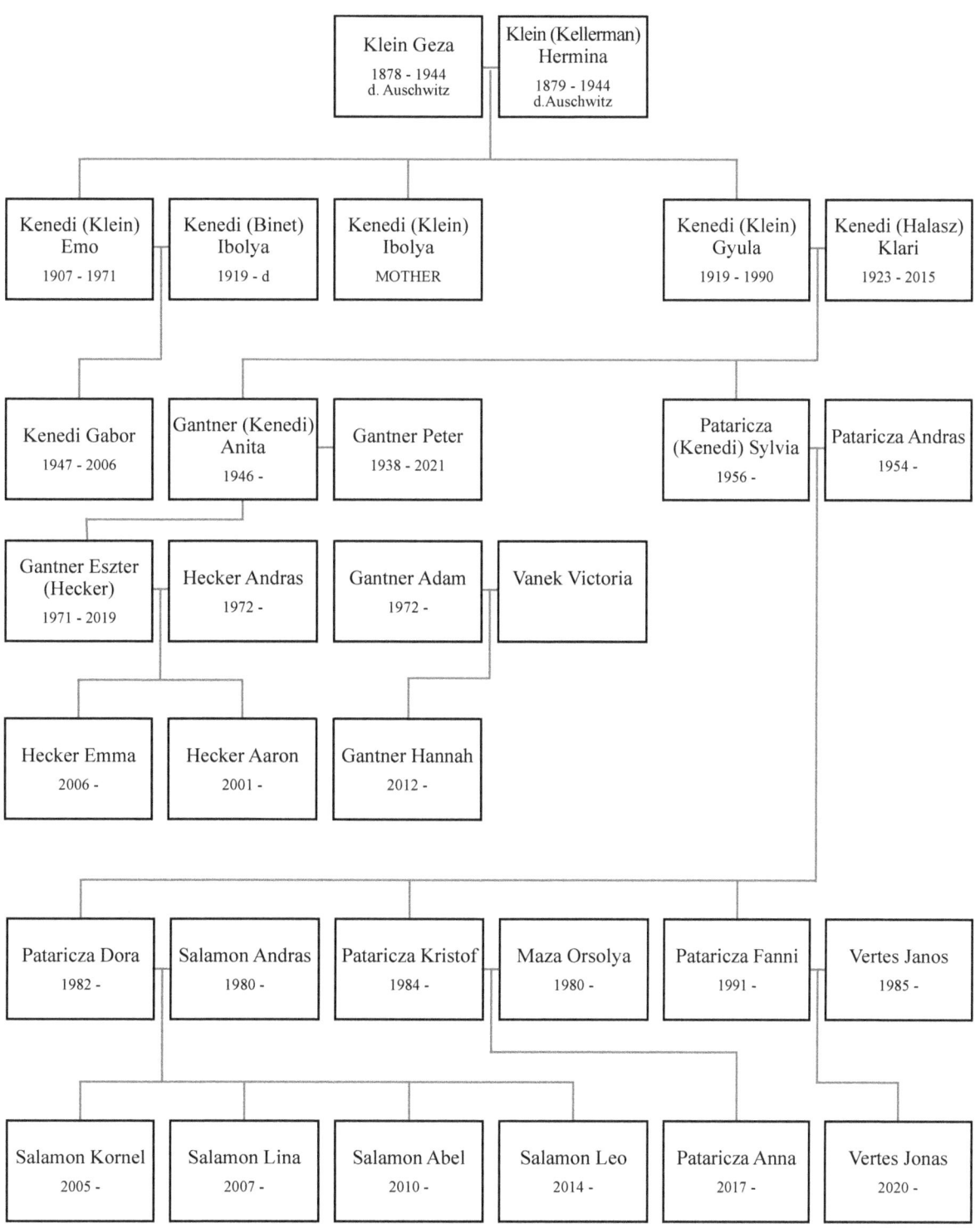

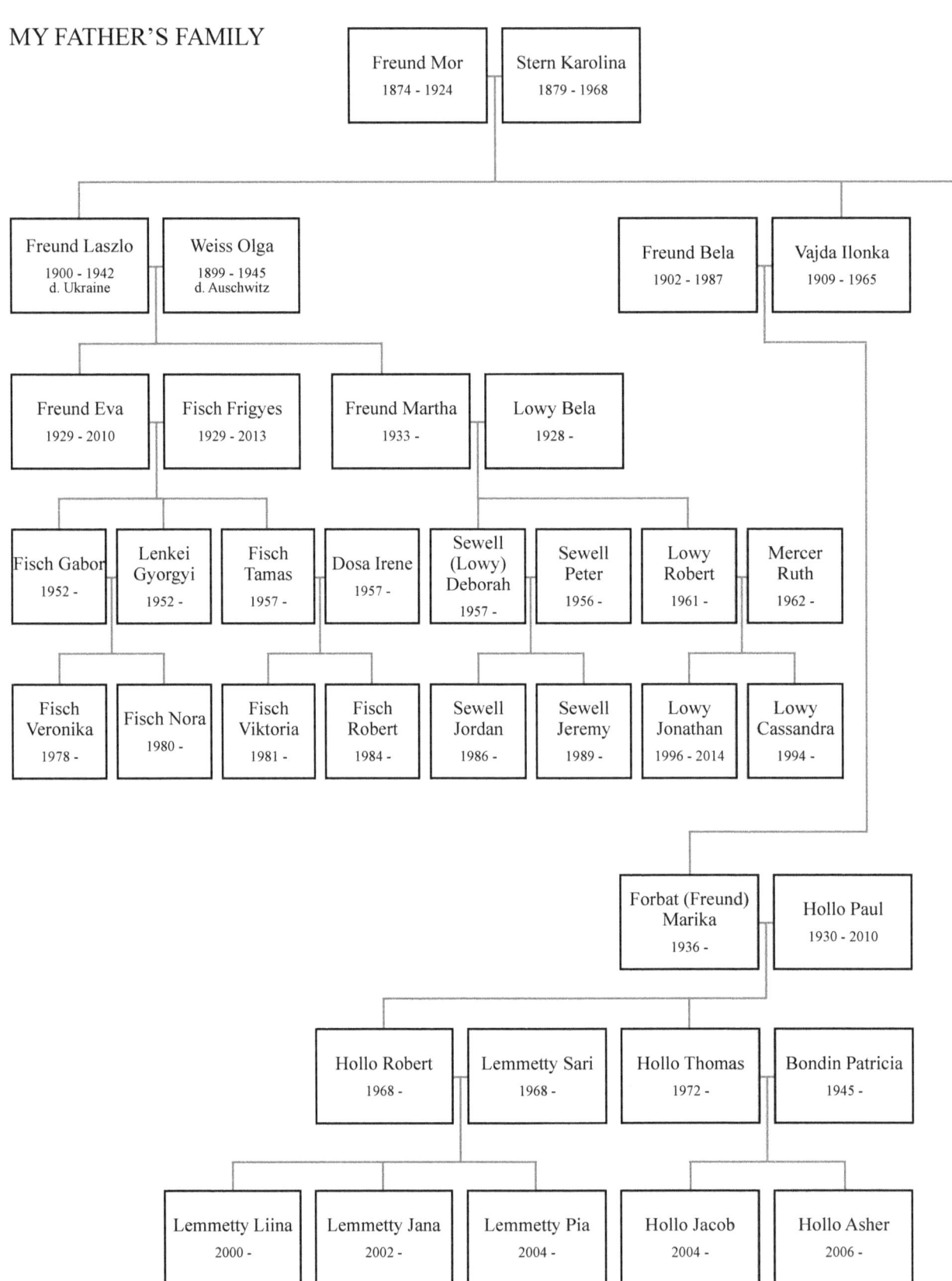

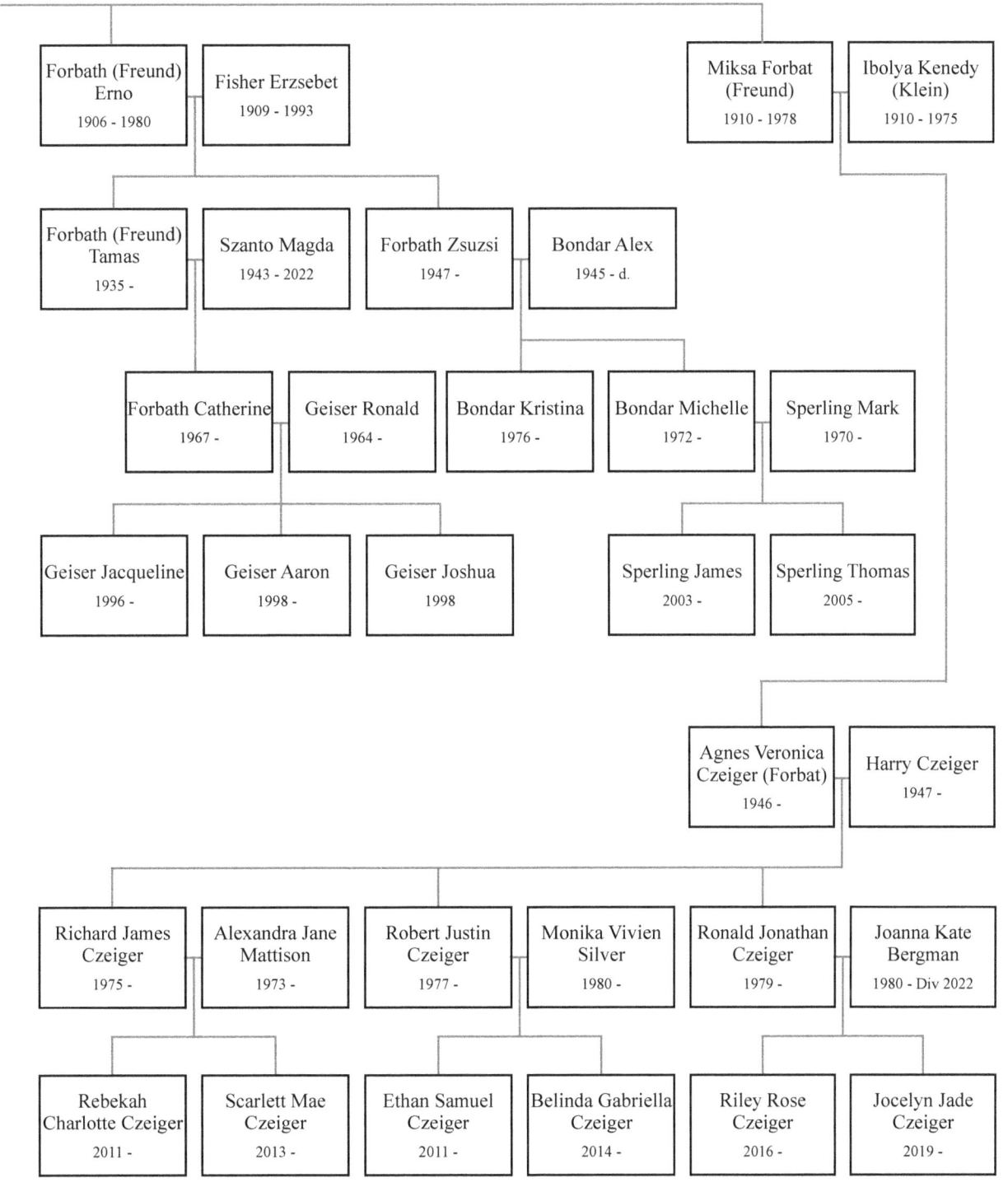

www.ingramcontent.com/pod-product-compliance
Lightning Source LLC
Chambersburg PA
CBHW041410300426
44114CB00028B/2970